Collected Courses of the Academy of European Law

Recueil des cours de l'Académie de droit européen

1991

The Protection of Human Rights in Europe

Vol. II Book 2

Edited by
Frank Emmert

European University Institute, Florence

Academy of European Law

Springer-Science+Business Media, B.V.

ISBN 978-94-017-1076-3 ISBN 978-94-017-1074-9 (eBook)
DOI 10.1007/978-94-017-1074-9

This publication should be cited as *AEL* Vol. II Book 2

Cover design: Francesco Cassese

Printed on acid-free paper

Originally published by Kluwer Academic Publishers in 1993.
Softcover reprint of the hardcover 1st edition 1993

General Table of Contents

Volume II Book 2
The Protection of Human Rights in Europe

Volume II Book 1
European Community Law

EMILE NOEL,
La Conférence intergouvernementale sur l'union politique européenne, à la veille du conseil européen de Luxembourg

OLE DUE,
Conférence Robert Schuman
Article 5 du traité CEE. Une disposition de caractère fédéral?

JOHN A. USHER, *General Course: The Continuing Development of Law and Institutions*

MICHEL WAELBROECK, *Règles de concurrence et concentrations*

JEAN-VICTOR LOUIS, *La Banque européenne pour la reconstruction et le développement. Aspects juridiques*

FRANCIS SNYDER, *The Common Agricultural Policy in the Single European Market*

L'Académie de droit européen

L'Académie de droit européen a été créée par l'Institut en 1990. Son activité principale consiste en l'organisation de cours d'été consacrés au droit des Communautés européennes et à la protection des droits de l'homme en Europe.

Elle offre l'opportunité de participer à des cours donnés par les plus grandes autorités mondiales en la matière. Les conférenciers présentent leur propre analyse et appréciation du droit communautaire, de la convention européenne des droits de l'homme et d'autres sujets concernant le droit européen. Les conférences, sous une forme révisée et plus détaillée, sont l'objet de cette publication.

Tous les cours sont en anglais ou en français. Les participants doivent maîtriser l'une de ces langues et avoir au moins une connaissance passive de l'autre. Ils doivent résider à Florence pendant la tenue de l'Académie et participer à l'ensemble de ses activités. La participation est ouverte tant aux étudiants ou enseignants en droit qu'aux juristes praticiens. Le nombre de participants est limité, et la sélection est faite sur la base des mérites respectifs des candidatures reçues.

Les participants qui possèdent déjà une connaissance approfondie dans les domaines du droit communautaire et des droits de l'homme peuvent demander à se soumettre à des épreuves écrites en vue de l'obtention du diplôme de l'Académie en droit européen. Ce diplôme est susceptible d'être délivré avec mention. Lors de la rédaction de leur candidature, les candidats sont donc appelés à préciser s'ils souhaitent se présenter aux épreuves du diplôme. Dans l'affirmative, ils doivent préciser dans le détail les enseignements qu'ils ont déjà suivis en droit communautaire et sur la convention européenne des droits de l'homme, ainsi que l'expérience qu'ils ont déjà acquise dans ces domaines.

Pour de plus amples informations, adressez-vous à

l'Institut universitaire européen

Académie de droit européen

Villa Schifanoia

Via Boccaccio, 121

I-50133 FIRENZE

Italie

(téléphone (055) 5092572/50921, fax 5092573)

The Academy of European Law

The Academy of European Law was established by the European University Institute in 1990. Its main activity is the holding of summer courses in the law of the European Community and the protection of human rights in Europe.

The Academy offers the opportunity of attending courses given by leading authorities from all over the world. Lecturers offer their own evaluation and analysis of Community law, the European Convention on Human Rights and other topics concerning European law. The lectures are published in the present annual publication.

All courses are held in English or French. Students must be fluent in one of these languages and have at least a passive knowledge of the other. Participants are expected to stay in Florence for the duration of the course and should attend all the courses. Participation in the summer session is open to law students, law teachers and those in legal practice. Enrolment numbers are limited and admission is based on merit.

A limited number of participants who already have some advanced knowledge in the fields of Community law and the law of the European Convention on Human Rights may request to sit a written examination. Successful candidates will be awarded the Diploma of the Academy in European Law. Exceptionally the Diploma may be awarded *cum laude*. Applicants should indicate if they wish to be candidates for the Diploma in their application. Those who wish to be considered for the Diploma must include in their applications details of courses they have already attended in Community law and on the European Convention on Human Rights together with other experience they have in these fields.

For further information please contact
European University Institute
Academy of European Law
Villa Schifanoia
Via Boccaccio, 121
I-50133 FIRENZE
Italy
(telephone (055) 5092572/50921, fax 5092573)

The Officers of the Academy

Advisory Committee

List of Principal Abbreviations
Table des principales abréviations

ABl.	Amtsblatt
ACP	Africa-Carribean-Pacific Countries (Lomé Conventions)
Ad.L.Rev.	Administrative Law Review
AEL	Collected Courses of the Academy of European Law
A.E.L.E.	Association européenne de libre échange
AETR	Accord européen relatif au travail des équipages des véhicules effectuant des transports internationaux par route
AFDI	Annuaire français de droit international
A.I.E.A.	Agence internationale de l'énergie atomique
AJCL	American Journal of Comparative Law
AJIL	American Journal of International Law
All ER	All England Law Reports
Annuaire	Annuaire de la CEDH
Appl.	Application (European Commission of Human Rights)
ArchVR	Archiv des Völkerrechts
ASDI	Annuaire suisse de droit international
ASE	Agence spatiale européenne
ASEAN	Association of South-East Asian Nations
ATF	Recueil officiel des arrêts du Tribunal Fédéral Suisse
BayVerfGH	Bayerischer Verfassungsgerichtshof
BEI	Banque européenne d'investissement
BERD	Banque européenne pour la reconstruction et le développement
BFH	Bundesfinanzhof
BGB	Bürgerliches Gesetzbuch
BGBl.	Bundesgesetzblatt
BGH	Bundesgerichtshof
BIRD	Banque internationale pour la reconstruction et le développement
Bull.EC Suppl.	Bulletin of the European Communities, Supplement
BVerfG (E)	Bundesverfassungsgericht (Collected Decisions)
BVerwG (E)	Bundesverwaltungsgericht (Collected Decisions)
BYbIL	British Yearbook of International Law
Camb.L.J.	Cambridge Law Journal
CanYIL	Canadian Yearbook of International Law

CCT	Common Customs Tariff
CDDH	Comité directeur des droits de l'homme
CDE	Cahiers de droit européen
CE	Communautés européennes
CECA	Communauté européenne du charbon et de l'acier
CEDH	Convention européenne des droits de l'homme
CEE	Communauté économique européenne
CEEA	Communauté européenne de l'énergie atomique
CES	Comité économique et social
CIJ Rec.	Cour international de Justice Recueil
CJCE	Cour de Justice des Communautés européennes
CJCE Rec.	Cour de Justice des Communautés européennes Recueil
CMLR	Common Market Law Reports
CML Rev.	Common Market Law Review
Colum.J.Trans.L.	Columbia Journal of Transnational Law
Com.CE Doc.	Document de la Commission européenne
Com.EDH	Commission européenne des droits de l'homme
Conseil CE Doc.	Document du Conseil européen
Corte Cost.	Corte Costituzionale
C.P.E.	Coopération politique européenne
CSCE	Conference on Security and Cooperation in Europe
DB	Der Betrieb
Declaration E.P.	Declaration of European Parliament
Debs. PE	Débats du parlement européen
Dec.	decision; décision
Dir.	directive
DÖV	Die Öffentliche Verwaltung
DR	Decisions and Reports of the European Commission of Human Rights
DS	Recueil Dalloz Sirey
DVBl.	Deutsches Verwaltungsblatt
EAEC/Euratom	European Atomic Energy Community
EBRD	The European Bank for Reconstruction and Development
EBU	European Broadcasting Union
EC	European Community
ECHR	European Convention on Human Rights
ECJ	European Court of Justice
ECLR	European Competition Law Review
ECOSOC	Economic and Social Council; Conseil économique et social

ECR	European Court Reports (Reports of the Court of Justice of the European Communities, Luxembourg)
ECSC	European Coal and Steel Community
ECU	European Currency Unit
EEC	European Economic Community (Treaty)
EFTA	European Free Trade Association
EG	Europäische Gemeinschaft
EGMR	Europäischer Gerichtshof für Menschenrechte
EHRR	European Human Rights Reports
EIB	European Investment Bank
EIRR	European Industrial Relations Review
EJIL	European Journal of Interntional Law
EKMR	Europäische Kommission für Menschenrechte
ELR	European Law Review
EMRK	Europäische Menschenrechtskonvention
EMS	European Monetary System
EP	European Parliament
EPC	European Political Cooperation
EP Doc.	European Parliament Document
EP Debs	European Parliament Debates
EPIL	Encyclopedia of Public International Law
ERTA	European Road Transport Agreement
ESA	European Space Agency
EuGRZ	Europäische Grundrechte Zeitschrift
EUI	European University Institute
EuR	Europarecht (Zeitschrift)
Eur. Bus. L. Rev.	European Business Law Review
Eur Court H.R.	European Court of Human Rights
Eur Comm H.R.	European Commission of Human Rights
EuZW	Europäische Zeitschrift für Wirtschaftsrecht
EWS	Europäisches Wirtschafts- und Steuerrecht
FAO	Food and Agriculture Organization
FIDE	Fédération internationale pour le Droit européen
F.M.I.	Fonds monétaire international
Fordham Int'l. L.J.	Fordham International Law Journal
Foro it.	Foro italiano
Foro pad.	Foro padano
Fs.	Festschrift
G.A. Res.	General Assembly (of the United Nations) Resolution; Résolution de l'Assemblée Générale des Nations Unies
GATT	General Agreement on Tariffs and Trade
Ga.J.Int'l. & Comp.L.	Georgia Journal of International and Comparative Law

Gazz Uff	Gazzetta Ufficiale
Giur. Cost.	Giurisprudenza Costituzionale
GRUR Int.	Gewerblicher Rechtsschutz und Urheberrecht, Auslands- und internationaler Teil
GSP	General System of Preferences
GYIL	German Yearbook of International Law
Harvard Int'l L.J.	Harvard International Law Journal
Harvard L. Rev.	Harvard Law Review
HCR	UN High Commissioner on Refugees; Haut-Commissaire des Nations unies pour les réfugiés
HRLJ	Human Rights Law Journal
HR Rev.	Human Rights Review
HZA	Hauptzollamt
IAEA	International Atomic Energy Agency
IAEO	International Atomic Energy Organization
IATA	International Air Transport Association
ICAO	International Civil Aviation Organization
ICJ Reports	International Court of Justice Reports
ICLQ	International and Comparative Law Quarterly
ILC	International Law Commission
ILM	International Legal Materials
ILO	International Labour Organization
ILR	International Law Reports
IMF	International Monetary Fund
ITU	International Telecommunications Union
IYIL	The Italian Yearbook of International Law
J. Common Mkt. Stud.	Journal of Common Market Studies
JCP	Jurisclasseur périodique
JDI	Journal de droit international
JOCE	Journal officiel de la Communauté européenne
JORF	Journal officiel de la République française
Journal of the ICJ	Journal of the International Commission of Jurists
JWT	Journal of World Trade
Law.Soc.Gaz.	Law Society Gazette
LDC	Less developed country
LIEI	Legal Issues of European Integration
LLDC	Least developed country
LQR	Law Quarterly Review
MEP	Member of European Parliament
MFN	Most Favored Nation
Mich.J.Int'l L.	Michigan Journal of International Law
Mich. LR	Michigan Law Review

MLR	Modern Law Review
MPE	Membre du Parlement européen
NATO	North Atlantic Treaty Organization
NGO	Non-governmental organization
NILR	Netherlands International Law Review
NJ	Nederlandse Jurisprudentie
NJW	Neue Juristische Wochenschrift
NLJ	New Law Journal
NVwZ	Neue Zeitschrift für Verwaltungsrecht
NYIL	Netherlands Yearbook of International Law
OAS	Organization of American States
OAU	Organization of African Unity
OCDE	Organisation de coopération et de développement économique
O.E.A.	Organisation des Etats américains
OECD	Organization for Economic Cooperation and Development
OJ	Official Journal of the European Community
O.L.P.	Organisation pour la libération de la Palestine
ÖJZ	Österreichische Juristen-Zeitung
ONG	Organisation non gouvernementale
O.N.U.	Organisation des Nations Unies
O.T.A.N.	Organisation du traité de l'Atlantique Nord
O.U.A.	Organisation de l'unité africaine
PCIJ Reports	Permanent Court of International Justice Reports
PE Doc.	Documents du parlement européen
PLO	Palestine Liberation Organization
P.V.D.	Pays en voie de développement
QB	Queen's Bench (U.K. Law Reports)
RabelsZ	Rabels Zeitschrift für ausländisches und internationales Privatrecht
RAE	Revue des affaires européennes
RBDI	Revue belge de droit international
RdC	Recueil des Cours de l'Académie de droit international de la Haye
RDE	Rivista di diritto europeo
RDH/HRJ	Revue des droits de l'homme/Human Rights Journal
RDI	Rivista di diritto internazionale
Reg.	regulation; règlement
Res.	resolution; résolution
RGDIP	Revue générale de droit international public
RHDI	Revue hellénique de droit international

RIDC	Revue internationale de droit comparé
RIW	Recht der Internationalen Wirtschaft
RMC	Revue du marché commun
RMT	Rechtsgeleerd Magazjin Themis
RSDIE	Revue suisse de droit international et de droit européen
RTDE	Revue trimestrielle de droit européen
RUDH	Révue universelle des droits de l'homme
SEA	Single European Act
Série A	Publication de la Com.EDH: Arrêts et décisions
Série B	Publication de la Com.EDH: Mémoires, plaidoiries, documents
SEW	Social-Economische Wetgeving
S.M.E.	Système monétaire européen
Stb	Staatsblad van het koninkrijk der Nederland
Syr.J.Int.L. and Comm.	Syracuse Journal of International Law and Commerce
UN	United Nations
UNCTAD	United Nations Conference on Trade and Development
UNESCO	United Nations Educational, Scientific and Cultural Organization; Organisation des Nations Unies pour l'éducation, la science et la culture
UNTS	United Nations Treaty Series
UNY	United Nations Yearbook
U.S.C.A.	United States Courts of Appeals
Va.J.Int'l.L.	Virginia Journal of International Law
Vand.J.Trans.L.	Vanderbilt Journal of Transnational Law
WEU	Western European Union
WIPO	World Intellectual Property Organization
WHO	World Health Organization
WuW	Wirtschaft und Wettbewerb
YB	Yearbook of the European Convention on Human Rights
YEL	Yearbook of European Law
ZaöRV	Zeitschrift für ausländisches öffentliches Recht und Völkerrecht
ZERP	Zentrum für Europäische Rechtspolitik
ZfZ	Zeitschrift für Zölle und Verbrauchssteuern
ZHR	Zeitschrift für das gesamte Handelsrecht
ZRP	Zeitschrift für Rechtspolitik

Winston Churchill Lecture on the Council of Europe

Academy of European Law (ed.),
Collected Courses of the Academy of European Law, Volume II, Book 2, 1–20.

On the Road to a European Constitutional Court

by

ROLV RYSSDAL

Biography

Born 27 October 1914 in Bergen, Norway

Education:

1939	–	Law degree (cand.jur.), University of Oslo

Main positions held:

1939-1940	–	Assistant Advocate, Oslo
1940-1941	–	Judge at the Office of the District Judge in Eiker, Modum and Sigdal
1941-1943	–	Legal Counsellor, Legal Division, Ministry of Supply
1945-1948	–	Acting State Advocate, Office of the Director General of Public Prosecutions
1947-1952	–	University fellowship in jurisprudence, University of Oslo
1948	–	Supreme Court Advocate
1948-1956	–	Private law practice as a Supreme Court Advocate in Oslo
1956-1964	–	Secretary-General, Ministry of Justice
1964-1969	–	Supreme Court Justice
1969-1984	–	Chief Justice of the Supreme Court
1973-present	–	Judge on the European Court of Human Rights, Strasbourg
1981-1985	–	Vice-President of the European Court of Human Rights
1985-present	–	President of the European Court of Human Rights

Introduction

Your invitation to me, as the President of the European Court of Human Rights, to conclude this year's study programme on the protection of human rights in Europe by delivering the prestigious Winston Churchill lecture is a great honour not only for me personally but for the European Court of Human Rights as a whole, and I should like to thank the European University Institute and its Academy of European Law most warmly for giving me this opportunity.

You are fortunate to have had the opportunity of following a week long general course on the protection of human rights in Europe given by my colleague and friend Carl Aage Nørgaard, the President of the European Commission of Human Rights. To speak after him, in order to bring to a close your study programme, makes my task in some respects easier because I can take it for granted that you now have a clear and comprehensive understanding of the guarantees and the functioning of the European Convention on Human Rights. On the other hand, it is, I must confess, not without a certain apprehension that I take the floor at this juncture because I am very well aware of how difficult it is to keep the attention of an audience which has had the privilege of hearing Carl Aage Nørgaard on more or less the same subject. There are however two factors which I hope will be of assistance to me. First, a Winston Churchill lecture, as I understand it, is required to offer a prospective view on the subject-matter, and I shall therefore concentrate on the future of human rights protection in Europe. Secondly, even if in so doing I deal with points already covered by the President of the European Commission, you may find some interest in hearing how they are viewed by the President of the second institution set up under the European Convention on Human Rights.

I.

1. More than forty years ago the European Convention on Human Rights and Fundamental Freedoms was signed in Rome. Thirty-seven years ago, nearly to the day, the European Commission of Human Rights held its first session and more than thirty-two years ago the European Court of Human Rights was established. Today, all the member States of the Council of Europe, with the temporary exception of Hungary and Czechoslovakia, have ratified the Convention, accepted the right of individual petition to the Commission and recognised the compulsory jurisdiction of the Court. Furthermore, in most of the Contracting States the legislative, executive and judicial branches of Government regularly consider the Convention and the case-law of the Court before embarking on action having repercussions on

the fundamental rights and freedoms of the citizen. In addition, the Court of Justice of the European Communities in Luxembourg treats the Convention as interpreted and applied by the Court in Strasbourg as an integral part of the law of the European Community.

The European Convention on Human Rights and Fundamental Freedoms of 4 November 1950, which, I would add in passing, served as a model for the American Convention of Human Rights and in certain respects also for the African Charter of Human and Peoples' Rights, is thus part of the constitutional landscape of modern Europe. By virtue of the Convention, the Contracting States undertake to secure to everyone within their jurisdiction those rights and freedoms which are laid down in the Convention itself or in its Protocols. To ensure that the engagements undertaken by the Contracting Parties are observed, the Convention set up control machinery and conferred on the Contracting States and individuals a right of application in respect of alleged breaches of the Convention. Such applications undergo first a preliminary examination in the Commission; thereafter they may be referred for adjudication to the Court which decides by a final and binding judgment not only as to the merits but also, where appropriate, on the award of 'just satisfaction' to the victim of a violation.

2. Women and men in our countries have become aware of the guarantees and the means of redress which the Convention offers them. Two sets of figures graphically illustrate this: the number of applications registered by the Commission was 390 in 1980, 596 in 1985 and 1,657 in 1990, while 8 cases were referred to the Court in 1980, 12 in 1985 and 61 five years later.

The reasons for such a substantial increase are doubtless manifold and careful analysis is needed to fully explain this progression. Evidently, it has something to do with the fact that over the last ten years more and more States have joined the Council of Europe and accepted the Convention, as well as the right of individual petition to the Commission and the compulsory jurisdiction of the Court. But there is also a more fundamental reason. It certainly cannot be said that the rights of the individual are today more frequently disregarded within the Council of Europe member States. Many of the applications to the Convention institutions may rather be explained by the fact that citizens, who are now generally more conscious of their individual rights than ever before, believe that a European remedy is the best remedy for their grievances. Indeed, it is not surprising that in our 'shrinking' and homogeneous society at the end of the 20th Century the citizen should seek this supranational route. This is an indication of the evolution that the Convention has undergone since its inception after the war as a response to the horror and terror which were experienced under Fascism and Nazism in Europe, and as a bulwark against new totalitarian regimes.

The Convention has become the embryo of a European Constitution, to borrow a formula used by Giulio Andreotti last year in Rome and by Francesco Cossiga when he visited our Court two months ago. Thanks to the firm anchoring of effective political democracy on our continent, the Convention institutions do not nowadays have to deal with gross violations of human rights as occurred in Europe in the 30's and 40's and still occur in too many parts of the world. The typical issue brought before the Commission and the Court is more of a constitutional nature: it embraces the age-long and sensitive problem of the balance to be struck between the general interest of the community and the protection of the individual's fundamental rights. This is how the Convention and its institutions contribute today to the process of creating the United Europe urged by Winston Churchill in 1947 and set into motion by Robert Schuman, Alcide De Gasperi, Paul-Henri Spaak and Konrad Adenauer.

3. It follows that all those who have responsibility for the functioning and operation of the Convention system, and in particular the member States of the Council of Europe, have a duty to look to the future and to develop ideas for ensuring that human rights protection in Europe remains effective beyond the end of the century. Two major events in recent times have made it abundantly clear that it has become a matter of urgency to reflect on the future of the European Convention on Human Rights. First, 40 to 45 years after the Second World War, the dissolution of the Soviet Empire following the unmasking of communist ideology opens the way for the unification of Europe as a whole. At the same time, as a result of the unflagging efforts of the Commission in Brussels under its President Jacques Delors, the European Community is beginning to move forward from economic cooperation and integration towards the goal of Political Union.

In view of those two developments – history may well confirm that the second was a major cause of the first –, the human rights' community of the European Convention has to confront three principal risks: firstly, the risk of a proliferation of international or European human rights protection systems; secondly, the risk of having a catalogue of human rights which is not adapted to present and future requirements; and finally the risk of a petrified organisational structure which is no longer able to afford adequate protection of the rights and freedoms guaranteed. These are genuine problems and have to be faced if we wish to save the Convention system from being bled dry. What better occasion than this Winston Churchill lecture to put forward once again before a prominent and highly qualified audience committed to the European process my modest thoughts on the challenges before us.

II.

4. Today the great majority of the Contracting States of the European Convention on Human Rights are at the same time Contracting Parties to the International Covenant on Civil and Political Rights and many of them have accepted the competence of the Human Rights Committee to receive communications by a State Party against another State Party under Article 41 of the Covenant and a right to individual petition in accordance with the provisions of the Optional Protocol to the Covenant. Those Convention States may therefore be required to answer for their decisions and actions not only in Strasbourg but also before the control body set up under the United Nations Covenant. Their authorities and in particular their courts have to apply the provisions of the Convention and those of the Covenant wherever these international treaties are part of the law of the land. This double jeopardy situation has not in fact led to confusion harmful to the (more binding) European system, probably because citizens wishing to lodge a human rights complaint against Convention countries still feel that their needs are best accommodated by the judicial process available under the European Convention.

The hard-earned achievements in the field of human rights protection in Europe are now under threat from two new ideas, whose proponents, I fear, fail to grasp the potential of thc European Convention on Human Rights. These ideas are: the setting up of a new international system of human rights protection within the context of the Conference on Security and Co-operation in Europe, and the move to provide the European Communities or the forthcoming Political Union with their own catalogue of human rights and freedoms.

5. Basket Three of the Final Act of the Helsinki Conference adopted on 1 August 1975 has undoubtedly played an essential role in the process of re-establishing democratic society in Central and Eastern Europe, not least because of its linkage with the other Baskets and despite its use of somewhat imprecise language. The political situation today is, however, rather different from the situation in 1975: Germany is reunited, Hungary and Czechoslovakia have become democratic States, joined the Council of Europe and signed the European Convention on Human Rights. Poland, it seems, will follow quite soon, while Yugoslavia, Roumania, Bulgaria and the Soviet Union, which have been granted special guest status with the Parliamentary Assembly of the Council of Europe, are endeavouring to establish political pluralism and to secure obedience to the rule of law. In these circumstances there is no need to develop the human rights programme of the Helsinki Conference into a new Pan-European system of collective enforcement. Winston Churchill's idea of setting up a Council of

Europe was intended to apply to the whole of Europe; equally the European Convention on Human Rights was seen by its founding fathers, and notably Pierre-Henri Teitgen, as a constitutional text for all the States on our continent. Joining the Council of Europe and acceding to the European Convention on Human Rights is the right path; which has already been taken by Hungary and Czechoslovakia and that is the way open to all the other States of Central and Eastern Europe which are determined to accept political democracy.

A further European system for safeguarding human rights would certainly have to be welcomed if integration into the already existing system of States from Central and Eastern Europe were not possible, or if the new system could provide markedly better protection than that available under our Convention. However, the adoption of the European Convention on Human Rights of 1950 was a unique development and indeed a revolution in international law, which came about as a result of a general feeling that, in view of the then recent history, protection of human rights could no longer be considered to be exclusively a matter between the citizen and his or her State. Today, when the Second World War and the holocaust are, for an increasing number of our fellow citizens, receding into history, any attempt to set up a new system for protecting human rights in Europe runs a serious risk of creating something which falls far short of the machinery of binding judicial review established by the Council of Europe Convention.

I would suggest that all those who doubt that it is possible to integrate the States of Eastern and Central Europe into the Convention system look to the examples of Hungary and Czechoslovakia. Those two States, which are receiving all possible technical assistance from the Council of Europe, are at present preparing themselves for early ratification of the Convention. It is not clear why the same should not be possible for other States from that part of Europe wishing to join the common European home. It may be necessary to wait a little longer for one State than for another, and indeed transitional arrangements may have to be made. The Paris Charter, which recognises the achievements of the Council of Europe in the field of human rights, speaks of 'new procedures', with reference to the 'involvement' of individuals in the protection of human rights, of 'services of experts' and, in particular, of a 'roster of eminent persons'. If this is meant to be a preparatory step to the integration of the States concerned into the European Convention system, the 'new procedures' and 'services of experts' should be linked to the Council of Europe, in which case the 'roster' could very well be composed of members of the European Commission and Court of Human Rights. In any event it is to be hoped that at the Third CSCE Conference on the Human Dimension in Moscow, the Council of Europe and its member States will proclaim unequivocally the vocation of the European Convention of 1950 as the human rights system for the whole of Europe.

6. A further problem arises within the context of the European Communities and the forthcoming Political Union. In the absence of a specific Community catalogue of human rights and fundamental freedoms, the Court of Justice in Luxembourg secures the protection of the individual, with reference, *inter alia*, to the European Convention on Human Rights and the case-law of the Court in Strasbourg. That pragmatic and flexible solution offers a good prospect of ensuring that the human rights standards within the European Community and those of the Convention community of States do not drift apart, but it evidently does not exclude the possibility of a conflict between the Strasbourg approach to the Convention and the Luxembourg approach.

One answer to the problem posed by the absence of human rights guarantees within the Community framework is the enacting of a specific catalogue of fundamental rights and freedoms for the European Community citizen. However, the result of such an enactment would be the development on our continent of two independent human rights orders, with all the damaging consequences that that would entail; consequences which inevitably follow the introduction of rival sets of rules in an otherwise homogeneous community; consequences which are especially detrimental in the field of human rights and freedoms. In any case, a catalogue of fundamental rights for the Communities and the Political Union would presumably not preclude the Convention institutions from reviewing, should the occasion arise, the compatibility of a Community measure with the Convention provisions. It is difficult to accept that the Contracting States of the Convention should be in a position to shed their Convention obligations simply as a consequence of transferring certain of their competences to an international organisation.

I gather that the European Commission of Human Rights adopts basically the same approach to this issue. However, I have some difficulty in reconciling with such an approach the Commission's recent decision that a complaint of breach of Article 6 of the Convention was incompatible *ratione materiae* with the Convention provisions on the ground that the Luxembourg Court, in the exercise of its jurisdiction to review Community measures from a human-rights standpoint, had found that the applicant had received a fair hearing.[1] Whatever the rationale for that decision I think that it must not be construed as generally barring the way to the Convention institutions for an applicant who complains of a breach of his human rights by a member State deriving from a Community measure. There is in any event a second situation where Community law can and indeed must come under the review of the Convention institutions; namely where refer-

1 Eur. Comm H.R., decision of 9 February 1990, application No. 13258/87, *M.* v. *Federal Republic of Germany*; for a brief discussion of this decision see also Frowein, *AEL* Vol. I Book 2, 306.

ence is made in the Convention to the law of the Contracting States, because in the EC member States Community law forms part of domestic law. Lawfulness of detention, lawfulness of interferences with the right to respect for private and family life, with the freedoms of thought, conscience and religion, of expression, of peaceful assembly and of association, or with the right of property – these are some of those areas where the Commission and Court in Strasbourg have to consider whether the measure complained of has a legal basis in domestic law and also, should the occasion arise, whether it has the substantive quality of a democratic 'law' required under the Convention.

Given that situation, it is not surprising that Jacques Delors, known as he is for his commitment to the idea of a united Europe and his far-sightedness, should have come back to a proposal launched several years ago: that the Community should accede to the Convention. This suggestion was endorsed in the Commission communication of 19 November 1990 on Community accession to the European Convention which emphasises that it has become increasingly difficult to separate the protection of human rights from Community activities. It is indeed understandable that the Community should wish to be present in the Convention institutions if in one way or another its measures are to be subject to their review.

Accession of the Community to the Convention is surely the right way. It would not only serve to fill the conspicuous gap in the Community's legal order in that the Community is not subject to the Convention's control mechanism, but would also be the surest way to avoid the separate development of two different European standards of human rights protection, in an area where common standards are essential.

7. It is true that the accession to the Convention of States from Central and Eastern Europe and of the European Community will expose certain weaknesses in the present Convention system and aggravate several problems which have been apparent for some time. The answer to those problems is a flexible adaptation of the Convention by way of additional and amending protocols.

III.

8. Forty years after the adoption of the Convention, the case-law of the European Court of Human Rights has addressed nearly all the provisions of the Convention. The fact that the Convention is worded in broad and general terms has enabled it to remain over the years a 'living instrument' which can be and is interpreted by the Court in the light of present-day con-

ditions. That approach, which makes it possible to adapt the Convention provisions, of course has its limits: new rights cannot be created by judicial interpretation of the Convention. To expand the existing catalogue of rights and freedoms, additional protocols to the Convention are needed. Four such protocols have been adopted since the Convention was signed in 1950; Protocol No. 6, which abolishes the death penalty at least in time of peace, is an important recent addition.

Technological, social and political development on our continent over the last few years has brought to light a number of gaps in the Convention's net of protection – albeit not genuinely new ones – to which an appropriate remedy on the European level seems possible only if further specific provisions are added to the Convention. The successful Seventh International Colloquy on the Convention organised last year by the Secretary General of the Council of Europe, Catherine Lalumière, together with the Nordic Institutes of Human Rights, was the occasion for an impressive analysis of those fields where future action of the Council of Europe is needed. It is to be hoped that the Council of Europe will now be given the necessary means to enable it to follow up with vigour the conclusions of that Colloquy, which I myself had the honour to present.

You will therefore forgive me if today I simply refer to the papers of the Colloquy and confine myself to a few remarks on three areas to which I attach special importance, namely treatment of prisoners, the protection of social and economic rights and the protection of minorities.

9. Treatment of prisoners and persons otherwise detained merits particular attention. It seems more than appropriate to dwell on this point here, on the home territory of our friend Antonio Cassese, who chairs the European Committee for the Prevention of Torture and Inhuman or Degrading Treatment or Punishment. I have just received the first general report of his Committee and should like to take this opportunity to congratulate him on the remarkable achievement involved in setting up the Committee in such a short time, but in particular on the efficiency with which the Committee has commenced its activities during its first year of existence.

The European Convention on Human Rights contains no specific provision regarding treatment of detainees comparable, for instance, to Article 10 of the UN Covenant on Civil and Political Rights. Article 3 of the Convention which prohibits torture and inhuman and degrading punishment and treatment will come into play in serious cases, but is probably of no assistance in relation to lesser problems concerning prison life. It is true that penitentiary administration in our countries has become more and more sensitive to the question of the day-to-day conditions of detention, which are dealt with in detail in the European Prison Rules. Those Rules are, however, not compulsory or binding in character. It is now generally accepted that prisoners need safeguards to protect them against the specific dangers to which they are exposed by reason of their being completely dependent on the persons who organise their everyday existence, by reason of their physical, social and legal situation.

Three years ago I was invited by the Steering Committee for Human Rights of the Council of Europe to an exchange of views on possible improvements to be made to the functioning of the Convention. On that occasion I expressed the opinion that the penal policy of our countries was now sufficiently uniform to warrant giving some of the European Prison Rules the form of a binding guarantee secured under the Convention. The question was subsequently taken up as one of the topics for consideration at the Seventh International Colloquy, to which I have just referred, where the discussions reiterated the call to reinforce, on the European level, the international protection of persons deprived of their liberty, in particular in relation to prison conditions. One view expressed by many of the participants at this Colloquy – including myself, I should add – was that thought should be given to the idea of drawing up an additional protocol providing for the inclusion in the European Convention of a provision modelled on Article 10 of the International Covenant. I am pleased to hear that last month the Steering Committee for Human Rights instructed a Sub-Committee to examine, as a matter of priority, the feasibility of preparing a draft protocol concerning conditions of deprivation of liberty and treatment of detainees.

10. More effective protection of social and economic rights represents one of the most important goals for the forthcoming years. Civil and political rights, on the one hand, and social and economic rights, on the other, are interdependent. The proper exercise of the first category of human rights is hardly conceivable if economic and social rights are not also protected.

It is true that social and economic rights are often considered to be of a different category from civil and political rights and therefore unsuited to be brought within the scope of the judicial mechanism of the European Convention. The Court itself answered that argument as early as 1979 in its much quoted *Airey* judgment, where it held that there was no water-tight division separating the sphere of social and economic rights from the field covered by the Convention. Indeed even the present catalogue of rights and freedoms protected under the Convention is not concerned solely with the *status negativus*, but includes certain rights which may be classified as social and economic guarantees. It suffices to mention the right to form and to join trade unions or the right of property. Several provisions of the Convention, such as Article 6 §3, give the individual a right to claim services or even payment from a Contracting State, while others have been construed by the Court as imposing on the State positive obligations. The democratic society which the Convention presupposes and is intended to secure, must clearly be a society which is committed to social responsibility and social justice. This is also evident from the Court's case-law, although the Commission and Court may not yet have exhausted this concept in relation to the interpretation and application of the rights and freedoms guaranteed under the Convention.

The failure of earlier attempts to add social and economic rights to the Convention should therefore not be discouraging. The Italian judge on the Court in Strasbourg, my friend Carlo Russo, suggested last year in Lund that the Council of Europe should undertake a thorough study to identify which rights in the Social Charter are today justiciable, and thus capable of being transposed into the Convention system of judicial protection. Judge Russo is doubtless right to advocate a move from generalities to concrete action in relation to specific economic and social rights. The right and freedom to exercise a profession as guaranteed under the constitutions of many member States of the Council of Europe could very well be a suitable subject for a first additional protocol to the European Convention on Human Rights in this field. It is to be hoped that Judge Russo's call will be heard and that the Ministerial Conference which is to be held in the autumn in Turin on the occasion of the 30th Anniversary of the signing of the Social Charter will take up this issue.

11. The protection of minorities, which hitherto was the subject of discussion in the member States of the Council of Europe only occasionally, has become a matter of major concern since the collapse of the communist regimes in Central and Eastern Europe. It was the CSCE which provided our sister States in that part of our continent with the opportunity to raise the matter of special guarantees for minorities.

We are now confronted with the question how to preserve, through international regulations, the identity of minorities and at the same time alleviate frictions between minorities and States. Here again the Seventh International Colloquy on the Convention gave a clear answer: non-discrimination and individual rights may not be sufficient to meet the needs of minorities: special rights and preferential treatment are necessary to afford minorities appropriate safeguards to preserve their own characteristics and traditions.

The European Convention on Human Rights as it now stands would not appear to be capable of addressing the problem of minorities in its entirety. There is nothing to preclude the insertion into the Convention, by way of an additional protocol, of those rights which are deemed necessary to ensure the protection sought. However, a detailed study of all the problems involved seems necessary before specific proposals as to the contents of such a Protocol can be made. If such a study concluded in favour of justiciable rights, the interests of a coherent and efficient European constitutional human rights order would require that preference be given to the well-established, existing Convention system, over new legal instruments and new control machinery.

IV.

12. Over the coming years we must therefore work towards supplementing the Convention where lacunae have become apparent. There is no doubt, however – and this is now generally accepted – that, parallel to that process of 'up-dating' the normative provisions of the Convention, a radical reform of its control machinery is necessary. The steadily increasing work-load of the Convention institutions makes it more and more difficult for members of the Commission and the Court to reconcile their duties in Strasbourg with their other activities. To take the example of my colleagues at the Court: they already need on average 135 days per year for their work in Strasbourg, and that figure is likely to increase. Up to now, in spite of its growing work-load, the Court has been able to decide cases brought before it within an average of some 12 to 15 months. However, there is an acute awareness that the length of the Strasbourg proceedings from the introduction of an application to the Commission until the final judgment of the Court is too long, and that the authority of the Convention will be jeopardised unless there is a radical change in the enforcement machinery. The challenge is to adapt the control machinery, taking due account of political developments in Central and Eastern Europe, to ensure that cases are processed within reasonable time. A revised Convention structure must have regard to these realities. Since the Court has not yet had the opportunity to discuss the question of reform, I will confine myself to the following tentative, personal observations on the three solutions which are under discussion. These are (1) that the Commission and the Court should become permanent; (2) the setting up of a two-court system and (3) the creation of a single court.

13. The first solution has an advantage which is by no means negligible: it could be achieved fairly easily and rapidly. To make the Commission and the Court permanent institutions, otherwise functioning within the present framework of the Convention, requires no more than adequate funding. It can also be expected that proceedings under the Convention would on the whole be shorter if the Commission and Court could sit on a permanent basis. However, the conferring of permanent status on the institutions will not in itself help to overcome the complexity of the present control machinery: under the Convention, two independent institutions were set up, one of

which is primarily competent to consider the admissibility of applications, while the other has jurisdiction to decide finally on the merits. To understand fully this special structure, it should be recalled that in 1950 the creation of a court as a control body under the Convention did not meet with the agreement of all the member States of the Council of Europe. Today one must ask whether it is really the best solution to continue with a system that requires cases to be examined by two institutions, one of which serves more or less as a filter for the other. Such separation involves a duplication of effort and an in-built factor of delay. It is also, of course, a drain on resources. Furthermore, with the likelihood that, after Hungary and Czechoslovakia, more new European democracies will join the Council of Europe and ratify the Convention, it may be questioned whether it is reasonable to envisage a permanent Commission and Court, each with perhaps thirty members.

14. Under the second solution the Commission would operate as a court of first instance. Individual applicants and States would be accorded the right to appeal to the Court against the Commission's decision, possibly subject to leave to appeal being granted, a decision which would obviously fall to the appellate court.

The introduction of such a system may have the advantage that it would not necessitate a complete remodelling of the Convention control machinery. Furthermore, an examination of a case at two levels of jurisdiction may enhance the quality and authority of the final decision. Nevertheless, I am afraid that I do not find this proposal convincing, although I believe that, at least to some extent, my friend Carl Aage Nørgaard is in sympathy with it.

The Strasbourg proceedings have to be seen as a last resort in human rights cases. As the Court has said many times, the Convention system is of a subsidiary nature: it is in the first place for the national authorities and in particular for the domestic courts in our countries to secure the protection of the human rights and freedoms set forth in the Convention. This is reflected in the rule that no State has to answer before the Convention bodies before it has had an opportunity to redress the alleged wrong within the context of its own legal order. The practical consequence of this pre-condition is that complaints lodged in Strasbourg will usually have been examined by two or more national courts and, in most Convention States, already under the very same provisions which are later at issue in Strasbourg. In this respect there is an important difference in relation to the usual situation in the European Communities. It is therefore misconceived to point to the establishment of a court of first instance in Luxembourg as a model to be followed in Strasbourg.

The setting up of a Convention control mechanism in the form of two courts – either both having full competence or one having full competence and the other being an appellate court with limited competence – is not likely to meet the challenge of dealing with cases within a reasonable time. It is significant that none of the Contracting States which have instituted a specific judicial mechanism of human rights protection have opted for a system with two levels of jurisdiction.

15. The third solution is the creation of a single court vested, as the courts on our continent traditionally are, with jurisdiction to decide on both the admissibility and the merits of a case brought before it. Such a reform of the control machinery, which would have the advantage of avoiding the delays inherent in a two tier system, would obviously be a radical and substantial one. It requires careful reflection, intellectual ingenuity and imagination. To mention only one aspect, it would be important to retain the possibility of a friendly settlement procedure, which has proved so valuable in proceedings before the Commission.

16. The question of reform of the Convention machinery was placed on the agenda of the Vienna Ministerial Conference in March 1985 which was followed by the productive colloquy which Olivier Jacot-Guillarmod organised in Neuchâtel two years later. Several years have passed since then and the enlargement and possible further enlargement of the Convention community following the recent political developments in Central and Eastern Europe have made it quite plain that a solution has to be found in the near future. The problem is currently under examination within the Council of Europe Steering Committee for Human Rights. Without underestimating in any way the difficulty of its task, I hope very much that the Committee will be able to report soon, so that Commission and Court will have sufficient opportunity and time to study and comment on the results of its work. The reform of the Convention system has indeed become a matter of urgency. In any event an appropriate solution will have to be found so as to maintain the effectiveness of the Convention system in the face of all the attendant difficulties, not least those which the growth and very success of the system are generating.

V.

This brings my observations to a close. My intention was to present to you some of the most important problems which we are facing today in the Convention community. Whether after the turn of the century the Convention system will remain the basic constitutional instrument for our Europe, which it is at present will depend on the response which we are able to give to those problems. Far-sightedness is needed and in this respect too there is no better example than Sir Winston Churchill who, at the very first session of the Consultative Assembly of the Council of Europe, on 17 August 1949, expressed the hope that 'once the foundation of human rights is agreed', 'a European Court might be set up, before which cases of the violation of these rights' 'might be brought to the judgment of the civilised world'. The Court exists today, as envisaged by Winston Churchill. It is now our responsibility to make sure that it will succeed on the way to becoming a European Constitutional Court.

General Course
The Protection of Human Rights in Europe

by

CARL AAGE NØRGAARD

Academy of European Law (ed.),
Collected Courses of the Academy of European Law, Volume II, Book 2, 21–97.

Table of Contents

Biography

Carl Aage Nørgaard.

Born: 15 September 1924.

1954: Candidatus juris (LL.M.), University of Aarhus.

1954-55: Law studies at Cambridge.

1955-64: Assistant Professor of Law, University of Aarhus.

1958-59: Law studies at Geneva.

1962: Dr Juris (*The Position of the Individual in International Law*).

1964: Professor of Law, University of Aarhus.

Member of the European Commission on Human Rights from 1973 to present and continuing. Vice-president from 1975 to 1981. President since 1981.

Member and chairman of various Danish Law preparing Committees.

Director of Institute of Public Law University of Aarhus 1964-86.

Independent legal adviser for the United Nations concerning the release of political prisoners in Namibia 1989-90.

Principal Publications

The Position of the Individual in International Law (1962).

Forvaltningsret. Sagsbehandling (Administrative Law Procedure) (1972, 2nd ed., 1981, 3rd ed., 1988) (together with J. Garde).

Administration og Borger (Administration and Citizen) (1973, 2nd ed., 1984, 3rd ed. 1988) (together with C.Haagen Jensen).

Author of a number of articles on Human Rights and on Danish Administrative law in Danish and international legal periodicals.

Introduction

The General Course on the Law of Human Rights in Europe at the second session of the Academy of European Law, European University Institute, Florence 1991, was attended by about 100 students mainly from European countries.

The group of students attending the course was not a homogeneous one. Some of the students had already studied Human Rights in detail whereas others had had little experience in this field. The aim, therefore, was to give, during 10 lectures, the inexperienced a basic knowledge and the experienced more profound insight.

In order to achieve this aim the first and rather extensive part of the course was devoted to a description of the practical daily work within Convention organs – especially the Commission – and their Secretariats.

The second part of the course dealing with the material rules of the Convention was based on the analysis of a number of illustrative cases without attempting to give a comprehensive description of the entire case-law. The purpose of presenting the rules of the Convention in this way provide both basic knowledge and an illustration of the methods of interpretation applied by the Convention organs. At the same time the development of the Convention institutions and the laws emanating from them became evident.

The present paper is not supposed to be a written repetition of what was said during the lectures. Nevertheless the main outline will be the same. As in the lectures, a considerable part of this study will be devoted to the practical daily work and the procedure followed by the Convention organs with special emphasis on important elements such as friendly settlement and interim measures.

The reason for this choice is that these problems have not been dealt with in the existing books and papers on Human Rights to the same extent as the case-law. Experience shows, however, that a detailed knowledge of the procedures is important, both for lawyers representing applicants, for government representatives, and for legal writers, and that lack of knowledge of the procedures sometimes creates unnecessary mistakes.

Instead of a chapter on the material rules and the case-law, the other main part of the present study will treat the question of the effect of the Convention and the case-law in the Member States of the Council of Europe. The reason for this choice is that the effects of the Convention and the case-law within the states appear to be a most important aspect of the whole Convention system, which has not been dealt with in the doctrine to the same extent as the material rules.

It is not the intention here to set up a bibliography in this field nor to refer extensively to the existing literature. As a few examples of the many outstanding textbooks, however, mention could be made of the late Sir James Fawcett's classical work: *The Application of the European Convention on Human Rights*; Frowein and Peukert: *Europäische Menschenrechtskonvention*; and the most recent text, Velu et Ergec: *La convention européenne des droits de l'homme*, which also contains a very extensive and useful up-to-date bibliography.

Before dealing with the main subject 'The Protection of Human Rights in Europe' the concept of Human Rights will briefly be discussed, followed by a very brief and by no means exhaustive description of the development of Human Rights and their protection on national and international level.

I. General Background

A. The Concept of Human Rights

The idea that every individual has some fundamental and inherent rights which should not be interfered with by those in power in the national states is not a new one. Without using the notion of Human Rights this idea has been expressed in legal texts dating nearly 4,000 years back, such as Hammurabi's famous laws from about 1700 BC. The same idea was expressed by philosophers such as Platon and Aristoteles and again in many religions, for instance in Christianity.

Today the concept of Human Rights may have many different meanings for different people in different contexts, and it would hardly be possible to find one generally accepted definition.

In colloquial language the term Human Rights seems to be a very popular one which is used more and more often, simply to describe something which a person using the term finds desirable. Some would, for instance, consider it a human right to have good railway connections with decent seats for all passengers. Others might claim a human right to have access to public libraries.

When the term Human Rights is used in professional or technical language it may have different meanings depending on its context. For instance, if a prisoner is kept in solitary confinement for a long period this may raise a problem of human rights seen from a legal point of view. At the same time the same phenomena may raise human rights problems from a medical, psychiatric point of view, a criminal preventive point of view, and a social point of view without the concept of Human Rights necessarily being applied with the same substantive elements.

In order to apply the concept of Human Rights as a legal term at least two conditions must be fulfilled. First, it must be possible linguistically to formulate the Rights as rules and, secondly, someone, typically the states, must be under a legal duty to respect the rules. To these two conditions it would, however, be desirable to add a third when applying Human Rights in a legal context; namely that the possibility to enforce the rules should exist.

Even if the concept of Human Rights is applied as a legal concept as, for example, in international legal texts and instruments, the concept covers a wide range of rights which differ widely with regard to clarity, responsibility and enforcement.

Human Rights are often classified in legal writings in three main groups.

1) Traditional civil and political rights such as the right to life, the right to personal liberty, and the right to freedom of expression.

   These rights are all individual rights, they can be and are clearly described in legal rules, the State normally is responsible for violation of these rights, and the rights can normally be enforced on the national level and often on the international level.

2) Economic and social rights, such as the right to a decent standard of living, the right to work, and the right to rest.

   Again these rights are individual rights, they can be and are formulated as legal rules, they are, however, only enforceable to a lesser extent than the rights in the first group.

3) The third group is composed of a number of essential, but different rights, such as the right to peace, the right to a fair distribution of natural resources between peoples, and the right to a decent environment.

   These rights can hardly be characterized as individual rights, but must be considered collective rights. They are not, and can hardly be, formulated as legal rules with the same precision as the first two groups, and they are at present enforceable to a much lesser extent than the first two groups.

The above mentioned three groups of Human Rights are often labelled as the first, second, and third generation of Human Rights. This terminology, although commonly used, does not appear to be an adequate one. The word 'generation' normally denotes the single steps in family descent or all persons born on about the same time. It is, of course, true that the three groups of rights have been recognized as such at different times, the political and civil rights first, and the third group most recently. The groups, however, continue to co-exist; the 'older' generations have not died out and been replaced by 'younger' rules.

The more important distinction seems to be the fact that there is a difference between civil and political rights and economic and social rights on the one hand, and the third group on the other. The two first groups are typically individual rights which in principle could be enforced by individuals, whereas the third group are typically collective rights.

A possible and perhaps more useful terminology would be to simply apply the term Human Rights to the individual rights, namely civil and political rights, and economic and social rights, and to introduce the term Rights of Mankind to describe the third group of rights, such as the right of peace, the right of self-determination, the people's right to the natural resources of their countries, and the right to a healthy environment.

The proposed terminology, however, does not imply any attempt to classify some rights as more important than others. Any such attempt seems useless. Which right is considered most important will probably depend on the situation at a given time in a given place. Beyond doubt, the right to peace may in some situations be more important than anything else, similarly for persons nearly dying from starvation the right to food may be more important than the right to freedom of speech.

As far as the traditional civil and political rights, as enforced for instance in Western Europe, are concerned, it is sometimes alleged that these rights are a luxury in a world where millions in other places are dying from hunger, and thousands are being innocently killed, tortured or ill-treated. It is probably true that the full enjoyment of many of the civil and political rights presupposes a certain economic and social development. On the other hand, civil and political rights also include such fundamental rights as the right to life and freedom from torture and ill-treatment. Secondly, the whole catalogue of civil and political rights are inseparably related to democracy, without these rights no true democracy can exist and only by true democracy everywhere it seems possible to secure all Human Rights and Rights of Mankind throughout the world.

B. National and International Protection of Human Rights

1. National

Until the 18th century the existence of Human Rights was recognized in continental Europe principally in philosophical and legal thinking. On the other hand in England the tradition of common law and particularly the tradition of the judges applying it brought a real protection of the individual against arbitrary acts of the King. As early as 1215 the Magna Carta ensured *inter alia* that unlawful arrest or punishment of a free man was prohibited, and this principle was re-confirmed in the famous Habeas Corpus Act of 1679.

Equipped with such ideas and traditions the American colonists expressed in the Declaration of Independence of 1776 and the Bill of Rights those freedoms which they considered to be the basic rights of man. Apart from the principles relating to a democratic order they were those freedoms which are recognized today as the basic Human Rights including the right to life, liberty, and security of person, the right of the accused in criminal proceedings, freedom of expression, freedom of religion, and of peaceful assembly.

At about the same time the French revolution produced in Europe a similar development, culminating in the French declaration of the Rights of Man of 1789, which contained more or less the same catalogue of rights and freedoms as the American Bill of Rights.

The 19th and the first half of the 20th century marked a period of recognition of such rights on a national level and their incorporation in the national constitutions. Thus a number of rights such as equality before the law, personal liberty, freedom of expression and of religion are included in the French Constitutional Charter of 1840. A catalogue of similar rights is to be found in the Belgian Constitution of 1831, in the Danish Constitution of 1849, in the German Constitution from the same year, and in the Austrian Basic Law of 1887, just to mention a few. Today practically all constitutions in the world contain references to Human Rights and many of them provide a machinery for their enforcement.

2. International

On the international level the protection of Human Rights was nearly nonexistent before the First World War. After that war, however, an important development commenced by the conclusion of several treaties which ensured for minorities a number of fundamental human rights such as the right to life and freedom, the right to free exercise of religion, and the right to elementary education in their own language. The most remarkable of these treaties from the point of view of the protection of Human Rights is the German-Polish Convention of 1922 on Upper Silicia because it contains a detailed system for the protection of the minorities' Human Rights based on individual petitions. Another notable treaty concluded in this period is the International Convention on the Abolition of Slavery and Slave Trade of 1926.

Most important for the development of the protection of Human Rights in the period between the two World Wars is probably the work performed by the International Labour Organization (ILO). Since its formation in 1919 the ILO has become responsible for the enforcement of more than 100 labour conventions ratified by the ILO member states. These conventions deal with the right to work as such, the right to just and favourable working and living conditions, including fair remuneration, protection of mothers and children, holidays, etc. They deal with trade union rights, the freedom from forced labour, and the equality of opportunity and treatment; that is, non-discriminination in employment. Since 1926 there exists a committee of experts on the application of conventions and recommendations which makes observations and other comments on annual government reports, and another committee on the application of conventions and recommendations which during the general conference of the ILO discusses the report of the committee of experts. The ILO Constitution (Article 26) also contemplates a formal inter-governmental complaints procedure and provides for the creation of a commission of inquiry which functions on a judicial basis.

The major development of the international protection of Human Rights began during and continued after the Second World War. The atrocities committed by Nazi-Germany made it clear that measures had to be taken in order to prevent the recurrence of such crimes, and to ensure the observance of fundamental rights and freedoms in the future. It was also clear that a system of international control and supervision was required to achieve that aim and that international organizations should play a major role in this context.

The General Assembly of the United Nations therefore approved in February 1946 a recommendation that a Commission on Human Rights should be established which should prepare an international Bill of Rights. This Commission began its work in 1947 and decided to proceed in three stages: to prepare a declaration, a convention, and a system of international control and supervision of Human Rights.

The Universal Declaration of Human Rights adopted on 10 December, 1948, by the General Assembly of the United Nations, is today the basic statement of general principles on which all other international Human Rights' instruments are built. Its 30 articles spell out the meaning of the phrase 'Human Rights and Obligations in the UN Charter' and constitute the law which all states should observe.

The next step to prepare a convention was concluded in 1966 by the adoption of the two covenants, the one on economic, social and cultural rights, and the other on civil and political rights which both entered into force ten years later in 1976. Both covenants also make provisions for a system of implementation and thus include the third step contemplated by the Human Rights Commission in 1947.

The main organs for the implementation of the United Nations' system for the protection of Human Rights are the United Nations Human Rights Commission which has existed since 1947, and the United Nations Human Rights Committee which started to operate in 1977. The UN Human Rights

Commission is composed of state representatives and it examines communications, about 30,000 a year, concerning particular situations which appear to reveal a consistent pattern of gross and reliably attested violations of Human Rights. The UN Human Rights Committee is composed of 18 members who sit on the Committee in their individual capacity. It started to operate under the Covenant on Civil and Political Rights in 1977. It examines the state reports submitted to it under Article 40 of the Covenant by holding hearings during which detailed questions are put to representatives of the State whose report is under examination. At the same time it examines individual complaints which have been submitted to it under Article 1 of the optional Protocol.

Apart from these activities of the United Nations themselves, a number of specialized agencies of the United Nations such as the International Labour Organization (ILO), the United Nations Educational, Social and Cultural Organization (UNESCO), the World Health Organization (WHO), and the Food and Agriculture Organization (FAO) engage in activities relating to the protection of Human Rights within their special fields.

3. Regional

Parallel to the activities on the world level, important systems for the protection of Human Rights have been set up in different regions.

The European Convention for the Protection of Human Rights and Fundamental Freedoms of 4 November 1950 will be dealt with in detail below.

In America a similar system was set up by the American Convention on Human Rights (Pact of San José) which was adopted on 22 November 1969 after a special conference sponsored by the Organization of American States (OAS).[1] This Convention is to some extent modelled on the European Convention. Thus the rights guaranteed are the traditional civil and political rights, and the system established for control and supervision with a Commission and a Court is reminiscent of the European system.

The Commission is composed of seven independent members acting in their individual capacity. It does not sit permanently but meets three or more times a year for sessions of approximately two weeks. The Commission is assisted by a permanent staff. The Commission's basic tasks are to deal with State applications and individual applications alleging violations of the Convention, the preparation of country reports of the general

1 Farer, 'Inter-American Commission on Human Rights', in R. Bernhard (ed.), *Encyclopedia of Public International Law* (hereinafter referred to as *Encyclopedia*), *Instalment 8*, 321, and Buergenthal, 'Inter-American Court of Human Rights', in *Encyclopedia, Instalment 8*, 324.

Human Right situation in particular countries, and general promotion of Human Rights by issuing publications and organizing seminars.

The Commission's function in dealing with the petitions submitted to it is to investigate the cases, and if a friendly settlement is not achieved to formulate its conclusions and recommendations. If the State fails to adopt the recommendations, the Commission may publish them along with its conclusions. Finally the Commission may also refer the case to the Inter-American Court of Human Rights.

A very important element in the Commission's work is the carrying out of on-the-spot investigations. During such on-site investigations the Commission receives individual complaints from the area and it speaks *inter alia* with applicants, representatives of professional and social organizations, lawyers, and governmental representatives.

The Inter-American Court of Human Rights is composed of seven independent judges and has both a contentious and an advisory jurisdiction. Under its contentious jurisdiction the Court deals with cases referred to it by States or by the Commission, after the Commission has examined the case. The Court's decisions are binding on the States concerned and in addition to deciding whether there has been a violation, the Court can award damages and indicate the measures that the State must take to remedy the violation.

The African Charter on Human and People's Rights has been prepared within the framework of the Organization of African Unity (OAU). It was adopted 27 June 1981 and entered into force in October 1986.[2] Although the African Charter is inspired both by the European and the American Convention and shows certain similarities with these conventions, there are also remarkable differences. The rights guaranteed in the African Charter include traditional civil and political rights and also economic, social, and cultural rights, such as the right to work, the right to health, and the right to participate in cultural life.

The Charter, however, does not only guarantee individual rights but also a special category of collective rights, namely 'People's Rights'. This includes the right of peoples to be treated on the basis of equality and not to be dominated by other peoples, the right to self-determination, to dispose of their wealth and natural resources, to develop their economic, social, and cultural conditions, and to enjoy peace and security and a satisfactory environment.

Besides dealing with these rights the African Charter also contains a special chapter on duties of the individual. These duties are not owed only to the State and society as a whole but also to other social institutions

2 Mbaya, 'African Charter on Human and People's Rights', in *Encyclopedia, Instalment 8*, 1.

within and beyond the State, to the family, and to private individuals. The duties include duties towards the family and respect for the maintenance of parents and duties owed to the State and the society; this latter category includes the duty to serve the national community not to compromise State security, the duty to preserve and strengthen social and national solidarity, national independence and territorial integrity, which includes contributing to the defense of the country, and the duty to work and pay taxes. Finally, it lays down duties towards the African Community as a whole such as a duty to preserve and strengthen positive African cultural values, and to contribute to the promotion of African unity.

The task of supervision and control is left to the African Commission of Human and People's Rights, but no court was created under the Charter. The Commission is composed of eleven independent members serving in their personal capacity. The Commission has different functions, firstly to promote Human and People's Rights by *inter alia* collecting information, arranging seminars, disseminating information, and if need be making recommendations to Governments. Secondly, to ensure the protection of Human and People's Rights according to the rules of the Charter, and thirdly, to interpret the provisions of the Charter on the request of a state or the OAU.

In order to ensure the rights of the Charter the Commission may receive communications from a state alleging violations of the Charter by another state. If the Commission, after having examined the complaint, does not succeed in reaching a friendly settlement, it shall prepare a report stating the facts and its findings. This report with the Commission's recommendations shall be sent to the Assembly of Heads of State and Government of the OAU.

The Commission may also receive communications other than state communications. With regard to such communications the Commission first decides which communications shall be considered. If the Commission after a preliminary deliberation finds that a communication relates to special cases which reveal the existence of a series of serious or massive violations of Human and People's Rights, the Commission shall draw the attention of the Assembly of Heads of State and Government to these cases. The Assembly may then request the Commission to undertake an in-depth study of such cases and present its report with its findings and recommendations to the Assembly. The Charter, however, does not provide for any decision binding on the states involved but only for the possibility to publish the Commission's report.

The purpose of the above brief survey of the American and African Conventions has been to indicate that there are both important similarities and differences between the three regional systems and to provide the actual background for the question whether it is desirable to have regional systems for the protection of Human Rights beside the universal United Nations' system. Although Human Rights in principle are and should be the same for every individual in the world, the historic, economic, and cultural backgrounds in various regions of the world are so different that Human Rights may be most efficiently secured and enforced under regional systems which for the time being accept these factual differences.

The oldest system, the European one, with detailed and refined rules for instance with regard to fair trial, might not be as effective today in the American or African states. On the other hand, the important practise with regard to on-the-spot investigations in the American system, which has proved most useful in dealing with serious mass-violations of Human Rights, will hopefully not be necessary as a general practice in Europe.

Turning to the African system, the inclusion of collective rights and social and economic rights in the Charter – understandable and natural against the historical background of this continent – must necessarily involve a less judicial and effective enforcement than under the more limited systems. In spite of the differences between the systems the important fact, however, remains that they are all inspired by the desire to create the best possible protection of Human Rights within the respective regions at a given time.

Given these similarities and differences in the face of the common goal it is obviously desirable that the organs of the three systems cooperate with the purpose of inspiring each other and learning from each other in order to improve the protection of Human Rights within their respective regions. Cooperation during recent years has involved not only exchange of all relevant documents, but also a number of meetings between members of the European Court and Commission and members of the Inter-American Court and Commission as well as with members of the African Commission. These meetings have proved most fruitful and a meeting between members of the organs of all three systems is planned to take place in Strasbourg in June 1992.

II. The European Convention for the Protection of Human Rights and Fundamental Freedoms

A. History and Development[3]

The statute of the Council of Europe of 5 May 1949 expressly recognizes the obligation of each Member State to respect Human Rights and fundamental freedoms. The states accept the principles of the rule of law and the enjoyment by all persons within their jurisdiction of Human Rights and Freedoms. (Statute Article 3).

As one of its first tasks the organs of the Council of Europe, namely the Consultative Assembly and the Committee of Ministers, commenced the work of elaborating the European Convention on Human Rights. As early as September 1949 the Consultative Assembly adopted a draft convention prepared by its legal committee on the basis of a report by P.H. Tietgen, the former French Minister of Justice.

The further elaboration of the Convention text took place in an expert committee under the Committee of Ministers, in a conference of senior officials, in the Committee of Ministers itself and in the Consultative Assembly. The Convention was signed in Rome on 4 November 1950 and entered into force on 3 September 1953 after having been ratified by ten states.

The European Convention on Human Rights consists of a preamble and 66 Articles. The first section (Articles 2-18) contains the material rights which are protected. Sections 2-4 (Articles 19-56) deal with the Commission and the Court, their composition, competence, and procedure. Section 5 (Articles 57-66) contains miscellaneous rules regarding ***inter alia*** reservations, ratifications, denunciations, and entry into force of the Convention.

In view of the speed by which the Convention was drafted, and in view of the development and changes in European society which have taken place during the last forty years, it is surprising how few changes and amendments to the Convention that have been adopted. The amendments have been made by 9 protocols out of which 8 have entered into force after a sufficient number of ratifications (which differ from protocol to protocol) has been deposited. Only Protocol No. 9 had not by the end of 1991 entered into force. Four Protocols (Nos. 1, 4, 6 and 7) add new material rights to those contained in the Convention, whereas the remaining 5 Protocols deal with changes in the procedures within the Convention organs.

In 1991 the Council of Europe had 26 Member States, out of which 23 have ratified the Convention. The three states, which have not yet ratified,

3 Frowein, 'European Convention on Human Rights', in *Encyclopedia, Instalment 8,* 184.

are the three newest Member States, namely Hungary, Czechoslovakia and Poland. They are, however, expected to ratify the Convention in the near future.

The European Convention on Human Rights is a treaty concluded under the rules of public international law. It creates obligations between the states who have ratified it. When it was signed more than forty years ago it heralded two important innovations in public international law:

Classic international law was the law between states. Consequently states were the sole subject of international law whereas no direct relation between that law and individuals existed. Although some developments had taken place in this century, especially after the First World War which in exceptional cases had given the individual a few limited rights under international law, it is still to be considered a remarkable innovation that Convention Article 1 makes it a duty under international law for the states to secure for everybody within their jurisdiction – including their own citizens – the rights and freedoms defined in the Convention.

The second important innovation – which was sensational forty years ago – was the creation of an international control machinery which can make binding decisions in cases concerning Human Rights, not only between states, but also between states and individuals in cases brought by individuals against states.

The question of the position of the individual in international law has been dealt with extensively in the doctrine of international law.[4] It is not the intention here to go through the doctrine or even try to give a summary of it. Apart from describing the actual position of the individual under various relevant treaties, much of the writings and discussions have been concentrating on questions of concepts and definitions such as the question of whether the individual is a subject of international law.

Before discussing the position of the individual under the European Convention on Human Rights it may, however, be useful to advance one or two definitions or descriptions of the subjects of international law, without in any way claiming that they are the only ones, or the only acceptable ones.

In order to be considered a subject of international law the individual must have directly under international law material or substantial rights or duties. Such material rights or duties, however, only become real legal rights if they are combined with sufficient procedural capacity. That is the capacity to enforce the international rights directly before an international court of law or to be held responsible for violating international duties before an international court of law.

4 See for instance C.A. Nørgaard, *The Position of the Individual in International Law* (1962).

If this definition is applied, the question of whether the individual is a subject of law under the European Convention on Human Rights is easy to answer. The first element in the definition creates no problem, the individual clearly has substantial rights directly under the Convention, but it is equally clear that the second condition is not fulfilled, as the individual has no capacity to enforce his or her rights directly before the European Court of Human Rights.

In order to give an adequate description of the position of the individual it is, however, not sufficient to only mention substantial rights and full procedural capacity. The question must be raised whether the individual although not having the perfect procedural position (namely to be able to personally enforce rights before an international court) nevertheless has certain possibilities to bring the question of an alleged violation of international rights before an international organ, for instance the right of petition under international law. The right of petition can be described as the capacity regulated by certain procedures to bring a petition to an international organ which must deal with the petition although it cannot – like a court – make a binding judgment.

The right of petition may differ in its content depending on the powers the organ dealing with the petition has under the treaty or convention by which the system has been established. It is, however, beyond doubt that an individual, who has a legally guaranteed opportunity to have the complaint dealt with by an international organ, has a better position than an individual who has a material international right but no avenue for enforcing the right before an international organ.

Under the most efficient petition systems such as the one established by the European Convention on Human Rights, the individual does not only have a real procedural capacity before the petition organ, here the Commission, but also a real and practical possibility to have his case finally decided by the Court. Although the applicant cannot himself bring his case before the Court this is in reality the situation because the Commission in practice as described below sends all real important cases to the Court. Whether the individual in such a position ought to be characterized as subject of international law or not is a matter of definition which shall not be pursued further.

Nevertheless Protocol No. 9 to the Convention for the Protection of Human Rights and Fundamental Freedoms was signed in Rome on 6 November 1990 when it enters into force, the position of the individuals will change also with regard to the question of the individual being subject of law under the Convention. The most important rules in the protocol are Article 3, which changes Article 44 of the Convention, and Article 5, which changes Article 48 of the Convention. Under the present rules only High Contracting Parties and the Commission can bring a case before the Court.

After the change also persons, non-governmental organizations, or groups of individuals having submitted a petition under Article 25 shall have their own right to bring the case before the Court.

The Protocol establishes, however, a special system for cases referred to the Court by individual applicants. According to Article 5, paragraph 2 such cases shall first be submitted to a panel of three judges and if the case does not raise serious questions affecting the interpretation or application of the Convention, and does not for any other reason warrant consideration by the Court the panel may by a unanimous vote decide that it shall not be considered by the Court. In that event the Committee of Ministers shall decide whether there has been a violation of the Convention or not.

It is regrettable that the protocol has not established full equality between the state and the individual with regard to bringing cases before the Court. Such equality could have been established either by having given the individual the right to bring the case directly before the Court without the special procedure before the panel, or alternatively by introducing a similar procedure for cases brought before the Court by states.

The introduction of the special rules in Article 5, paragraph 2 for dealing with cases brought before the Court by individual applicants makes it difficult to foresee how much the protocol will change the position of the applicant in practice. In view of the Commission's present practice for sending cases to the Court, it is difficult to imagine that the Commission would not send a case to the Court if it raises a serious question affecting the interpretation or application of the Convention, or if it for any other reason warrants consideration by the Court. Whether in practice there will be any real difference with regard to which cases will be decided by the Court will depend on whether the panels will follow the Commission, especially with regard to the question whether a case for any other reason warrants consideration by the Court. Nevertheless, the protocol marks an important improvement in the legal position of the individual as a subject of international law. When the protocol enters into force the individual applicant will have the capacity to bring any application, which has been declared admissible by the Commission, before the Court and it is for the Court itself sitting as a panel to decide whether the case shall be considered by it.

B. The Convention Organs

1. The Commission

The Commission consists of a number of members equal to that of the High Contracting Parties. Consequently, there should in 1991 be 23 members. However, so far no member from San Marino has been elected and there are therefore currently only 22 members. The members, who shall be of high moral character and either possess qualifications required for appointment to high judicial office or be persons of recognized competence in national or international law, are elected by the Committee of Ministers of the Council of Europe by an absolute majority from a list of three names put forward by each Member State's delegation to the Consultative Assembly. They are elected for a period of six years and may be re-elected. During the term of office they cannot be removed against their will.

No two members of the Commission may be nationals of the same state and in fact the Commission has always been comprised of one member from each state party to the Convention. This does not, however, mean that members are or can be considered as representing their national states. They sit on the Commission in their individual capacity and shall not hold any position which is incompatible with their independence and impartiality as members of the Commission or the demands of this office. This means that members may not receive instructions either from their state, or from any other institution or person. Against this background it can be concluded that the Commission is an independent and impartial organ composed of lawyers chosen for their personal qualifications.

The Commission does not sit permanently and all members have their domicile in their home-countries. At present, however, the Commission meets for eight sessions of two weeks per year. Besides the regular sessions, individual members will be in Strasbourg acting as the Commission's delegates in cases before the Court, and members may also have to participate in investigations of special cases which take place outside the normal sessions. Besides the work in Strasbourg, members will have to devote a considerable amount of time, normally up to sixteen weeks per year, for the preparation of cases to be dealt with during sessions. Consequently, although membership of the Commission is not a full-time task Commission work will occupy members for considerably more than half of the normal working year.

The Commission is assisted by a permanent secretariat of more than 50 persons out of which some 30 are highly qualified lawyers from the different Member States. The secretariat is composed in such a way that it is able to deal with applications in the languages of all Member States.

2. The Court

The Court is composed of a number of judges equal to the number of members of the Council of Europe and thus by the end of 1991, the Court had 26 judges. The fact that the number of judges is higher than the number of members of the Commission is due to the fact that three states, namely Hungary, Czechoslovakia and Poland are members of the Council of Europe, whereas they have not yet ratified the Convention, therefore no members of the Commission are appointed in respect of those three states. The members of the Court are elected from a list of three names presented by each of the Member States by the Consultative Assembly of the Council of Europe by majority of votes cast. The Court cannot include more than one national from each state. On the other hand, there is no rule according to which the judges must be nationals from any of the Member States. At present there is no member of the Court who is a national of Liechtenstein because the Consultative Assembly of the Council of Europe has elected a Canadian judge in respect of that state.

The judges must be of high moral character and must either possess the qualifications required for appointment to high judicial office or be jurisconsults of recognized competence. They are elected for nine years and may be re-elected. The judges are independent and may not receive any instructions either from states, organizations, or anyone else. It follows from the rules of the Convention that the Court fulfills all the necessary conditions to be a proper international court of justice.

The Court does not sit permanently but meets in sessions, at present ten to eleven sessions normally of one week's duration. Like the Commission, the Court is assisted by a permanent staff consisting of about 25 persons out of which about 15 are highly qualified lawyers.

3. The Committee of Ministers

The Committee of Ministers is one of the principal organs of the Council of Europe, and is established by the statute of the Council; which also fixes its competence. The Convention on Human Rights makes the Committee of Ministers the third organ entrusted with control and supervision under the Convention.

The Committee of Ministers was in 1991 comprised of 26 members, namely the minister for Foreign Affairs of each Member State. Normally the ministers only meet twice a year, and the more frequent meetings of the Committee are attended by ambassadors of the signatory states in their capacity as permanent representatives at the Council of Europe. The Committee of Ministers is consequently a political organ where the permanent representatives act on the instructions from their Governments.

C. The Function and Procedure of the Convention Organs

1. The Commission

The tasks of the Commission are to receive state and individual applications alleging breaches of the Convention and to decide whether an application is admissible or not. In admissible cases it shall undertake an examination of the case in order to establish the facts and at the same time place itself at the disposal of the parties with a view to secure a friendly settlement. If a case is not settled the Commission shall draw up a report on the facts of the case and state its opinion as to whether the facts found disclose a breach of the Convention. The report shall be transmitted to the Committee of Ministers with such proposals as the Commission thinks fit. After having sent the report to the Committee of Ministers, the Commission can decide to refer the case to the Court. Further, the Commission assists the Court through its delegate taking part in the proceedings, and it assists the Committee of Ministers in determining the amount of compensation for damage resulting from a violation of the Convention. Finally, according to its rules of procedure, the Commission may decide to apply interim measures until it has finally decided the case.

(a) Inter-state Applications

Two groups of applications can be brought before the Commission, namely state applications and individual applications. So far the Commission has dealt with 18 state applications which can conveniently be grouped into six complexes:

- two cases brought by *Greece* v. *United Kingdom* in 1956/57 concerning the situation in Cyprus: they were resolved in 1959 by the Zurich and London agreements;[5]
- one case brought in 1960 by *Austria* v. *Italy* in connection with certain criminal proceedings concerning a murder in South Tyrol: it ended with a decision that no violation had occurred;[6]
- five cases brought in 1967 and 1970 by *Denmark, the Netherlands, Norway and Sweden* v. *Greece* alleging numerous violations of the Convention by the then Government of the Colonels: it ended with a finding of violations in April 1970 when Greece had already resigned from the Council of Europe and denounced the Convention. As is well known, Greece joined the Council of Europe again in 1974 and is also now again a High Contracting Party to the Convention;[7]
- two cases brought in 1971 and 1972 by *Ireland* v. *United Kingdom* in relation to the situation in Northern Ireland: in January 1978 the Court held that there had been a practice of inhuman treatment at certain detention centres in the autumn of 1971, but otherwise found no breaches of the Convention;[8]

5 Application No. 176/56 and No. 299/57, Yearbook of the European Convention on Human Rights, 2, 182 and 186.

6 Application No. 788/60, YB 6, 742 and 796.

7 Application Nos. 3321/67 – 3322/67 – 3323/67, 3344/67 and 4448/70, YB 11, 690 and 737, YB 12, 108, YB 13, 108 and 122.

8 Application Nos. 5310/71 and 5451/72, YB 15, 92 and 255. ECHR, judgment of 18 January 1978, Series A, No. 25.

- three cases brought in 1974, 1975, and 1977 on behalf of the *Republic of Cyprus* v. *Turkey* relating to the situation on the island produced by the Turkish military intervention in 1974: the first two cases were terminated by a decision of the Committee of Ministers in January 1979 urging the parties to resume inter-communal talks.[9]

  In the third case the Commission adopted its report in October 1983, but the Committee of Ministers has not yet taken any decision in the case;
- five cases brought in 1982 by *Denmark, France, the Netherlands, Norway, and Sweden* v. *Turkey* alleging a number of violations of the Convention after the military had taken power in Turkey in September 1980. The case ended by a friendly settlement in 1986.[10]

(b) Individual Applications

Individual applications can only be brought against contracting states which have made a special declaration under Article 25 accepting individual petitions. Since 1989, however, all 23 contracting states have made such declarations.

An application may be introduced through a lawyer, but most applications are introduced without any formalities by a simple letter from the individual applicant addressed to the Commission. In 1991 the Commission received more than 5,000 such communications and since 1955 the total number exceeded 57,000.

As the Commission can be and frequently is approached by private individuals without support of legal counsellors, it is understandable that a great number of these complaints fall outside the Commission's competence, or do clearly not raise any question of a violation of the Convention. These may, for instance, be complaints against states not parties to the Convention, against private persons, or complaints of violations of rights which are not protected by the Convention. In such cases the Commission's secretariat will inform the applicant that the application has not formally been registered and explain the reason for it, and also, when appropriate, explain to whom, for instance a national ombudsman, the applicant should address the complaint. Also in cases where the application clearly does not fulfill the conditions for admissibility, for instance because of non-compliance with the six-month-rule, or because local remedies clearly are not exhausted, the secretariat will inform the applicant about this without registering the application.

In the majority of these cases the applicant will accept the secretariat's explanation and not pursue the case. It is, however, important to note that

9 Application Nos. 6780/74, 6950/75 and 8007/77, YB 18, 82 and YB 21, 100.
10 Application Nos. 9940-44/82, DR 35, 143 and DR 44, 31.

the secretariat has no power to dismiss an application. If, therefore, the applicant in spite of the explanation given by the secretariat wishes to have the case dealt with by the Commission, an application form will be sent to him or her with a request to fill out the form and to submit the relevant information and the relevant national decisions such as judgments in the case. Upon receipt of the form and documentation, the application will be formally registered.

In cases where the application from the outset seems to raise problems under the Convention, the applicant in the first letter from the secretariat is requested to fill in the application form, and after its receipt the application will be registered. In 1991 1,648 applications were registered and since 1955 altogether 19,216 have been registered.

When an application has been registered a member of the Commission is appointed as rapporteur in the case. The task of the rapporteur together with the member of the secretariat dealing with the case, is to make a report to the Commission with a statement of the facts of the case and a proposal as to whether the case should be declared inadmissible, or communicated to the Government concerned and further investigated.

If the rapporteur considers an application clearly inadmissible, his report will contain only a short note stating the relevant facts, and a short draft decision which does not repeat the facts but only the reasons for rejecting the application. He will further propose that the application be dealt with by a Committee of three members. If the rapporteur considers the case to be inadmissible, but that it nevertheless raises problems which warrant a more detailed report and discussion in the Commission, the report will be presented in the form of a draft decision with a detailed statement of the facts and a fully reasoned draft decision. If the rapporteur considers that the case is not inadmissible but raises problems of violations of the Convention, the report will contain a detailed statement of the facts and an analysis of the legal questions involved and a proposal to communicate the application to the Government concerned. The two last groups of cases – so-called ordinary cases – will be dealt with by the plenary Commission or by a Chamber.

Two to three weeks before each session of the Commission copies of the reports prepared by the rapporteurs for the session will be sent to each member of the Commission, normally two to three hundred reports per session, in order to give the members sufficient time for preparation. At the beginning of the session the Commission may, at the request of any member, decide that an application which the rapporteur has proposed should be dealt with by a Committee, or be dealt with by the plenary Commission. If no such decision is taken, the cases are dealt with by the Committees. The possibility to decide on applications in Committees is a new one, introduced by Protocol No. 8 which entered into force on 1 January 1990 as an amendment to Article 20.

A Committee can by a unanimous vote declare an individual application inadmissible or strike it off the list of cases if that decision can be made without further examination.

The Commission has set up six Committees, each composed of three members drawn by lot. At each session three Committees will sit simultaneously and deal with the Committee cases allocated to them. The Committees have already proved to be a valuable innovation in the efforts to speed up the treatment of minor cases. The basis for the Committees' decisions is the reports in the cases but the Committees will also, if necessary, have available during their discussions the full case file with all documents. They will also have the opportunity to ask for further clarification or information from the member of the secretariat dealing with the specific case. When a Committee unanimously decides that an application is inadmissible, the draft decision will be adopted and communicated to the applicant. If no such unanimous decision is possible the case will be sent back to the rapporteur, who will prepare a more elaborate report which will be dealt with by the plenary Commission or a Chamber at the following session.

It is difficult to estimate how many cases will be decided by Committees per year, but based on the short experience thus far it does not seem unlikely that between 70% and 80% of the applications will be decided in Committees.

Applications which the rapporteur has proposed to be dealt with as ordinary cases will – as mentioned above – be examined by the plenary Commission or by a Chamber. Like the Committees, Chambers are an innovation introduced by Protocol No. 8 as an amendment to Article 20. According to this rule which also entered into force on 1 January 1990 the Commission may set up Chambers, each composed of at least seven members. The Chambers may examine individual applications which can be dealt with on the basis of established case-law, or which raise no serious questions affecting the interpretation or application of the Convention. In 1990 the Commission set up two Chambers composed by ten and eleven members respectively. Each Chamber is presided over by one of the Commission's Vice-presidents – the President not being member of any Chamber. Besides the ordinary members of the Chambers, the member of the Commission elected in respect of the state against which the application has been lodged always has the right to sit on the Chamber when that case is being considered. The composition of the Chambers will be changed every three years at the same time as the election of the President and the two Vice-presidents.

During the preparation of the protocol, it was agreed that although it was for the Commission to decide which cases should be sent to a Chamber, the parties to the case should be consulted before the Commission's decision. The procedure for sending cases to Chambers has therefore during the first two years been as follows: All ordinary cases started in the plenary Commission, and when the Commission decided to communicate a case it considered at the same time whether the case should remain with the plenary after communication, or whether it might be dealt with by a Chamber. In the last case the parties were requested to inform the Commission if they had any objection to the case being dealt with by a Chamber. In practice very few reasoned objections were received. The formal decision to send a case to a Chamber was then taken on the proposal by the rapporteur when the observations from the parties had been received.

The cases are distributed between the Chambers in such a way that any case in principle is sent to the Chamber in which the national member has his seat. The cases which in the first periods have been sent to and decided by the Chambers have mainly been applications alleging violations of Article 6, due to extensive length of procedure, and other groups of cases falling within areas where a clear case-law has been established.

During the year 1991 the Commission realized that the system according to which all ordinary cases should start in the plenary Commission, and that cases were only sent to Chambers after the applicant and the respective Government had been consulted, was unnecessarily complicated and time-consuming. With the agreement of the Governments the following procedure was therefore introduced from 1992:

When the rapporteur makes his report and proposal in an ordinary case he proposes at the same time whether the case shall be dealt with by the plenary Commission or by a Chamber. If the proposal is to send the case to the plenary, the plenary may deal with the case or decide to send the case to a Chamber. Cases which the rapporteurs have proposed should be dealt with by a Chamber are nevertheless sent to all members of the Commission in order to give them the opportunity to consider whether the case should be dealt with by a Chamber or by the plenary. At the first day of the session where the case is to be examined, any member may propose that the case, instead of being examined by a Chamber as proposed by the rapporteur, should be examined by the plenary and the plenary will then decide this question.

If a case which is dealt with by a Chamber is communicated for observations, the parties at this stage have the opportunity to request that the case be examined by the plenary. If such a request is received it will be considered and decided upon by the plenary. Finally a Chamber – as a Committee – may at any time relinquish jurisdiction in favour of the plenary which may also order the transfer to it of any case dealt with by a Chamber or a Committee.

In the rapporteur's proposal on the case he may – apart from the question of Chamber or plenary – propose that the application be declared inadmissible. After having been discussed in the Chamber or the plenary as the case may be, the proposal will be voted upon. If the proposal is adopted either unanimously or by majority, the text of the attached draft decision will be discussed and adopted, if necessary with amendments. The decision which is communicated to the applicant will state whether the decision is unanimous or taken by a majority. In the last situation it will, however, not be revealed how many members have voted for and against the decision, and it is not possible to attach dissenting opinions to decisions on admissibility.

If the rapporteur's proposal to declare an application inadmissible is rejected, the Commission or the Chamber may instruct the rapporteur to prepare a new draft which would lead to inadmissibility, but based on other grounds than the first proposal. However, in most cases where the rapporteur's proposal to declare the application inadmissible is rejected, the Commission will decide to communicate the application to the Government concerned and ask for their observations.

The second group of ordinary cases are applications where the rapporteur considers that the application raises problems of violations of the Convention or that it – at least based on the information available at this stage – should not be declared inadmissible. The rapporteur will in his report to the Commission propose that the application be communicated to the responsible Government with a request for their observations, and he will normally also propose questions which the Government is specifically requested to answer. If the rapporteur's proposal is adopted, possibly with amendments to the questions, the Government will be requested to submit its answers, normally within a time limit of eight weeks.

When these observations are received the secretariat will immediately forward them to the applicant who will be invited to submit observations and comments. At this stage of a case the applicant will normally need the assistance of a lawyer. If the applicant is not already represented by a lawyer the secretariat will advise him or her to seek legal assistance and inform the applicant about the opportunity to obtain free legal aid from the Council of Europe if his or her general economic situation makes this necessary. When the applicant has submitted the necessary information about his or her financial situation and this has been verified by the national authorities the Commission will grant free legal aid if the conditions are fulfilled. The sums granted as free legal aid are rather moderate, but have nevertheless in practice made it possible for applicants to be represented by lawyers.

In some applications a number of violations are alleged. If some of the allegations are clearly inadmissible but others deserve communication, the Commission in most cases decides to communicate only the part of the application which raises problems, and will only ask questions concerning this part and will not at this stage formally decide to declare the remainder inadmissible. The understanding being that these allegations will be declared inadmissible in the final decision on admissibility covering the whole case which is taken after the communication.

The Commission may, however, in such situations decide to take a partial decision if this is considered more convenient in order to clarify matters for the applicant and the Government. A partial decision will formally declare the inadmissible complaints inadmissible and adjourn the remainder until the necessary observations have been received, and a second decision declaring this part admissible or inadmissible can be taken.

When in a communicated case the observations, from both the government and the applicant have been received, the rapporteur prepares a new report which is sent to all members with copies of the parties' observations. The report will include a proposal either to declare the application inadmissible, for instance because it may now have been clarified that local remedies have not been exhausted, or a proposal to declare the application admissible, or if the case needs further clarification a proposal to hold an oral hearing.

Based on the rapporteur's analysis of the case and the parties' observations the plenary Commission or a Chamber will take its decision. If the case is declared inadmissible this is the final decision against which no appeal exists. If the case is declared admissible the Commission or the Chamber will proceed to an examination of the merits of the case. (In the following discussion the word 'Commission' is used for both 'plenary Commission' and 'Chamber').

If the Commission decides to hold an oral hearing the parties will be invited to appear before the Commission at a later session and address normally both the admissibility and the merits of the case. In most cases the Commission will at the same time draw the parties' attention to problems which the Commission wishes the parties to consider.

At the hearing the Government will be represented by its agent assisted by civil servants or by a practising lawyer. The applicant will in practise be represented by a lawyer and may also be present personally, but will only exceptionally be allowed to address the Commission. The parties will normally address the Commission in one of the official languages, English or French, but if they so wish, they may also use their national language in which case the necessary interpretation will be provided.

Usually the parties are awarded half an hour each for pleading the case. After this first round members of the Commission will, if needed, orally put questions to the parties and after a short break both parties have about 15 minutes each to answer the questions and to make their final submissions. The time allotted for the oral presentation may be considered rather short. It must, however, be taken into consideration that before an oral hearing takes place the Commission has dealt with the case twice and that all members have in their files the substantial written submissions in the case. Experience shows that the time awarded for the 'first round' is sufficient for a concise and concentrated presentation of the case and the relevant arguments and submissions. Secondly, a very important part of the hearing is often the questions put to the parties and their answers.

After the hearing the Commission will immediately commence its deliberations on the case during which the members in order of seniority, starting with the youngest member, will express their opinion as to whether the application is admissible and, if so, also a provisional opinion as to whether a breach of the Convention has taken place. The opinions expressed by the members during the deliberations are not binding, a member may thus change their opinion due to arguments advanced by other members. After the deliberation a formal binding vote on the admissibility is taken, and if the application is declared admissible a provisional – not binding vote – is taken on the question of violation of the Convention. The parties will then be informed about the decision on admissibility and confidentially about the Commission's provisional opinion regarding violation. The last information is given as a guidance for friendly settlement negotiations (see below).

(c) The Admissibility Decision

The Commission can only declare an application admissible if a number of conditions are fulfilled. With regard to inter-state applications the conditions are that all domestic remedies have been exhausted and that the application is lodged within 6 months from the date on which the final national decision in the case was taken (Article 26).

In order to declare an individual application admissible the Commission must satisfy itself that the following conditions laid down in Articles 25, 26, and 27 are fulfilled, namely that:

1) the applicant can claim to be a victim of a violation of one of the rights set forth in the Convention,
2) the application is not anonymous.
3) the application is not substantially the same as a matter which has already been examined by the Commission.

4) the application is not incompatible with the provisions of the Convention.
5) the application is not manifestly ill-founded.
6) the application is not an abuse of the right of petition.
7) domestic remedies have been exhausted.
8) the application is submitted within 6 months from the date of the final national decision.

The first and fundamental condition is that the applicant – be it an individual, a non-governmental organization or a group of individuals – can claim to be the victim of an alleged violation. This excludes applications being brought by third persons or organizations who are not themselves affected by an alleged violation. An *actio popularis* is clearly inadmissible; it is not enough to allege that acts of a general nature made by a state (in particular legislative measures or administrative practices), which may be considered incompatible with the Convention, might in the future affect the individual concerned. An individual applicant – unlike a contracting state – cannot challenge legislation or other general acts as such. The complaint must be based on a concrete case with direct repercussions on the applicant's personal situation. Normally such a case will only arise where the legislation or practice is in fact applied to the applicant.

There are, however, situations where the legislation or practice complained of are of such a nature that either their mere existence involves a direct interference with the individual's right, for instance penal legislation outlawing homosexual acts. An individual can also claim to be a victim if it can be presumed that legislation might have been applied to him without he being informed thereof. This can be illustrated by the *Klass* case.[11] The facts of the case were briefly as follows. Five German lawyers had complained that their telephones had been secretly surveyed. The relevant German authorities had refused to inform the applicants whether their telephones in fact had been tapped. Referring to legislation according to which in some cases it was possible to undertake surveillance without informing the person against whom this measure had been applied, the applicants alleged that their rights under Article 8 to private life and correspondence had been violated. They argued that it was likely that a surveillance of their telephone conversations had taken place because they in their professional capacity, *inter alia* as defence lawyers, had contact with persons who might be considered dangerous for the society. The German Government submitted that the case was inadmissible because the applicants could not prove that they had been surveyed at all.

11 Application No. 5029/71, European Commission of Human Rights. Decisions and Reports 1, 20 (hereafter DR) ECHR, judgment of 6 September 1978, Series A, No. 28.

The Commission declared the case to be admissible because the applicants must be considered as if they were victims. Under the procedure before the Court the Commission submitted that the applicants could claim to be direct victims of a possible violation because the mere fact that the applicants had reasons to believe that their telephone conversations were surveilled, meant that they were in practice limited in their use of the telephone. During the procedure the German Government now informed the Court that the applicants' telephones never at any time had been surveilled and that the applicants therefore could not claim to be victims. The Court, however, found that applicants in special situations could claim to be victims of a violation due to the mere existence of a possible secret surveillance.

According to Article 25, applications can be brought by three types of individual applicants: any person, non-governmental organizations, and groups of individuals. Insofar as natural persons are concerned, the Convention does not make any distinction with regard to their legal capacity. Therefore children and minors can also be applicants,[12] as well as persons placed under guardianship.[13] They may be represented before the Convention organs by parents or guardians or sometimes even by persons who do not have this right under national law.[14]

Non-governmental organizations, for instance private associations, can complain about the rights of the association as such. A trade union can for instance complain against a violation of trade union rights under Article 11. On the other hand, an association cannot complain on behalf of its members. For instance an association of divorced fathers cannot complain that their members do not have adequate rights to visit their children who are in the custody of their mothers. The word 'non-governmental' means that a public corporation participating in the exercise of state power cannot bring an application. Therefore, regional administrations cannot lodge applications, even if they concern their property or civil rights.[15]

Of the remaining seven conditions for admissibility, in practice the most important ones are that the application is not incompatible or manifestly ill-founded, the rule of non-exhaustion, and the 6 months rule.

An application can be incompatible and thus outside the Commission's competence for different reasons. It is incompatible *ratione personae* if it is brought against a state which has not ratified the Convention such as a

12 See, e.g., *Marckx* case, judgment of 13 June 1979, ECHR (1979) Series A, No. 31.

13 See, e.g., *Winterwerp* case, judgment of 24 October 1979, ECHR (1979) Series A, No. 33.

14 See, e.g., *Nielsen* case, judgment of 28 November 1988, ECHR (1988) Series A, No. 144.

15 See, e.g., Application No. 15090/89 *Ayuntamiento de Madrid* v. *Spain*, Dec. (7 January 1991).

non-European state or against a private person, for instance a practicing lawyer.

An application is incompatible *ratione temporis* if it is brought against a state which has ratified the Convention but the allegations concern facts which have occurred before the ratification. A number of states having ratified the Convention did not accept individual applications until some years later. In such situations the states have normally limited their declaration under Article 25 to facts which have occurred after the date of the declaration with the effect that applications related to facts before that date have been considered incompatible *ratione temporis*. If, however, the state has ratified the Convention and some years later made the declaration accepting individual applications without limiting the declaration to facts occurring after the deposition of the declaration (for instance France ratified the Convention in 1974 and made its declaration under Article 25 without limitations in 1981), the situation is different. In such cases an application relating to facts after the ratification but before the declaration will not be incompatible *ratione temporis*. However, the 6 months rule will result in certain limitations with regard to admissibility, because an application can only be brought after the deposition of the declaration and it must at the same time be brought within 6 months from the final national decision in the case. In other words, cases in which the final national decision has been taken more than 6 months before the deposition of the declaration will be inadmissible.[16]

An application is incompatible *ratione materiae* if it concerns a violation of a right which is not protected by the Convention, for instance the right to work or the right to equal payment for equal work. The decision, especially as to whether a right is covered by the rules of the Convention or not, sometimes involves difficult and fundamental legal problems such as whether an unborn child's right to life is protected by Article 2 of the Convention.[17] Similarly, the question of whether certain relations between persons can be considered as family-life and protected or not by Article 8 may raise serious problems.

The purpose of the rule requiring the exhaustion of domestic remedies in Article 26 is to give the respondent state an opportunity of retracing the alleged wrong by domestic means within the framework of its own legal system. The remedies to be exhausted in principle comprise the entire system of legal protection which means that the complaint must be brought before the highest possible legal authority in the country, typically the highest court, before an application is lodged. However, only the effective or sufficient remedies need to be exhausted. Thus it is not necessary to bring a com-

16 Application No. 9587/81, DR 29, 228 (*X.* v. *France*, 1982).
17 Application No. 8416/78, DR 19, 244 (*X.* v. *United Kingdom*, 1980).

plaint before a national ombudsman because a national ombudsman will not have the competence to cancel or change the impugned decision. If there are doubts whether a particular remedy is effective, the applicant is required to use that remedy.[18] It is therefore in principle for the applicant to prove the ineffectiveness of an existing remedy and the applicant cannot in this respect invoke a lack of legal knowledge.[19] This rule, however, is not without exceptions. The Commission has held that if there are serious doubts as to the effectiveness of a remedy invoked by a Government, it is for the Government to show the effectiveness of the remedy.[20]

An applicant will be absolved from using a remedy if it can be shown that the remedy in question is doomed to failure having regard to the established case-law of domestic courts,[21] or having regard to decisions in parallel cases.[22] Finally an applicant will not, in order to exhaust domestic remedies, have to apply for extraordinary national remedies such as the reopening of a case which has already been finally been decided by the courts.

Besides the rule of exhaustion of domestic remedies Article 26 stipulates that the Commission may only deal with an application if it is introduced within 6 months from the date on which the final domestic decision was taken.

It is understandable that a certain time limit is laid down in the Convention in this respect. If this was not so the Commission might be faced with applications relating to events which had occurred many years ago, and it might be very difficult or even impossible to establish the facts of the case.

The 6 months are calculated from the final ordinary national decision whereas later extraordinary national remedies are not taken into consideration. If, for instance, an applicant has sought to have the case re-opened on the national level and this has been refused, the 6 months will still be calculated from the last ordinary decision, and not from the later date of the decision not to re-open the case.

An application is considered to have been introduced on the date of the first letter from the applicant to the Commission in which the applicant clearly specified his or her complaint. The fact that further information and documentation may be necessary, and that an application form must be completed, will often mean that the application is not formally registered until after the expiration of the 6 month limitation period. This will not affect the admissibility.

18 Application Nos. 5577-5583/72, DR 4, 4 (*Donnelly and others*).
19 Application No. 3040/67, YB 10, 518 (*X.* v. *Federal Republic of Germany,* 1967).
20 Application Nos. 8805-8806/79, DR 24, 144. (*De Jong and Baljet*).
21 Application No. 10103/82, DR 39, 186 (*Farragut*).
22 Application No. 8191/77, DR 14, 186 (*Campbell*).

There can, however, be exceptions to this normal situation. If an applicant has introduced his or her complaint within 6 months from the final decision, and has been requested by the Secretariat to submit further information or to complete the application form within a short time limit, and the applicant does not respond until 3-4 years later without any justification for this delay, the Commission may then declare the application inadmissible under the 6 month rule.

One of the most important rules to be applied in the procedure on admissibility is that the Commission shall declare an application inadmissible if it is manifestly ill-founded. This means that the merits of the application are considered at the first stage of the proceedings, and in many cases the Commission takes a final and binding decision to dismiss the case at this early stage.

The rule that applications shall be declared inadmissible if they are manifestly ill-founded and the way in which this rule in practice has been applied has sometimes been criticized as not being in conformity with the main idea of the Convention, namely to protect the individual. On the face of it this criticism might appear to be not without substance. However, in order to see whether the rule and practice in question are against the interest of the individual it is appropriate to look at the cases declared manifestly ill-founded. They can be divided into two groups.

The first and by far the biggest one is the group of applications which are declared manifestly ill-founded by a unanimous decision of a Committee. In this group of applications many different complaints can be found. For instance those from prisoners who, without any substantiation, claim that they have not committed the crime for which they are sentenced by the national court and for which they are serving their sentence, or from persons who claim – again without any substantiation – that they are constantly supervised by the authorities using all kinds of existing or non-existing electric devises. A possibility to declare such cases inadmissible as manifestly ill-founded protects the whole system from being overburdened with cases that lack substance. It seems also to be in the interest of the applicants that their complaints are dismissed without further investigations which raise unjustified hopes for them.

The second group of manifestly ill-founded applications are those which are declared inadmissible after further investigations. If an application is communicated because the facts cannot be sufficiently clarified by the information submitted by the applicant, the observations from the Government and the answers from the applicant sometimes make it clear that no possible violation of the Convention can have taken place, and the application will consequently be declared inadmissible as manifestly ill-founded. It also happens that it is necessary to hold an oral hearing with the parties in order to clarify all matters in a case and that after the oral hearing the application is found to be manifestly ill-founded. It is mainly with regard to the two last situations that the possibility of declaring an application manifestly ill-founded has been criticized, the argument against the existing practice normally being: How can an application be manifestly ill-founded when it has been necessary to have lengthy written and maybe oral submissions to reach that conclusion? The application may be ill-founded, it is said, but that certainly cannot be 'manifest' since a lengthy procedure has been necessary and by such a decision the applicant is barred from any possibility of having the case brought before the Court at a later stage.

Although such criticism may be understandable it is not necessarily justified. The situation could be, for instance, that when the application was first examined by the plenary Commission or a Chamber, there might have been a proposal to declare it manifestly ill-founded and the Commission might even have been inclined to do so. Nevertheless, during the discussions in the Commission some doubt could have been expressed, for instance regarding relevant facts of the case, and in order to avoid any injustice the Commission might have decided to ask for observations and to proceed with the case. If then during these proceedings the facts become absolutely clear and the Commission is convinced that there is no violation, the case is then declared inadmissible as manifestly ill-founded. It is true that this leaves the applicant without any opportunity of having his case examined by the Court, but again, is it in the interest of the applicant to go on with the case for two or more years to get a final judgment that there is no violation, when the Commission is already convinced that this will be the result?

The Commission is not only criticized for declaring too many cases inadmissible as manifestly ill-founded but is sometimes also criticized for declaring too many cases admissible. The argument on which this criticism is based is that the purpose of the Convention when adopted after the Second World War was to secure the *fundamental* principles and the basic ideas in the democratic parliamentarian states of Europe, and not to introduce a new possibility for complaints for anyone who in a concrete situation might feel himself injured or wrongly treated.

In this connection the practice of the Supreme Court of the United States of America as explained by the Court's President Taft in 1925 has been mentioned. President Taft said:

> The function of the Supreme Court is conceived to be not the remedying of particular litigants' wrong but the consideration of cases where decisions involve principles, the application of which is of wide public or governmental interest.

It has been suggested that similar considerations apply to the organs of the European Convention.[23]

It can, however, hardly be correct that the Convention organs are or should be limited to dealing only with complaints which involve principles, the application of which is of wide public or governmental interest. It may well be that the Commission declares applications admissible which do not raise questions of principle and is correct in doing so.

The Convention does not contain any rule according to which cases can be declared inadmissible because they do not raise matters of principle and that, in a way, is sufficient to answer the criticism mentioned above. It should be added, firstly, that if such a principle were to be applied it would seriously invalidate the position of the individual and invalidate the credibility of the Convention and its organs. Secondly, it would in practice be very difficult to make a distinction between cases where a violation might have taken place which involve matters of principle and which do not. For example: a child in country X has been taken into public care and the parents in an application allege that by this decision their family rights have been violated. After examining the legal rules and the practice followed by the authorities in the said country the Commission finds that the law and practice in general are in perfect conformity with the rules of the Convention and thus no matter or principle of wide public interest seems to be involved. Nevertheless, from the investigation it appears that in the concrete case something has gone wrong in the national authorities' handling of the case with the result that in this concrete – maybe exceptional case – the parents' right to family life seems to have been violated. It would be difficult to imagine a system for the protection of human rights under which such a case should be declared inadmissible because no matter of important principle is at issue.

The Convention does not lay down any specific order in which the conditions for admissibility shall be examined. Before declaring an application admissible the Commission, however, will always have to satisfy itself that all conditions are fulfilled. If only one condition is not fulfilled the application must be declared inadmissible. If one condition – be it a formal one such as exhaustion of national remedies or a material one such as being manifestly ill-founded – is clearly not fulfilled the Commission will normally as a matter of expediency declare the application inadmissible for that reason without examining the remaining conditions which may raise more complicated problems.

Besides the possibility of declaring an application inadmissible the Commission may also dismiss an application by striking it out of its list

23 Sørensen, 'Generel orientering om den europæiske Menneskerettighedskonvention', 50 *Nordisk Tidsskrift for International Ret* (1981) 99.

of cases. Before 1 January 1990 when Protocol No. 8 entered into force the Convention did not contain any rule regarding striking cases out of the list. There was in practice a need for such a possibility when an applicant wished to withdraw the application or where the circumstances, in particular the applicant's failure to provide information requested or to observe time limits led to the conclusion that the applicant did not intend to pursue the case. Thus the Commission introduced several years ago in its rules of procedure a special rule which permitted striking a case out of the list.

By Protocol No. 8 a new Article 30 was inserted in the Convention. According to this Article an application may be struck out of the list if the applicant does not intend to pursue his application, or the matter has been resolved or if for any other reason established by the Commission it is no longer justified to continue the examination of the application. Both under the former rule and the present one the Commission, however, could not strike a case out of the list if respect for Human Rights required its continued examination. If a case is struck out of the list the Commission can always decide to restore it to the list if it considers that the circumstances justify such a course. This may, for instance, be the case if the applicant shows that he has withdrawn the application by a mistake or a misunderstanding. The new rules cover generally the same situations as the old ones. They add the possibility to strike a case out of the list for *any other reason* established by the Commission when it is no longer justified to continue the examination of the case. The new rule could be considered to give a very wide discretion for the Commission to strike a case out of the list. It is, however, evident that the rule must be applied restrictively and it has during the first two years only been used three times. One of the cases may illustrate situations where the rule may be applied:

A Pakistani family living in Norway complained of the Norwegian authorities' intention to expel them to Pakistan. They claimed that such an expulsion would amount to inhuman treatment and invoked in this context Article 3 of the Convention. After the case had been communicated the applicants informed the Commission that they had been granted a visa for Austria and that they could apply for asylum in Austria. The applicants furthermore submitted that they were prepared to take advantage of the offer made by the Austrian authorities. Nevertheless, the applicants requested the Commission to decide whether it would be contrary to the Convention to deport them to Pakistan. The Commission decided to strike the application out of the list of cases by referring to Article 30, paragraph 1(c) of the Convention as the applicants no longer ran the risk of being deported to Pakistan as they could go to Austria whenever they liked and apply for asylum there. In these circumstances the Commission found that a continued examination of the petition was no longer justified. Furthermore, it found no special circumstances regarding respect for Human Rights which required the continuation of the examination of the application.[24]

(d) Friendly Settlement[25]

When an application has been declared admissible it is the duty of the Commission 'to place itself at the disposal of the parties with a view to securing a friendly settlement of the matter on the basis of human rights as defined in the Convention' (Article 28(b)).

As envisaged by the Convention friendly settlement is an important feature in the work of the Commission and during the years a considerable number of individual applications have been settled by friendly settlements.

The Commission only deals with friendly settlement in the formal sense after an application has been declared admissible. This does not mean, however, that the parties cannot come to an agreement before that decision is taken. On some occasions it has happened that, following the Commission's decision to communicate a case, the Government's representatives have contacted the applicant with a view to settling the dispute between them outside the proceedings before the Commission. When this has succeeded, both sides subsequently notified the Commission, whereupon the Commission, after having satisfied itself that the settlement has been reached on the basis of respect for Human Rights, can strike the case out of its list.

Cases in which a friendly settlement has been secured before the case was declared admissible are nevertheless rare. More important is the friendly-settlement procedure in cases which have been declared admissible. Here one can identify three stages: the decision of the parties to try to reach a settlement, the negotiations, and the Commission's decision accepting the agreement between the parties.

The decision to settle a case rests with the parties, and particularly for the respondent Government it involves a political decision. The Commission may, however, influence the decision through its provisional opinion as to the merits of the case, which is normally communicated in confidence to the parties. This provisional opinion is provided for in Rule 47 of the Commission's Rules of Procedure and is intimated to the parties for friendly-settlement purposes only. It in no way binds the Commission, although a clear tendency shown in the provisional opinion is seldom overturned in a final decision. It is difficult to know how much a provisional opinion of violation induces the authorities of the respondent state to seek a

24 Application No. 16022/90.

25 See Krüger and Nørgaard, 'Reflections Concerning Friendly Settlement Under the European Convention on Human Rights', in F. Matscher and H. Petzold (eds), *Protecting Human Rights: The European Dimension* (1988) 329.

friendly settlement; or how much a possible dislike for publicity on these matters or the high costs of being required to defend the case before the Court of Human Rights may influence the decision.

Presumably all these factors play a role, most significantly perhaps the possibility of being found in breach of the Convention by the Court at the end of a lengthy procedure. On the other hand, a decision to seek a friendly settlement may also be influenced by the fact that the Court in a previous case has already held that similar circumstances amount to a breach of the Convention. An offer to settle the case on terms similar to the previous judgment of the Court might simply be a recognition of that fact. Another factor that might guide the parties' attitude towards settlement is whether the matter can be solved by a mere payment of a sum of money as opposed to, for instance, a change in administrative practice or even legislative reform. Generally, it appears that it is easier to reach a settlement where only money is involved. Nevertheless, there have been settlements in which the Government undertook to introduce new legislation or change an administrative practice (see below p. 79).

If both sides have declared their willingness to settle the case, the second stage begins: the friendly-settlement negotiations. Sometimes these negotiations are conducted entirely by the parties themselves, and the Commission is informed of the result. More frequently the parties and in particular the responding Government request the Commission to assist in the negotiations. In that case the Commission normally instructs its Secretary to make contact with both sides and evaluate the prospects of a settlement. As a rule the Secretary first asks the applicant what he wants to obtain and to specify his claim which is then communicated to the Government.

The course of the negotiations may be such that the parties never actually meet, the Secretary acting as intermediary throughout. Alternatively it may be advisable to call a meeting of the parties in order to promote discussion of the matter between the parties themselves. Such meetings are normally convened by the Commission and presided over by a delegate of the Commission.

In the course of the negotiations it may well become obvious that a settlement on the terms put forward by the respective parties cannot be secured, but that both sides are still willing to reach agreement. In such a situation the Commission may take the initiative and propose a settlement to the parties. Normally such proposals are made on a take-it-or-leave-it basis and concern a settlement on financial terms only. The Commission will be inclined to make a proposal where the negotiations have taken a long time and the point has been reached where a decision must be made whether or not a settlement can be secured. In this context it is important that a balance be kept between the time spent in search of a settlement and the need to terminate the case within a reasonable time.

At the end of the negotiations there is a final stage: the Commission's approval of the parties' agreement. In this context the Commission must have regard to the so-called 'general interest', i.e. the European *ordre public* which may go beyond the interest of the particular applicant. The legal basis for the Commission's jurisdiction in this context is the requirement in Article 28, paragraph 1(b) that the Commission shall secure a friendly settlement "on the basis of respect for Human Rights as defined in this Convention'.

Although there has been no case so far in which the Commission has refused to accept the agreement reached between the parties, the importance of the Commission's role in this domain must not be underestimated. It is obvious that where the settlement has been achieved in collaboration with the Commission no problem would normally arise. Here the Commission will have defended the general interest at an early stage, making it a feature of the settlement negotiations from the very beginning. It is not so obvious where the parties have negotiated the settlement themselves. There has been at least one case where a settlement reached between the parties without the assistance of the Commission raised problems with regard to the Commission's acceptance of the settlement.

The case[26] concerned an applicant who was a Jordanian citizen living in Sweden. When the Swedish Government in 1989 decided to expel him to Jordan, the applicant asked the Commission to stop the expulsion. The Commission indicated to the Government that by applying Rule 36 of its Rules of Procedure (see below) it would be desirable that the expulsion did not take place before the Commission had had the opportunity to examine the application. The applicant was, however, nevertheless expelled to Jordan where he was arrested and allegedly maltreated. Shortly after he came back to Sweden and a friendly settlement was agreed between him and the Government according to which the applicant *inter alia* was granted permission to reside in Sweden permanently, received an ex gratia payment of 100,000 Swedish Kroners and had his travel costs and legal costs paid by the Government.

The settlement did, however, not mention the fact that the applicant had been expelled in spite of the indication under Rule 36. Therefore the Secretary of the Commission contacted the agent of the Government on this problem and in reply received the following statement from the Swedish Government:

26 Application No. 15658/89 *Mansi* v. *Sweden*. Report of the Commission (9 March 1990). To be published in DR.

> The Government regrets that Mr. Mansi was expelled to Jordan after the indication under Rule 36 of the Rules of Procedure of the Commission had been given by the President of the Commission that he should not be expelled.[27]

This statement was included in the Commission's report in the case where the Commission found that:

> having regard to Article 28, paragraph 1(b) of the Convention and to the statement made by the Government with regard to the indication under Rule 36 a friendly settlement had been secured on the basis of respect for Human Rights as defined in the Convention.[28]

The rules regarding friendly settlement also apply to interstate applications and one such case has in fact been settled, namely the interstate case brought by *Denmark, France, the Netherlands, Norway, and Sweden* v. *Turkey*. In this case the settlement negotiated by the parties assigned a special role to the Commission in that a provision was made for a series of reports by Turkey, followed by a dialogue with a delegation from the Commission, and terminating with a common final report. In this situation the Commission defined its own role, and the possibility cannot be excluded that a settlement on the terms envisaged by the parties would have failed if the Commission had not been prepared to play the role which the settlement assigned to it.[29]

Friendly settlement is part of a judicial process. Like a final judgment it terminates the dispute between the parties, but unlike a judgment it leaves neither a winner or a looser. Both sides will normally have gained something as a result of the settlement. Otherwise they would probably not have entered into one. It is for that reason, perhaps, that it is often the most satisfactory termination of a legal dispute regarding alleged violations of the Convention.

(e) Investigations

When an application has been declared admissible the Commission shall, with a view to ascertaining the facts, undertake together with the parties an examination of the case and if need be an investigation for which the states concerned shall furnish all necessary facilities (Article 28, 1(a)). In the large majority of cases the examination of the application and the establishment of the facts is carried out on the basis of the written material provided by the parties and in some cases supplemented by their oral pleadings and submissions. In some cases it has, however, been necessary to make further investigations by taking evidence, by hearing witnesses or by inspecting

27 Ibid., at para. 17.
28 Ibid., at para. 18.
29 Application Nos. 9940-44/82, DR 44, 31.

certain localities such as prisons or other places where applicants have been detained.

The most extensive investigation in the Commission's history was the investigation in the case of *Ireland* v. *the United Kingdom* regarding the allegation that the UK had violated in Northern Ireland a number of rights protected by the Convention.[30] Evidence was taken on the allegations under Article 3 and Article 14, and 36 witnesses were heard in Strasbourg. For security reasons a number of witnesses could, however, not be heard in Strasbourg as their lives might have been in danger if their identity became publicly known. The Commission therefore made an agreement with the Norwegian Government who provided the necessary facilities at Sola Military Airbase at Stavanger where sufficient security arrangements were established. At the Airbase another 77 witnesses were heard during periods of altogether about 5 weeks' duration. Finally 5 witnesses were heard in London.

At the same time as investigating the interstate case the Commission also took evidence in seven individual applications in the case of *Donnelly and others* v. *the United Kingdom*[31] in which the applicants alleged similar violations of Article 3 in Northern Ireland. The Commission heard evidence from 41 witnesses in this case. The hearing of a number of witnesses including four applicants took place in Strasbourg. Three applicants who were in detention were heard in prison in Northern Ireland and other witnesses were heard in Great Britain.

In a number of more recent individual applications the Commission has both heard witnesses and inspected places of detention where applicants have alleged that violations of the Convention have taken place.

(f) Interim Measures[32]

The need for measures to protect a party in a pending case against irreparable damage, which may occur before a final binding judgment in a case can be pronounced, is well known both in national and international legal systems. The domestic law often recognizes the need to stop the execution of the decision or order which has been challenged in subsequent court proceedings until these proceedings have been terminated. There are normally two ways in which this can be achieved at the domestic level. One is to give suspensive effect to the measures under attack on the introduction of the court proceedings; the other is to make an interim order to the effect that the

30 Application No. 5310/71. Commission's Report ECHR, Series B. No. 23, vol. 1.

31 Application Nos. 5577-5583/72, DR 4, 4.

32 See Nørgaard and Krüger, 'Interim and Conservatory Measures Under the European System of Protection of Human Rights', in M. Novak, D. Steurer and H. Tretter (eds), *Progress in the Spirit of Human Rights. Festschrift für Felix Ermacora* (1988) 109.

status quo ante should be preserved. Both have the purpose of preventing irreparable damage while the judicial proceedings are going on.

In the area of fundamental rights protection, whether on the domestic level or on the international level, the introduction of proceedings normally does not have suspensive effect. On the other hand, most domestic systems provide for the possibility of interim measures to be ordered by the judge where it is considered that otherwise irreparable damage will be done or an irreversible situation created.

The Convention does not contain any rule on suspensive effect or interim measures. It appears that the matter was never considered at the time the Convention was drafted as there is no mention of it in the Preparatory Works or elsewhere in discussions on the Convention at this time. As early as in 1960 the need for interim measures as part of the Convention system became apparent. By that time a few applications had been brought in which the applicant complained about his or her imminent expulsion from the territory of one of the Convention states to a country where he or she feared reprisals on political grounds. The applicants in these cases alleged that the removal to their home countries would subject them to the risk of persecution for their political opinions, including treatment which was contrary to the Article 3 prohibition on torture and inhuman and degrading treatment.

In dealing with such cases the Commission gradually elaborated on the reasons why it considered that in expulsion cases an issue could arise under Article 3 of the Convention. It emphasized in the first place that there was no right under any of the provisions of the Convention for a foreigner to stay or to reside in a particular country. On the other hand, where there was a justified fear that the applicant would be subjected to treatment contrary to Article 3 in the state to which he was expelled, the Commission examined the complaint against expulsion or extradition under that provision. In doing so the Commission was well aware of the fact that it was not the situation in the state which had decided to expel the applicant that was the subject of its examination, but the situation in the country to which he would be expelled. Nevertheless, the Commission considered that if a Government bound by the Convention decides to expel or extradite a person in a situation where the government is or ought to be aware of the serious risk of the person in question being tortured or severely ill-treated in the country of destination – not bound by the Convention – the expelling state itself may thereby commit an act which constitutes inhuman treatment in violation of Article 3.

In cases of this kind it is evident that if the expulsion has taken place and the person has been killed or tortured in the country to which he was expelled the damage is irreparable. Therefore the need for interim measures became more and more apparent. In the beginning the Commission obtained the Governments' cooperation in an unofficial way. It instructed its Secretary in a given case to contact the Government concerned and to ask that no expulsion be effected pending the examination of the application by the Commission. In practically all cases the Government agreed and throughout the 1960's and 1970's there were numerous cases in which a temporary stay of the execution or the deportation order was granted by the domestic authorities.

This positive reaction by member states encouraged the Commission to formalize this practice in the sense that in 1974 it introduced a new rule in its Rules of Procedure. This was Rule 36 which states that the Commission or, where it was not in session, its President 'may indicate to the parties any interim measure, the adoption of which seems desirable in the interest of the parties or the proper conduct of the proceedings before it'.

The Commission has received an increasing number of requests under Rule 36 every year (for example in 1991, there were 296 requests). The demand by applicants that the Commission should intervene pending the examination of the application has a wide range. Many of the requests concern expulsion or extradition, both in the context of a complaint under Article 3 of the Convention, and a complaint under Article 8. However, other cases may also concern a request for release from prison pending the decision on a complaint regarding unfair trial or unlawful detention; or even a request to stay the execution of the demolition of a building pending the decision on a complaint regarding expropriation or failure to grant a building permit.

It is true that the terms of Rule 36 are very broad when they speak of measures 'desirable in the interest of the parties and the conduct of the proceedings'. Nevertheless, the Commission has given a narrow interpretation to the Rule. Thus, an indication for interim measures is given only in very specific cases which satisfy the criteria established by the Commission over the years.

In the first place an indication under Rule 36 is only given where it is apparent that *irreparable damage* would result from the execution of the decision concerned. This is the case where expulsion or extradition is imminent and it is alleged that the applicant will be treated contrary to Article 3 in the receiving state. An indication under Rule 36 would be refused, for instance, where a proposed expulsion is not imminent or where the violation alleged is not one under Article 3 of the Convention, but falls to be considered under Article 8 and relates to separation of family, or where the expulsion is proposed to a country other than that in which the applicant fears persecution.

Secondly, the indication for an interim measure is given only where there is *a high degree of probability* that a violation of Article 3 of the

Convention is likely to occur. This is perhaps the most difficult assessment to make. It requires an applicant to state their case in a credible manner and possibly also to present some evidence showing the danger of life or limb to which he or she may be exposed if expelled or extradited to the particular country concerned. In this context it would not be sufficient if the applicant simply alleged that there was an armed conflict in the receiving state and that he or she was an opponent of the ruling government. It would be necessary for the applicant to show in a credible way that he or she was personally at risk.

It is often stated that it is practically impossible for an applicant to provide evidence of the risk involved when they have fled a country in haste under the threat of an immediate arrest and where documents and papers about their involvement are left behind or are simply not available. Of course, the Commission takes these factors into account when considering a request for interim measures and has been able to make the necessary assessment on the basis of the information which it has at its disposal through the applicant or otherwise.

The Commission has never given an indication under Rule 36 where the receiving state was a member of the Council of Europe which has recognized the Right of Individual Petition under Article 25 of the Convention. The reason for this is that in such a case a complaint can be lodged directly against the receiving state. This follows from the fact that the actual risk of treatment allegedly contrary to Article 3 does not exist in the state which orders the expulsion or extradition, but in the receiving state which is itself bound by the Convention and has recognized the competence of the Commission under Article 25.

A further problem may arise when an applicant has left his country under completely normal circumstances, but due to involvement in political activities abroad fears political persecution upon return to his or her home country. In such a case the seriousness of the risk of treatment contrary to Article 3 must again be sustained in a convincing way. It may also be of relevance whether the activities engaged in were legal or illegal in the host country. Similar considerations arise where the deportation is a result of a conviction for a criminal offence in the host country.

An indication under Rule 36 is normally addressed to the Government but it is also possible to address such an indication to the applicant although this seldom happens in practice. A situation where this was necessary arose in 1983 in a case concerning the Federal Republic of Germany where the applicant alleged that if extradited he would be treated contrary to Article 3 of the Convention in the receiving state. The Commission gave an indication to the Government to suspend the applicant's extradition until it had had an opportunity to examine the application at the next session. The Government complied but urged the Commission to decide quickly as it was no longer possible under German law to keep the applicant in detention pending extradition. The Government maintained that if released he would abscond. In these circumstances the Commission gave an indication under Rule 36 to the applicant that:

> if he was released he should remain at the disposal of the German authorities pending the decision which the Commission might take at its session commencing 2 May 1983.[33]

Requests under Rule 36 are often extremely urgent and are consequently dealt with by the Commission or its President very quickly, often within days and sometimes within hours. It is, however, important that applicants or their lawyers submit the request as soon as the final domestic decision has been taken, and in sufficient time before the execution of the order so that an intervention by the Commission is still possible. Requests which arrive at the Commission's secretariat 'at the last minute' carry the risk that the indication comes too late. A certain time is required for the secretariat to prepare the case, and when the Commission is not in session to communicate with the Commission's President. It should also be possible for the Commission to obtain some information on the matter, for instance by contacting the agent of the Government informally to enquire about the Government's intentions. Secondly the request must be in writing and contain full information as to the background of the dispute and the grounds of the complaint. A telephone communication may serve as an announcement of the request, but it cannot as such set in motion the procedure under Rule 36. On the other hand, a telex or telefax communication is sufficient, provided it contains adequate information on the applicant's situation, on the nature of his fears and the risks involved.

The Court may also apply interim measures.[34] According to Rule 36 of the Rules of Court the President of the Court may indicate to any party or to the applicant any interim measures which it is advisable for them to adopt. When the case is before a Chamber, the Chamber or its President shall have the same power.

This rule has only been applied very rarely because the need for interim measures will normally exist at the introduction of an application or even earlier, and will consequently normally arise before the case is brought before the Court. If, however, the Commission has applied its Rule 36, adopted its report and brought the case before the Court, there may still be a need for interim measures because, for instance, the question whether an intended extradition or expulsion would be in violation of Article 3 has not

33 Application No. 10308/83, DR 36, 209 (*Altun*).

34 See Berger, 'Le règlement amiable devant la Cour européenne des droits de l'homme', in F. Matscher and H. Petzold (eds), *Protecting Human Rights. The European Dimension* (1988) 55.

finally been decided. As the Commission's indication under its Rule 36 cannot apply after the case has been sent to the Court, it may be necessary for the Court to apply its Rule 36.

This was the situation in the *Soering* case[35] in which the Commission had applied Rule 36. On 25 January 1989 the Commission brought the case before the Court and on 26 January, following a request for interim measures made by the Commission and the applicant, the Court applied its Rule 36 and indicated to the United Kingdom Government that it would not be advisable to extradite the applicant pending the outcome of the proceedings before the Court.

In such situations it could, however, happen that there might be a few days delay from the time when the Commission's indication under Rule 36 elapses and until the President of the Court could make his recommendation under Rule 36 with the risk – at least theoretically – that an applicant might be extradited or expelled during such an interval. This risk has, however, been eliminated by the Court's adoption of an amendment to Rule 36 which entered into force on 1 April 1989. The amendment (Rule 36, paragraph 2) states that in cases where the Commission pursuant to its Rule 36 has indicated that an interim measure is desirable, its adoption or maintenance shall remain recommended to the parties after the case has been brought before the Court unless the President decides otherwise.

The *Soering* case is an important leading case because it is the first case in which the Court has had the opportunity to deal with the Commission's case-law according to which a person's deportation or extradition may give rise to an issue under Article 3 with regard to the deporting state where there are serious reasons to believe that the individual will be subjected to treatment contrary to Article 3 in the receiving state. The Court, after having analyzed the question, confirmed this case-law by saying that:

> In sum the decision by a Contracting State to extradite a fugitive may give rise to an issue under Article 3, and hence engage the responsibility of that State under the Convention, where substantial grounds have been shown for believing that the person concerned, if extradited, faces an real risk of being subjected to torture or to inhuman or degrading treatment or punishment in the requesting country.[36]

The facts of the case were that a German national, Mr. Soering, was detained in a prison in England pending extradition to the United States of America to face charges of murder in the state of Virginia. He alleged a violation of Article 3 because if extradited to the United States of America he would be faced with the risk of being subjected to the so-called 'death row

35 *Soering* case, judgment of 7 July 1989, ECHR (1989) Series A, No. 161.
36 Ibid., at para. 91.

phenomenon' as he might be sentenced to death and thereafter kept in prison for up to 8 years before execution.

The Commission had by a vote of 6 to 5 found that the extradition would not constitute a violation of Article 3, mainly because:

> In the circumstances of the present case the Commission does not consider that the conditions of detention on 'death row' or the execution procedures attain a level of severity contrary to Article 3 of the Convention.[37]

The Court, however, found that:

> having regard to the very long period of time spent on death row in such extreme conditions with the ever-present and mounting anguish of awaiting execution of the death penalty, and to the personal circumstances of the applicant, especially his age and mental stage at the time of the offence, the applicant's extradition to the United States would expose him to a real risk of treatment going beyond the threshold set by Article 3. A further consideration of relevance is that in the particular instance the legitimate purpose of extradition could be achieved by another means which would not involve suffering of such exceptional intensity or duration.[38]

The Court then unanimously held that:

> in the event of the Secretary of State's decision to extradite the applicant to the United States of America being implemented, there would be a violation of Article 3.[39]

The question as to whether an indication under Rule 36 is legally binding on states has remained unsolved. The reason for this being that Governments as a rule abide by an indication under Rule 36. This practice had found support in Recommendation No. R (80) 9 adopted by the Committee of Ministers of the Council of Europe on 27 June 1980 concerning extraditions to states not party to the Convention. In this Recommendation governments of member states are advised:

> to comply with an interim measure which the European Commission of Human Rights might indicate under Rule 36 of its Rules of Procedure as, for instance, a request to stay extradition proceedings pending a decision on this matter.[40]

There has been no expulsion case and only one extradition case (the above-mentioned *Soering* case) in which it has been finally established that a proposed extradition would be in violation of Article 3. The reason for this is that following an indication under Rule 36 the Government either reconsid-

37 *Supra* note 35, at para. 143.
38 *Supra* note 35, at para. 111.
39 Judgment's conclusion.
40 YB 23, 78.

ers its position with regard to the expulsion and decides that the applicant may stay on, for the time being or indefinitely. If this is the case the application before the Commission is either withdrawn and then struck out of the list, or it is declared inadmissible on the ground that the applicant can no longer claim to be a victim of the violation alleged. Alternatively, in the subsequent proceedings, the Government may show that the applicant's claim of treatment contrary to Article 3 of the Convention in the receiving state is manifestly ill-founded leading to a decision by the Commission to declare the application inadmissible and consequently the lifting of the Rule 36 indication.

Up till 1989 no Government had ever refused to comply with an indication under Rule 36 in expulsion cases. As far as extradition cases are concerned there has been one case where the Government considered that it could not abide by the indication given by the Commission. This was a very special case of an extradition to the United States for an offence which carried a mandatory sentence of 50 years' imprisonment. The applicant alleged that if convicted the sentence to be imposed would constitute inhuman or degrading punishment in violation of Article 3. The Government found itself in conflict with its own domestic law if they abided by the indication and they proceeded to extradite the applicant. The Commission subsequently declared the application inadmissible but reminded the respondent Government of the established practice to take account of such indications under Rule 36.[41]

In 1989, however, the Swedish Government refused to follow indications under Rule 36 in two expulsion cases. The first case, *Mansi* v. *Sweden*,[42] was as mentioned above terminated by a friendly settlement. In this case the Government formally declared that it regretted that the applicant had been expelled after the indication under Rule 36 had been given that he should not be expelled. Although this declaration was important it does not necessarily mean that the Government considered itself legally bound by an indication under Rule 36.

In the case of *Cruz Varas and others* v. *Sweden* the applicants Hector Cruz Varas, his wife, and their son were all Chilean citizens living in Sweden. After the Swedish authorities had decided to expel the family they filed an application and a Rule 36 request with the Commission on 5 October 1989. In the morning of 6 October the Commission decided that it was desirable not to deport the applicants to Chile until the Commission had had an opportunity to examine the case at its session in November. The Swedish authorities were immediately informed of the indication and were aware of it when they decided not to stay the enforcement of the expulsion.

41 Application No. 11615/85. To be published in DR.
42 Application No. 15658/89. To be published in DR.

Mr. Cruz Varas was deported to Chile the same afternoon. His wife and their son went into hiding in Sweden.

The Commission continued its examination of the case and found in its report of 7 June 1990[43] that although Mr. Cruz Varas had been ill-treated in Chile during a period ending in January 1987, the political situation in Chile had considerably improved between that time and the time of the expulsion in 1989. There did not exist in October 1989 a real risk that Mr. Cruz Varas would again be exposed in Chile to treatment contrary to Article 3. The Commission concluded by 8 votes to 5 that there had been no violation of Article 3. With regard to a complaint under Article 8 the Commission found unanimously that there had been no violation of this provision either. The important question, however, remained whether Sweden by not complying with the indication under Rule 36 had violated the Convention. The Government submitted that an indication under Rule 36 is a non-binding recommendation and that the Convention does not oblige the state to follow such an indication given by the Commission.

The Commission examined the question under Article 25 of the Convention according to which Governments which have accepted the right of individual petitions 'undertake not to hinder in any way the effective exercise of this right'. The Commission noted that before the present case no state had ever failed to comply with an indication given by the Commission in expulsion cases. The Commission had been seized with 182 requests to apply Rule 36 in expulsion cases and had given an indication in 31 of these cases.

In the present case the Commission considered that:

> to deport Mr. Cruz Varas although an indication under Rule 36 had been given frustrated its examination and thereby rendered his right of petition ineffective. Such an action is in the Commission's opinion contrary to the spirit of the Convention and is incompatible with the effective exercise of the right to petition guaranteed by Article 25, paragraph 1 of the Convention. These considerations apply notwithstanding the fact that the Commission has after a full examination of the merits of the complaint under Article 3 of the Convention concluded that there has been no violation of that provision.[44]

The Commission concluded by 12 votes to 1 that Sweden had failed to comply with its obligations under Article 25, paragraph 1 of the Convention.

The case was referred to the Court and the Swedish Government in July and August 1990 respectively and the Court gave its judgment on 20 March 1991.

43 *Cruz, Varas and others* case, judgment of 20 March 1991, ECHR (1991) Series A, No. 201, 42.

44 *Ireland* v. *United Kingdom, supra* note 30, at para. 122.

The Court referred to its statement in the *Soering* case (see above) according to which an extradition may incur the liability of the extraditing state under Article 3:

> where substantial grounds have been shown for believing that the person concerned, if extradited, faces a real risk of being subjected to torture or to inhuman or degrading treatment or punishment in the requesting country.[45]

The Court considered that the same principle applied to expulsion decisions and to cases of actual expulsion. In the present case the Court, however, like the Commission by 18 votes to 1 found that there had been no violation of Article 3 and unanimously that there had been no violation of Article 8.

On the crucial question whether a Rule 36 indication is binding and whether Sweden was consequently in breach of the Convention by not complying with the Commission's indication, the Court disagreed with the Commission and held by 10 votes to 9 that there had been no violation of Article 25, paragraph 1.

The Court noted that unlike other international instruments the Convention does not contain a specific provision with regard to interim measures. It further noted that the Parliamentary Assembly of the Council of Europe in a recommendation had called on the Committee of Ministers to draft an additional protocol which would empower the Convention organs to order interim measures.

> The Committee of Ministers subsequently decided that the conclusion of such a protocol was not expedient on the grounds *inter alia* that the existing practice of the Commission in requesting governments to postpone the measures complained of work satisfactorily.[46]

The Court observed that Rule 36 is only a Rule of Procedure and that:

> in the absence of a provision in the Convention for interim measures an indication given under Rule 36 cannot be considered to give rise to a binding obligation on Contracting Parties.[47]

After having examined Article 25, paragraph 1 the Court found that:

> it would strain the language of Article 25 to infer from the words 'undertake not to hinder in any way the effective exercise of this right' an obligation to comply with a Commission indication under Rule 36.[48]

45 *Supra* note 43, at para. 69.
46 Ibid., at para. 96.
47 Ibid., at para. 98.
48 Ibid., at para. 99.

The Court considered that 'the power to order binding interim measures cannot be inferred from either Article 25, paragraph 1 in fine or from other sources'[49] such as the practice of Governments to comply with Rule 36 indications or general principles of international law. The Court added, however, that where a state did not comply with a Rule 36 indication 'any subsequent breach of Article 3 found by the Convention organs would have to be seen as aggravated by the failure to comply with the indication'.[50]

The nine members of the Court being in the minority in a joint dissenting opinion found like the Commission that there had been a violation of Article 25. The minority said *inter alia:*

> The protection under the Convention would be meaningless if a State had a right to extradite or expel a person without any prior possibility of clarification – as far and as soon as possible – of the consequences of the expulsion. The Court has repeatedly underlined that 'the object and purpose of the Convention as an instrument for the protection of individual human rights require that its provisions be interpreted and applied so as to make its safeguards practical and effective.' (See the *Soering* judgment of 7 July 1989, Series A, No. 161, 34, para. 87). This basic principle must be kept in mind when we consider the procedural guarantees contained in the Convention.[51]

Before reaching its conclusion the minority said that:

> it is in our view implicit in the Convention that in cases such as the present the Convention organs have the power to require the parties to abstain from a measure which might not only give rise to serious harm but which might also nullify the result of the entire procedure under the Convention.[52]

The *Cruz Varas* case has been dealt with at some length because the issue of that case is of fundamental importance for the effective functioning of the Convention system. It is to be hoped that Governments will continue the practice of complying with Rule 36 indications also after the judgment mentioned above.

(g) Article 31 Reports

When an application has been declared admissible and if it is not settled the Commission will, after having examined the facts and merits of the case proceed to elaborate its report under Article 31 of the Convention. In the report the facts of the case are stated as well as the Commission's opinion as to whether the facts found disclose a breach by the state concerned of

49 Ibid., at para. 102.
50 Ibid., at para. 103.
51 *Supra* note 43, Joint dissenting opinion, at para. 1.
52 *Supra* note 43, Joint dissenting opinion, at para. 3.

its obligations under the Convention. Besides the majority opinion individual opinions of members of the Commission may be stated in the report.

When the report has finally been adopted it is sent to the Committee of Ministers and to the state concerned who shall not be at liberty to publish it. The report is, however, not sent to the applicant at this stage. In transmitting the report to the Committee of Ministers the Commission may make such proposals as it thinks fit, for instance proposals regarding economic compensation to the applicant in case the Commission has found a violation. At this stage the Commission will normally not be in possession of the information necessary to propose an exact amount of compensation to the applicant. A practice has therefore been developed according to which the Commission, in cases where a violation has been found, makes a standard proposal to the Committee of Ministers in which it proposes that compensation as well as legal costs should be paid to the applicant. At the same time the Commission offers its assistance to make precise proposals at a later stage (see below under Committee of Ministers).

After the report has been sent to the Committee of Ministers and when it concerns a state which has recognized the Court's compulsory jurisdiction under Article 46, the Commission decides within a period of 3 months whether or not to bring the case before the Court. The case may also be submitted to the Court by the state whose national is alleged to be a victim, by the state which referred the case to the Commission, and by the state against which the application has been lodged. In practice the great majority of cases brought before the Court are brought there by a decision of the Commission.

2. The Court[53]

According to Article 44 only the High Contracting Parties and the Commission shall have the right to bring a case before the Court. The states which can bring a case before the Court are the state whose national is alleged to be a victim, the state which refers the case to the Commission and the state against which a complaint has been lodged. A case can only be brought against a state which has accepted the Court's compulsory jurisdiction under Article 46. Since 1990 all 23 states bound by the Convention have made such declarations.

When a case has been brought before the Court a chamber of 9 judges is constituted to deal with the case. Members of the Chamber are *ex officio* the Court's President or Vice-president and every judge who holds a nationality

53 See Ganshof van der Meersch, 'European Court of Human Rights', in *Encyclopedia, Instalment 8*, 192.

of a party. The remaining members and a number of substitutes are drawn by lot among the judges (Rules of Court. Rule 21).

A Chamber, however, may at any time relinquish jurisdiction in favour of the Plenary Court if the case raises serious questions affecting the interpretation of the Convention. The relinquishement is obligatory when a resolution of such questions might have a result which is inconsistent with a previous judgment (Rule 51). Chambers have so far relinquished jurisdiction in 48 cases.

As mentioned above, only the Commission and states can bring a case before the Court. The fact that the individual applicant does not have this capacity, however, does not in itself solve the question regarding the position of the applicant when a case has been brought before the Court. This question is not clearly answered by the Convention and has been dealt with in detail both in the Commission and the Court and in numerous articles in the legal doctrine.[54] In the text of the Convention there is a discrepancy between the English and the French text of Article 44. According to the English text only states and the Commission 'shall have the right to bring a case before the Court', whereas in the French text the same 'ont qualité pour se présenter devant la Cour'.

In the very first case decided by the Court, the *Lawless* case, this problem was raised and the Court found that it followed from Article 44 that only states and the Commission had the right to bring a case before the Court as well as the right to appear before it.[55]

This situation, of course, was not satisfactory. Before the Commission the applicant, through his lawyer or personally, had the opportunity to plead his case and the Commission might have expressed the opinion that he had been the victim of a violation of the Convention. Before the Court the applicant had no legal right to present his case, although the Court might finally conclude that he was the victim of a violation and even recognized him by awarding compensation to him under Article 50 as 'the injured party'.

The Court seems to have been clearly aware of the unsatisfactory solution and observed that the Commission's delegate had the full opportunity to submit the applicant's observations to the Court and that the Commission was free to establish contact with the applicant or his lawyer in order to make it possible for its delegate to present the applicant's point of view to the Court.[56]

54 See J. Velu et R. Ergec, *La Convention européenne des droits de l'homme* (1990) 976-987 with further references.

55 *Lawless* case (Preliminary objections), decision of 14 November 1960, ECHR (1960) Series A, No. 1, 15.

56 *Lawless* case, judgment of 7 April 1961, ECHR (1961) Series A, No. 2, 24.

The next important step in the development in this matter was in the case of *De Wilde, Ooms and Versyp*, where the question was raised whether the Commission's delegate could be assisted by the applicant's lawyer so that the lawyer could take the floor in the pleadings before the Court. The Court in its decision on this matter based itself on its rule of procedure according to which the Commission's delegate could be assisted by anyone of the delegate's choice and found that this rule did not forbid the delegate from having the assistance of the applicant's lawyer. The Court emphasized, however, that the applicant's lawyer assisting the delegate of the Commission was acting on and talking under the control and responsibility of the delegate.[57]

In the following decade the delegate was in practically all cases assisted by the applicant's lawyer or in some cases even by the applicant himself, who, at the request of the delegate, was given the floor after the delegate to present his observations and submissions. In practice the rule that the applicant or his lawyer was acting under the control and responsibility of the delegate did not raise serious problems although it might sometimes have been considered slightly embarrassing. The applicant's lawyer would thus naturally without any difficulty have the opportunity to present points of view which might not be in conformity with the Commission's opinion. The delegate's control and responsibility in reality did not seem to be necessary as the system developed.

However, the position of the applicant in a case before the Court, could still not be considered satisfactory. By its revised Rules of Court which entered into force 1 January 1983 the Court managed in a remarkable way to give the applicant a position before the Court which comes very close to that of a party and the Commission. The 1983 rules are in this respect more or less the same as the present rules of Court – as in force from 30 June 1990 – which in detail lay down the rights of a party, of the Commission's delegate and now also of the applicant. In these rules the term 'party' is still reserved for the state or states which are applicant or respondent parties.

The main innovations for the applicant are that when a case is brought before the Court the applicant is asked whether he wishes to take part in the proceedings before the Court and if so to name the advocate or any other person appointed by him as his representative (Rule 33 paragraph 3(d)). Having answered this request in the affirmative, the applicant's representative may submit written memorials and observations, he can appear before the Court at the oral hearing and take the floor. He will, of course, during

57 *De Wilde, Ooms and Versyp* (Preliminary objections), decision of 18 November 1970, ECHR (1970) Series A, No. 12, 8.

the proceedings receive relevant information and observations in the same way as the party.

Apart from the important fact that the applicant cannot bring a case before the Court, the only difference between the applicant and a party is that only a party has the right to raise preliminary objections before the Court (Rule 48); neither the Commission nor an applicant have this right. It is, however, difficult to imagine that the Commission or an applicant could have any interest in raising such objections.

Secondly, only a party or the Commission, but not the applicant, can make a request for an interpretation or revision of a judgment (Rules 57 and 58). It can, of course, not be ruled out that an applicant has an interest in an interpretation or revision. On the other hand, as an applicant cannot bring a case before the Court it seems logical that he cannot ask for a 're-opening' of a decided case either. It might also give rise to abuse if applicants had this right. In fact it happens not so seldom that an applicant who has lost a case before the Court complains to the Commission and asks the Commission to request an interpretation or revision without giving any real substantiation for the request.

In the proceedings before the Court the party or parties (i.e. the state or states involved) shall be represented by the agent who is normally assisted by advocates or advisers. The Commission shall be represented by a member of the Commission as delegate and the applicant by an advocate or any other person approved by the President of the Court. The President may also allow the applicant to present his own case (Rules 28-30).

The proceedings before the Court normally consist of an exchange of written memorials between the party or parties, the applicant, and the delegate of the Commission. At the oral hearing which takes place after the exchange of memorials, the President prescribes the order in which those appearing before the Court shall be called upon to speak. Normally the delegate of the Commission speaks first and presents the case on the basis of the Commission's report which is sent to the Court and made public as soon as the case is referred to the Court. Secondly, the lawyer for the applicant pleads the case, and thirdly, the representative of the respondent Government. After the hearing, the Court will normally give its judgment within a few months.

Although the Convention does not contain any specific rule regarding friendly settlement of a case before the Court such settlement is possible and in fact 29 cases (including 14 Italian length cases which were settled at the same time) have been settled before the Court. If the parties inform the Court that they have reached a settlement of a case and the settlement is consonant with the general interest attaching to observance of Human Rights, the Court in a judgment strikes the case out of the list (Rule 49).

The large majority of cases, however, are terminated by a final and binding judgment, finding a violation or no violation. As at the end of 1991 the Court had found violations of one or more articles in 174 cases, and in 107 of these cases Article 6 was violated. In 56 cases the Court found no violation, and 31 of these concerned Article 6. In cases where the Court finds a violation it will also decide whether compensation according to Article 50 shall be paid. Compensation can be awarded for pecuniary or non-pecuniary damage and for reimbursement of cost and expenses, normally lawyers' fees. Just satisfaction of a pecuniary nature has been awarded in 143 cases.

3. The Committee of Ministers[58]

The Committee of Ministers has two main functions within the field of Human Rights. Firstly, when the Commission has adopted its report under Article 31 it is sent to the Committee of Ministers, and if the case is not brought before the Court within 3 months, the Committee of Ministers under Article 32 decides by a majority of 2/3 of its members whether there has been a violation of the Convention. This decision which is taken in the form of a resolution is binding upon the States, and the Committee of Ministers supervises the execution of its decision.

Secondly, the Committee of Ministers shall according to Article 54 supervise the execution of the judgments of the Court.

When the Committee of Ministers has found a violation it would often be appropriate also to decide that the respondent state should pay just satisfaction to the injured party. According to Article 50 the Court is competent to grant such satisfaction, whereas the Convention does not contain a similar rule with regard to the Committee of Ministers.

For many years the unsatisfactory situation prevailed that the Committee of Ministers did not decide on the question of pecuniary compensation. There is, however, for the Committee of Ministers a possibility to grant compensation according to the rule in Article 32, paragraph 2 pursuant to which the Committee of Ministers, when a violation has been found, shall prescribe a period during which the States concerned must take the measures required by the decision of the Committee of Ministers. This rule must be interpreted as also giving the Committee of Ministers the competence to decide on granting just satisfaction.

In order to fix compensation the Committee needs the observations from the injured applicant and the respondent state. As the individual applicant

58 See J. Velu et R. Ergec, *supra* note 54, at 1089-1128 with further references and Hondius, 'The Other Forum' in F. Matscher and H. Petzold (eds), *Protecting Human Rights: The European Dimension* (1988) 245.

has no procedural standing before the Committee, a satisfactory procedure was difficult to establish in order to solve this problem. The problem was solved in 1987 when the following new procedure was introduced. When the Commission has sent a case to the Committee of Ministers it may according to Article 31, paragraph 3 make such proposals as it thinks fit. Under this rule the Commission can make proposals for compensation in cases where it has found a violation. At this stage, the Commission, however, does not know whether the Committee of Ministers will follow the Commission's opinion although the Committee does so in the great majority of cases. Secondly, the Commission normally has not at this stage the information from the parties which is necessary in order to propose a concrete amount of compensation and legal costs.

The new procedure agreed upon is the following: When the Commission sends a case, in which it has found a violation, to the Committee of Ministers it will make a general proposal that compensation and costs shall be paid to the applicant and at the same time offer its assistance to the Committee of Ministers in proposing the exact amount later.

When the Committee has found a violation in the case it will inform the Commission and ask the Commission for its exact proposal. The Commission then requests the applicant to submit and specify his claim for compensation and costs. At the same time, the Commission's report which is not yet public and not known to the applicant is communicated to him as the necessary basis for his claim. The applicant is, however, obliged to keep the report confidential until it is made public at a later stage. After having received the applicant's claim and the respondent Government's comments on the claim, the Commission will make its precise proposal to the Committee of Ministers which then can make its decision on just satisfaction. So far the decisions of the Committee of Ministers have followed the proposals from the Commission. During the few years of its existence this system – although complicated – has functioned satisfactorily.

The fact that the Committee of Ministers makes binding decisions regarding violations of the Convention when a case is not brought before the Court has often been criticized, mainly for two reasons. Firstly, it is said that the Committee of Ministers as a political organ composed of representatives of Governments acting under instruction from their respective Governments should not take decisions which ought to be of a purely legal nature. Secondly, because the procedure before the Committee is totally devoid of any equality of arms. Neither the applicant nor the Commission takes part in the proceedings whereas a representative of the respondent Government participates both in the deliberations and the vote. A third reason for criticism namely that the Committee of Ministers did not award just satisfaction has disappeared after 1987 as mentioned above.

It is true that the role of the Committee of Ministers is not consonant with a modern judicial system for the protection of Human Rights and several proposals have been made throughout the years for changing the system in this respect, for instance simply by making the Commission's report binding if the case is not sent to the Court. At present, however, intense negotiations are taking place with a view to a possible reform of the existing system for the control of Human Rights (see below), and no doubt the functions of the Committee of Ministers will be carefully considered in these negotiations.

D. Effects of the Convention System in the Member States[59]

1. General

The European system for the protection of Human Rights includes today – apart from the Committee of Ministers – a Court with 26 judges, a Commission with 22 members, all of whom work more than half time within the system, and a Registry, and a Secretariat with more than 50 full time occupied lawyers. Against this background it is justified to ask whether the Convention and the decisions of its organs have had and have any real effect within the member states.

Firstly, all states have before ratifying the Convention and accepting the right of individual petition under Article 25 and the Court's jurisdiction under Article 46 carefully scrutinized the conformity of their national legislation with the Convention, and in nearly all countries legislation has been changed in order to comply with the requirements of the Convention at this stage. Similarly, in most Convention states any proposed new legislation is carefully examined before it is submitted to parliament in order to secure conformity with the rules of the Convention.

Secondly, it is possible that the mere existence of a legal right for the individual to complain to an international control organ has a preventive effect in the member states so that possible violations are avoided. Although such an effect is often mentioned and clearly cannot be excluded, it is evident that it can hardly be proven by objective criteria.

Thirdly, and more concretely, it is a fact that national courts in an increasing number of cases apply the rules of the Convention and the practise from the Convention organs. Naturally, this is especially so in the countries which have incorporated the Convention into national law, i.e. all the member states apart from Great Britain, Ireland, Norway, Sweden, Iceland, and until 1 July 1992 Denmark. But even in these countries, where the courts are not directly bound to apply the Convention, the courts have in an

59 See J. Velu et R. Ergec, *supra* note 54, at 1043-1088 with further references.

increasing number of cases nevertheless applied the rules of the Convention in the interpretation of national law. To further improve this effect it is to be hoped that the Convention before too long will be incorporated into the national law of all Convention states. In Denmark a new statute by which the Convention was incorporated into Danish Law entered into force 1 July 1992. In Norway a similar proposal appears to be under preparation.

Fourthly, the most obvious general effect of the decisions taken by the organs in Strasbourg is the number of changes in the legislation of the member states. The number of changes in the individual member states amounts to about 100. In addition, there has been an impressive number of changes in national jurisprudence and administrative practise. Changes of legislation and changes of the practice have occurred in some cases as an element of a friendly settlement concluded before the Commission or the Court, in other cases as a result of decisions by the Commission which has been confirmed by the Committee of Ministers, and last but not least as a result of decisions by the Court. It will not be possible here to mention all the relevant cases and changes, but a number of examples may illustrate this important effect of the functioning of the system.

2. Friendly Settlements which have Resulted in Changes of Legislation

When the Commission has declared an application admissible the first task is to try to reach a friendly settlement between the applicant and the respondent state. Throughout the years several applications have been settled, in most cases in the way that the state pays a sum of money in compensation to the applicant. Before accepting a settlement between the parties it is, however, the Commission's duty to secure that the settlement has been concluded on the basis of respect for Human Rights. If the application shows a defect in the national system it may therefore be necessary as part of the friendly settlement to secure that a change of the legislation in the respondent state takes place.

In a case against Austria[60] which was settled in 1981 the applicant had been convicted by the regional court of Vienna sitting as a jury court of the crime of aggravated robbery with deadly issue. The court pronounced the sentence of 10 years imprisonment. This judgment was subject to appeals, both by the applicant and by the prosecution. The applicant claimed, *inter alia*, the existence of grounds for extraordinary mitigation which would have justified a sentence of below the 10 years. The prosecution in its appeal considered that the sentence was too lenient and claimed a higher sentence. When the case was dealt with by the Supreme Court the applicant was in prison. In that situation the court could have granted permission for

60 Application No. 8289/78, DR 25, 182 (*Peschke*).

the accused person to be present during the court hearing; the accused person, however, was refused to be present in spite of his lawyer's protest. In its sentence the Supreme Court rejected the applicant's appeal from the sentence but upheld the prosecution's appeal adding 2 years to the original 10 years' sentence.

Before the Commission the applicant complained that his exclusion from the hearing at the Supreme Court was in violation of Article 6 of the Convention. After having declared the application admissible, the Commission commenced friendly settlement negotiations. As part of the settlement the Government undertook to propose changes to the Code of Criminal Procedure to the effect that an accused who is under arrest must at his request be brought before the court to attend the hearing which deals with an appeal lodged to his detriment. Secondly, by an act of grace the applicant's prison sentence should be reduced from 12 years prison to 10 years. The proposed change of legislation was adopted shortly after and the applicant's sentence was changed to 10 years' imprisonment.

Another interesting example of important changes in national law as part of a friendly settlement took place in two cases against Iceland, which were settled in 1990.[61] Before 1990 the Icelandic legislation contained a special rule for the treatment of minor criminal cases in all parts of the country except in the capital, Reykjavik. According to this rule minor criminal cases were dealt with by the local chief of police or his substitute, who functioned both as prosecutor and judge in the case.

In 1986 and 1987 the Commission received applications from two persons who in different parts of Iceland had been sentenced for minor criminal offences under the existing system. Both applicants alleged violations of Article 6 because their cases had not been decided by an impartial and independent judge. In the pleadings before the Commission the Icelandic Government in both cases submitted that the Icelandic system, where investigative and judicial powers were combined, had historical and geographical origin and they emphasized that the conditions prevailing in Iceland were significantly different from those in other member states of the Council of Europe. These particular Icelandic conditions formed the background for the legal system and the applicant's cases should in the Government's opinion, be seen in this light.

The Commission, however, declared both applications admissible in October 1987 and in December 1989 respectively. In the first of the two cases (the *Kristinsson* case) the Commission did not succeed in obtaining a settlement and found in its report that from March 1989 that Article 6 had

61 Application No. 13291/87 *Sverrisson* v. *Iceland*. Com. Rep. of 6 February 1990, to be published in DR and *Jon Kristinsson* case, judgment of 1 March 1990, ECHR (1990) Series A, No. 161-B.

been violated. In April 1989 the Commission brought the case before the Court and the report was published.

In the second case (the *Sverrisson* case) the applicant and the Government concluded a friendly settlement before the Commission in December 1989. The settlement contained the information that a new bill in respect of separation of district judicial and administrative powers had been enacted and approved by the President on 1 June 1989. This enactment, which will enter into effect on 1 July 1992, provides that police administration from that date will be in the hands of district executive agents to be titled magistrates, and that district court judges, independent and separate from the executive branch of Government, will resolve issues relating to criminal charges. Secondly, the Government reimbursed the applicant with his costs in the case.

The settlement was important and in general acceptable, the only problem being that the change of the legislation will only take effect more than two years later. However, before the Commission accepted the friendly settlement a new development took place. In January 1990 the Supreme Court of Iceland quashed a judgment in a similar case from another district criminal court and referred that case back to retrial on the ground that the judge concerned was both deputy county magistrate and head of the district police which had conducted the investigation. In its decision the Supreme Court took account of the Commission's report from March 1989 in the *Kristinsson* case. As a result of the judgment the President of Iceland a few days later in January 1990 issued a provisional Act which as an interim measure creates new posts of district court judges. After this development the Commission in February 1990 approved the friendly settlement agreed upon by the parties in December 1989.

In the first of the two cases, which as mentioned above was brought before the Court, friendly settlement negotiations between the applicant in the case and the Icelandic Government took place at the same time and a friendly settlement similar to that in the second case before the Commission was concluded between the parties. This settlement was approved by the Court in March 1990 and the case was struck out of the Court's list of cases. The two cases are important because they illustrate that through friendly settlement negotiations it is sometimes possible to achieve rather fundamental changes in the legal system in a member country. At the same time the cases are interesting because the Supreme Court in a country, which has not incorporated the Convention into its national law, applied a decision from the Commission as the basis for annulling a court decision which was in full conformity with Icelandic law, as it was hitherto understood and interpreted.

As a last example of a friendly settlement which has resulted in important changes in national law mention ought to be made of one, or rather three cases against Sweden.[62] The cases were all brought before the Commission by the same applicant.

The applicant had been arrested on 5 May 1978. He was later transferred to a police-station about 600 km away where he was questioned by the police. Having been informed about the arrest the public prosecutor, without having herself heard the applicant, two days later on 7 May decided that the applicant's provisional detention should continue. The applicant was then for the first time brought before a judge on 12 May, 7 days after the arrest. The judge then decided to detain him on remand.

In his application to the Commission the applicant alleged a violation of Article 5, paragraph 3 according to which everyone arrested shall be brought promptly before a judge or other officer authorized by law to exercise judicial power. In its report the Commission found that Article 5, paragraph 3 had been violated because the public prosecutor who decided on the detention two days after the arrest had not herself heard the applicant and secondly because the public prosecutor did not fulfill the requirements of an 'officer authorized by law to exercise judicial power' within the meaning of Article 5, paragraph 3. Next the Commission found that the 7 days which had elapsed from the arrest of the applicant until he was brought before a judge did not fulfill the requirement that the arrested person promptly shall be brought before a judge.

The case was subsequently brought before the Court of Human Rights where it was terminated with a settlement in 1984. As part of the settlement the Swedish Government had informed

> the Commission for Revision of Certain Parts of the Code of Judicial Procedure about the report of the European Commission of Human Rights and asked the Swedish Commission to propose and work out the details for such amendments to the Code as required in order to put it beyond any doubt that it is in conformity with Article 5, paragraph 3 of the Convention. A Government Bill on the basis of this proposal can be expected as soon as possible in accordance with the provisions of the Swedish Instrument of Government.[63]

The Government further paid a pecuniary compensation of 5,000 Swedish Crowns to the applicant.

A friendly settlement was approved by the Court in October 1984 by 4 votes against 3, which in itself is unusual as settlements are normally approved unanimously. The minority found that although the settlement would appear to satisfy the individual interest of the applicant, the decision to strike the case out of the list did not seem to be consonant with a general

62 Application No. 8582/79. *Skoogström* case, judgment of 2 October 1984, ECHR (1984) Series A, No. 83. Application No. 12867/87 and 14073/88. Com. Rep. of 8 March 1989, *Skoogström* (II and III) v. *Sweden*, to be published in DR.

63 Ibid., at para. 22.

interest attaching to the observance of Human Rights, an interest which the Court was responsible for safeguarding. The minority found that the settlement should not be approved as it did not indicate the nature of the amendments that would be made to the Code of Judicial Procedure, or when these amendments will be proposed.[64]

Changes in the legislation were, however, adopted in December 1987 and entered into force in April 1988:

> It follows from the new rules that where a person has been arrested and provisionally detained by order of the public prosecutor, a request for his detention on remand shall be submitted to the court on the same day as the provisional detention was ordered or, at the latest, on the following day. Where there are special reasons, the request may be postponed up to the third day after the provisional detention order (Chapter 24, section 12 of the Code). The court shall hold a hearing regarding the request for detention on remand on the same day as the request is received or, at the latest, on the following day. If there are special reasons, the hearing may be postponed, but it must never be held later than 96 hours after the arrest (Chapter 24, section 13 of the Code).[65]

Before these amendments had entered into force the same applicant was, however, again arrested on 14 January 1987 and not brought before a judge until 7 days later on 21 January. After having been released the applicant was again arrested on 16 April 1987 and was not brought before a judge until 6 days later on 22 April.

In both of these cases the applicant again complained to the Commission alleging a violation of Article 5, paragraph 3. These two cases were settled before the Commission in March 1989, with a pecuniary compensation to the applicant and reference was made to the above-mentioned amendments to the Swedish Code which had now entered into force.

3. Reports of the Commission and Resolutions by the Committee of Ministers which have Resulted in Changes of Legislation

As examples of this situation two of the rare cases in which a violation of Article 12 has been found might be illustrative. In 1975 an applicant complained that he was refused permission by the Home Secretary to get married when he was serving a long-term prison sentence in the United Kingdom. He claimed that such refusal constituted a breach of Article 12 of the Convention. A similar case was introduced in 1977 by another prisoner who was serving a life-sentence in the United Kingdom.[66]

64 Ibid., at para. 11.

65 Quoted from Com. Rep. on Application Nos. 12867/87 and 14073/88 (*Skoogström*).

66 Application Nos. 7114/75 and 8186/88. Com. Rep. of 13 December 1979, *Hamer* v. *United Kingdom*, DR 24, 5 and Com. Rep. of 10 July 1980, *Draper* v. *United Kingdom*, DR 24, 73.

In its report from 1979 and 1980 respectively the Commission found that the fact that national law did not allow the applicants to marry in prison and that the Home Secretary or prison authorities would not allow their temporary release so that they could marry elsewhere constituted an interference with the exercise of the applicants' right to marry. The Commission further found that the imposition by the state of any substantial period of delay on the exercise of this right in general must be seen as an injury to its substance and that the applicants' ability to exercise their right to marry was substantially delayed by the continued effects of the national law and administrative action. In both cases the Commission unanimously found that the applicants' right to marry as guaranteed by Article 12 had been violated. The Committee of Ministers agreed with the opinion expressed by the Commission.

During the examination of the cases the Committee of Ministers was informed that the Government of the United Kingdom had changed its practice with regard to the marriage of prisoners serving a determinate custodial sentence and that a decision had been taken to prepare legislation to amend the marriage laws so as to allow prisoners to be married in prison. Subsequently such legislation has been passed.[67]

4. Court Judgments which have Resulted in Changes of Legislation

A very important number of changes of national legislation (about 70) has occurred as a result of judgments from the court. Many of the changes have concerned procedural matters after the Court has found violations of Article 6, but some judgments have also resulted in remarkable changes in legislation in other important areas.

The question of impartiality of courts was at issue in the case of *Hauschildt* v. *Denmark*. The applicant complained of a violation of Article 6 and alleged that he had not had a fair trial before an impartial court because the same judges who had on several occasions decided his detention on remand later decided the merits of his case and sentenced him to five years' imprisonment. The Commission found, by 9 votes to 7, that there had been no violation of Article 6. The Court, however, with 12 votes to 5, found that Article 6 had been violated.[68]

In the judgment the Court analyzed the Danish system in general and found that:

67 Committee of Ministers Resolutions DH (81) 4 and 5, YB 1981, Part Two, Chapter III, p. 462 and 464 (*Draper* and *Hamer*).

68 *Hauschildt* case, judgment of 24 May 1989, ECHR (1989) Series A, No. 154.

> the mere fact that a trial judge or an appeal judge in a system like the Danish, also makes pre-trial decisions in the case including those concerning detention on remand cannot be held as in itself justifying fears as to his impartiality.[69]

In the special circumstances of the present case the Court came to a different conclusion because several of the decisions to prolong the detention on remand had been based on the Administration of Justice Act, section 762 (2) which requires that the judge be satisfied that there is a 'particularly confirmed suspicion' that the accused has committed the crime with which he is charged. The Court therefore found that the difference between the issue the judge has to settle when he is applying this section and the issue he will have to settle when giving judgment at the trial becomes tenuous. In the circumstances of the case the impartiality of the tribunal was therefore capable of appearing to be open to doubt, and the applicant's fears in this respect could be considered objectively justified. Consequently there had been a violation of Article 6 of the Convention.

After the case had been declared admissible by the Commission on 9 October 1986 but before the judgment in the case, the Danish Administration of Justice Act was amended by a statute of 10 June 1987. According to the change no one shall act as judge in the trial if at an earlier stage of the proceedings he has ordered the person concerned to be remanded in custody *solely* under section 762 (2). The new statute was shortly after interpreted by the Danish Supreme Court in another case.[70] The question again was whether a judge could be considered impartial as judge at a trial when he had earlier decided on detention on remand of the accused. The judge had in his decisions on detention on remand based the decisions on a combination of grounds, one of them being 'particularly confirmed suspicion' according to section 762 (2) of the Administration of Justice Act, but also on other grounds such as risk of collusion.

The Supreme Court, after analyzing the *Hauschildt* judgment, held that this judgment must be interpreted in such a way that it will not ordinarily be consistent with Article 6 of the Convention that a judge, who prior to the trial has ordered detention under section 762 (2) either solely or in connection with other grounds for detention, participates at the hearing of the case. The judge therefore should be regarded as being disqualified. The Supreme Court, in other words, interpreted the Danish statute of 10 June in the way that the word 'solely' in fact did not only mean 'solely' but also 'in connection with other grounds'.

As a result the Danish Administration of Justice Act was again amended in June 1990. According to this amendment a judge cannot act in a trial if he at an earlier stage of the proceedings has ordered the person

69 Ibid., at para. 50.
70 *Ugeskrift for Retsvæsen* (1990) 13.

concerned to be remanded in custody and if the decision of detention on remand is based on a particularly confirmed suspicion alone, or together with other reasons for detention.[71]

The case is remarkable for two reasons. Firstly, because the first change of the Danish legislation took place on the basis of the Commission's decision to declare the application in the *Hauschildt* case admissible before any decision on the merits had been taken. Secondly, because the Supreme Court in a country which has not yet incorporated the Convention into national law used the judgment from the Court of Human Rights to interpret the national legislation in such a way that it in fact changed the national legislation in order to bring it in full conformity with the Court's decision.

In Dutch law an important change of legislation regarding access to court in certain administrative cases has taken place as a result of the Court's judgment in the *Benthem* case.[72] The applicant had complained of a violation of Article 6, alleging that his case had not been heard by an independent and impartial tribunal. The applicant had applied for a license to operate an installation for the delivery of liquid petrol gas for motor vehicles. The license had been granted by the municipal authorities under certain conditions, but on appeal by the Regional Health Inspector to the Crown the decision to grant the license was quashed. There was no further appeal against this decision.

Before 1980 the Crown (the King or the Queen together with the responsible minister) gave rulings in administrative litigation which were brought before it on appeal. The Crown, however, did not take a decision until the Administrative Litigation Division of the Council of State had investigated the matter and prepared a draft decision. The Crown was not under a duty to follow the advice from the Administrative Litigation Division, but nearly always did and this practice was followed in the present case.

A crucial problem before the Convention organs was whether Article 6 was applicable to the case or not. Once the applicability of Article 6 had been established, the Court also concluded that Article 6 had been violated. The Court found that the Crown could not be considered a tribunal in the sense of Article 6 as it did not fulfill such essential requirements as independence and impartiality, and that the Crown decision constituted an administrative act emanating from a minister who was therefore responsible to Parliament.

As a result of the judgment an important provisional act was adopted which entered into force on 1 January 1988. The act regulates proceedings in matters of litigation where the Crown has thus far been competent, and it gives a power of decision to the Administrative Litigation Division of the

71 Committee of Ministers Resolution DH (91) 9. To be published in the YB.
72 *Benthem* case, judgment of 23 October 1985, ECHR (1985) Series A, No. 97.

Council of the State which can henceforth act as a tribunal within the meaning of Article 6 of the Convention.[73]

As an illustration of more specific, but still important changes of national law relating to fair trial mention can be made of two subsequent changes in German law regarding payment of interpretation in criminal cases. According to Article 6, paragraph 3(e) of the Convention everyone charged with a criminal offence has the right to have the free assistance of an interpreter if he cannot understand or speak the language used in court. According to German law as it stood before 1980, the services of an interpreter were always provided by the court if an accused in a criminal case had not mastered the German language. If, however, an accused was convicted he would have, as part of the costs of the proceedings, to pay the costs for the interpretation.

In the case of *Luedicke, Belkacem and Koç*[74] the three applicants who had been found guilty of criminal offences and had been ordered to pay costs, including costs for interpretation, complained of a violation of Article 6, paragraph 3(e). Before the Convention organs the German Government submitted that Article 6 only secured that interpretation should be provided for *ex officio* and when necessary, and that no advance payments for the costs could be claimed from the accused, whereas it did not prevent him from being charged with such expenses once he had been convicted. The applicants submitted that interpretation costs could never be charged to them. Both the Commission and the Court unanimously found a violation in the case, because it would run contrary to the ordinary meaning of the word 'free' (*gratuitement*) and to the object and purpose of Article 6 if the rule in question were to be reduced to the guarantee of a right to a provisional exemption from payment and if it did not prevent the domestic courts from making a convicted person pay the interpretation costs. As a result of the judgment the German legislation was amended by an act of 18 August 1980 so that persons convicted in criminal cases would not be charged with interpretation costs.[75]

The new legislation, however, only applied to ordinary criminal cases and not to cases which were decided under the Regulatory Offences Act. Under this act an administrative authority can fine persons who have committed minor offences such as traffic offences. Persons fined, however, can lodge an objection to such decisions in which case the matter will be tried before a court.

73 Committee of Ministers Resolution DH (88) 6. To be published in the YB.

74 Case of *Luedicke, Belkacem and Koç*, judgment of 28 November 1978, ECHR (1978) Series A, No. 29.

75 Committee of Ministers Resolution DH (83) 4, YB 1983, Part Two, Chapter IV, p. 19 (*Luedicke, Belkacem and Koç*).

In the *Öztürk* case[76] the applicant had been fined DM 60 on the grounds that he had committed a traffic offence. He lodged an objection against the fine but at a hearing before a district court he withdrew it, and as result the fine became payable. Subsequently he was ordered to pay, apart from the fine, the costs of the proceedings, including interpreter's fee of DM 63.

Before the Commission the applicant complained of a violation of Article 6, paragraph 3(e). The main problem in the case was whether a person like the applicant, who has been charged and fined for a traffic offence, could be considered as being charged with a criminal offence within the meaning of Article 6. The Court found that the Article was applicable as it would be contrary to the object or purpose of Article 6 if the state were allowed to remove from the scope of this Article a whole category of offences merely on the ground of categorizing them as petty. The Court, however, pointed out that it did not follow from this that the very principle of the system adopted in the matter by the German legislature was being put in question:

> having regard to a large number of minor offences, notably in the sphere of road traffic, a contracting state may have good cause for relieving its courts of the task of their prosecution and punishment. Conferring the prosecution and punishment of minor offences on administrative authorities is not inconsistent with the Convention, provided that the person concerned is enabled to take any decision thus made against him before a tribunal that does offer the guarantees of Article 6.[77]

Having found Article 6 applicable the Court found on the basis of the judgment in the *Luedicke, Belkacem and Koç* case a violation of Article 6, paragraph 3(e).

After the judgment the German legislation was again amended by an act of 15 June 1989 which entered into force on 1 July 1989. According to these amendments, in criminal proceedings or in court proceedings under the Regulatory Offences Act, interpretation costs shall be payable by an accused or other person concerned who does not understand German only if these costs are imposed on him by the court on the grounds that he had incurred them unnecessarily by his own default or in another culpable manner.[78]

Judgments in which violations of Article 8 have been found have resulted in changes of legislation in several countries in many different areas of life, for instance changes in the rules regarding prisoners' correspondence

76 *Öztürk* case, judgment of 21 February 1984, ECHR (1984) Series A, No. 73.
77 Ibid., at para. 56.
78 Committee of Ministers Resolution DH (89) 31. To be published in the YB.

in United Kingdom,[79] decriminalization in Northern Ireland of homosexual acts in private between consenting males aged 21 or over,[80] and new rules regarding interception of telephone conversations in the United Kingdom[81] and France.[82]

In Belgium the judgment in the *Marckx* case[83] resulted in a number of important changes to the legislation. The applicant in this case was an unmarried mother who complained on her own behalf and on behalf of her daughter, born out of wedlock, of several violations of Article 8, Article 8 in conjunction with Article 14, and Article 1 of the first Protocol alone and in conjunction with Article 14.

The main problem in the case was that before 1987 children born out of wedlock and their mothers were in several respects treated differently from children born in wedlock and their mothers. The birth of a child born out of wedlock did thus not in itself establish any family relations between the mother and the child. In order to establish family ties the mother had formally to recognize the child before a public authority, moreover, even after recognition had taken place, the child did not have any legal family relations with the mother's family. With regard to right of inheritance there were fundamental differences between a child born out of wedlock and a child born in wedlock. Before recognition the first had no right of inheritance whatsoever from her mother, and even after recognition the right was limited; nor had the child any rights of inheritance from the mother's family.

In a very detailed judgment the Court found violations on 9 counts regarding the Articles invoked. It may be justified to summarize the Court's judgment in the way that the main violation was a discrimination between a child born out of wedlock and her mother on the one hand, and children born in wedlock and their mothers on the other.

As rather fundamental changes of Belgian legislation were necessary it took some years before they were adopted, but by an act of 31 March 1987 amending various legal provisions concerning affiliation, the Belgian legislation was brought into compliance with the Convention as interpreted by the European Court of Human Rights in the *Marckx* case. In particular, as regards the violation concerning the manner of establishing maternal affiliation, the new act provides that a child's mother is the person so designed in its birth certificate. Recognition by the mother is therefore no longer nec-

79 *Silver and others* case, judgment of 25 March 1983, ECHR (1983) Series A, No. 61. Committee of Ministers Resolution DH (85) 15.

80 *Dudgeon* case, judgment of 22 October 1981, ECHR (1981) Series A, No. 45. Committee of Ministers Resolution DH (83) 13.

81 *Malone* case, judgment of 2 August 1984, ECHR (1984) Series A, No. 82. Committee of Ministers Resolution DH (86) 1.

82 *Kruslin* and *Huvig* cases, judgments of 24 April 1990, ECHR (1990) Series A, No. 176.

essary. The act further lays down the general principle of equality of the different methods of affiliation and finally, the different treatment of children born out of wedlock and in wedlock with regard to inheritance has been abolished.[84]

The legal position and the rights of children are not separately protected by the Convention. Nevertheless these questions have been dealt with in a number of cases. The *Marckx* case is probably the most important, but also the cases regarding corporal punishment in British schools which resulted in changes of the legislation ought to be mentioned.

In state schools in the United Kingdom, before 1987, school teachers were permitted to administer corporal chastisement in moderation as disciplinary measure. Excessive, arbitrary or cruel punishment by a teacher or its infliction for an improper motive would constitute an assault and could give rise to a civil claim for damages or to prosecution for a criminal offence. In the 1970's the Commission received a number of applications from parents who complained of a violation of their rights as parents and of the rights of their children because the children had been or at least ran the risk of being corporally punished. The punishment often took the form of striking the palm of the pupils hand with a leather strap and could also take the form of canning the pupil on other parts of the body.

The leading case on this issue is the case of *Campbell and Cosans*[85] which was decided by the Court in 1982. Ms. Campbell's nine year old son was attending a state school where corporal punishment was permitted. The responsible educational authorities had refused to guarantee that her son would not be subject to corporal punishment which, however, had never been used on him.

Ms. Cosans had a fifteen year old son who was suspended from school because he had refused to accept corporal punishment for having misbehaved. Four months later the educational authorities decided to lift the suspension on the condition *inter alia* that the applicant's son would accept the rules and disciplinary regulations of the school. The authorities, however, would not undertake to refrain from punishing him physically in the future. Ms. Cosans therefore refused to send him back to school. As a consequence the suspension was not lifted and Ms. Cosans' son never returned to school as he ceased to be of compulsory school age four months later.

Both applicants submitted on behalf of their sons that the use or threatened use of corporal punishment constituted a violation of Article 3 of the Convention. They further submitted that the refusal of the responsible au-

83 *Marckx* case, judgment of 18 June 1979, ECHR (1979) Series A, No. 31.
84 Committee of Ministers Resolution DH (88) 3.
85 *Campbell and Cosans* case, judgment of 25 February 1982. ECHR (1982) Series A, No. 48.

thorities to exempt their children from corporal punishment violated their rights as parents under Article 2 of the first Protocol according to which the State had the duty to respect the rights of parents to ensure education and teaching in conformity with their philosophical convictions. Finally, Ms. Cosans on behalf of her son submitted that his rights under the first sentence of Article 2, according to which no person shall be denied the right to education, had been violated because he had been suspended from school for nearly a whole school year as a result of his refusal to accept corporal punishment.

The Court found that the treatment of the two boys, who in fact were not corporally punished, did not constitute torture or inhuman treatment, nor could the treatment be considered degrading as the boys had not undergone – in the eyes of others or in their own eyes – severe humiliation or debasement. Consequently the Court and the Commission found no violation of Article 3.

With regard to the parents' complaint of a violation of Article 2 of the protocol the Court found that the state's function and responsibility with regard to education also extended to question of discipline. Secondly, the Court found that the parents' views opposing corporal punishment as a disciplinary measure in schools were sufficiently fundamental and serious to amount to 'a philosophical conviction'. The Court consequently, like the Commission, found a violation of Article 2 of the protocol. With regard to Ms. Cosans' sons' suspension from school the Court found that the suspension was motivated by his and his parents' refusal to accept corporal punishment and that his return to school could only have been secured if his parents had acted contrary to their philosophical convictions as protected by Article 2. Therefore Article 2 was also violated in this respect.

Due to divergent opinions prevailing in the United Kingdom with regard to corporal punishment, it took some time before legislation forbidding corporal punishment was adopted. However, in 1986 an education act was adopted which provided for the abolition of corporal punishment in state schools. The act entered into force at the beginning of the following school year in August 1987. The act applied in respect of pupils at schools maintained by local education authorities and certain other schools for which the state provides financial assistance, and in respect of pupils at independent schools any of whose fees are paid out of public funds.[86] The act, however, did not abolish corporal punishment in purely private schools. Recently, the Commission received an application from a mother of a child attending a private school who complained about the risk of corporal punishment at that school. The application is pending before the Commission at present.

86 Committee of Ministers Resolution DH (87) 9. To be published in the YB.

The Court's judgments have not only had the effect in several cases that the legislation in the respondent state has been changed; in some cases other Governments have realized that the legal situation in their countries was not in conformity with the Convention as interpreted by the Court in a judgment against another state. This situation may be illustrated by the case of *Young, James and Webster*.[87]

The three applications in the case were brought in 1978 and 1979 by three persons who had been employed by British Rail for several years (Mr. Young since 1972, Mr. James since 1974 and Mr. Webster since 1958). In 1975 British Rail concluded a 'closed shop' agreement with three trade unions providing that membership of one of those unions was a condition for employment. The three applicants failed to satisfy this condition and were dismissed in 1976. In their applications they submitted that their rights under Articles 9, 10, 11 and 13 of the Convention had been violated. The essential complaint was that dismissal of the applicants was alleged to be in violation of the right to freedom of association enshrined in Article 11. The Court therefore did not find it necessary to also examine the case under Articles 9, 10 and 13. With regard to the main complaint the Court found by 18 votes to 3 that there had been a breach of Article 11 of the Convention.

The Court was of the opinion that even if no general rule against compulsory membership were contained in the Convention, it did not follow that each and every mandatory measure requiring a worker to join a particular trade union was compatible with Article 11. The Court said:

> the situation facing the applicants clearly runs counter to the concept of freedom of association in its negative sense. Assuming that Article 11 does not guarantee the negative aspect of that freedom on the same footing as the positive aspect, compulsion to join a particular trade union may not always be contrary to the Convention. However, a threat of dismissal involving loss of livelihood is a most serious form of compulsion and, in the present instance, it was directed against persons engaged by British Rail before the introduction of any obligations to join a particular trade union. In the Court's opinion such a formal compulsion in the circumstances of the case, strikes at the very substance of the freedom guarantied by Article 11. For this reason alone, there has been an interference with that freedom as regards each of the three applicants.[88]

In the United Kingdom changes to the Employment Act had already taken place in 1980 and the provisions of the Employment Act of 1982 relating to the closed shop provides that the dismissal of an employee in circumstances similar to those under which Mr. James, Mr. Young and Mr. Webster were

87 *Young, James and Webster* case, judgment of 13 August 1981, ECHR (1981) Series A, No. 44.

88 Ibid., at para. 55.

dismissed is to be regarded as an unfair dismissal. An employee dismissed in these circumstances is therefore entitled to a remedy under British law.[89]

The judgment, however, also had effects outside the United Kingdom. In Denmark the question of the validity of closed shop agreements in the labour market had over the years been a rather sensitive matter and in some areas closed shop agreements did exist. However, after the judgment the Danish Social Democratic Government, which in general was not opposed to closed shop agreements in 1982 introduced a bill on protection against dismissal on the ground of association relations. In the introduction of the bill the minister of labour stated that he considered that Danish law did not fully secure all aspects of negative freedom of association as confirmed by the judgment from the Court of Human Rights. In the Government's opinion it was obvious that Denmark should respect its obligations under the Convention and for that reason alone the act was proposed. According to the act, which was adopted after long debate in Parliament, an employer is not allowed to dismiss an employee simply because the employee is member of an association or a specific association, or because the employee is not member of any association or a specific association.

The purpose of mentioning the above examples of changes of national legislation as a result of friendly settlements or decisions from the organs of the Convention has been to illustrate that the Convention and the practise often have consequences in the member countries which go far beyond the concrete case. The Convention and the control system has thus become a practical reality which affects and secures the position and daily life of individuals in Western Europe.

E. The Future

The very substantial increase in the number of applications submitted to the Commission especially within the last three years has – as mentioned earlier – created difficulties for the Convention organs to cope with the case load and decide the applications within a reasonable time. The capacity of the Commission has been considerably increased by the changes to the Convention of 1990 which introduced Committees of three members and Chambers. In order to give full effect to the increase of the Commission's capacity an adequate increase of the permanent staff in the secretariat is an absolute precondition, and it is to be hoped and expected that this will be accepted by those responsible for budgetary matters. Under this condition it is to be expected that the organs with the present structure and the present case load will be able to cope with their task.

89 Committee of Ministers Resolution DH (83) 3, YB 1983, Part Two, Chapter IV, p. 14 (*Young, James and Webster*).

The present situation may, however, rapidly change when – as expected – a number of Central and East European countries become members of the Council of Europe within the next few years and ratify the Convention on Human Rights. Against this background it is understandable that the problem of the future structure of the control system has become a central issue for the Council of Europe and the problem is at present being examined and intensively discussed in the relevant organs of the Council. Many proposals and possibilities have been floated, and it appears that at present at least three main ideas are being discussed. They may be summarized as follows.

The first one would be to uphold the present structure with a few adjustments including perhaps some changes to the role of the Committee of Ministers and the possibility of increasing the number or length of the Court's and the Commission's sessions. This solution has the advantage that the possibility to negotiate friendly settlements in the confidential and informal way which exists today would be upheld. Secondly, at a time where a number of new states are expected to join the Council, it may be an advantage to keep a system which has proved its efficiency and which new member states have the opportunity to know and evaluate. The solution has the disadvantage that – even with a certain increase of session days – it might within a few year's time hardly be possible to decide within a reasonable time limit the increased number of applications that must be expected.

The second possibility which has been proposed, is to create a new organ – a Court – instead of the present Commission and Court. This new Court should as the first and only organ deal with all applications from the introduction to the final binding judgment. The Court should be composed of members working full-time as judges in Strasbourg and having no other occupation. The advantage of this solution would be that the new Court would be able to deal with and decide a relatively high number of cases each year and that the procedures, compared with the present system, could be simplified and made less time consuming. The solution has the disadvantage that the full-time judges could hardly keep the same close contact with daily life in their own countries as the members and judges have under the present system. Secondly, there would be no possibility of appeal even in cases of fundamental importance.

A third possibility involves a combination of the two first, namely the creation of a new Court but combined with a Court of Appeal which would deal with only a limited number of cases involving fundamental or important problems of interpretation of the Convention. Appeal should only be possible after the granting of a special leave to appeal and the Court of Appeal might not necessarily have to be a full-time organ. Compared with the second proposal this solution has the advantage that the possibility of appeal exists without necessarily demanding two full-time organs. The disadvantage, of course, is that the system will be more complicated and in some cases more time consuming.

The description above of the various ideas for the future structure has deliberately been very brief, and no opinion as to which solution might be considered to be the most adequate one has been expressed. A more detailed analysis would, of course, show further advantages and disadvantages of the different possibilities and other solutions than those mentioned above. An expert group under the Steering Committee on Human Rights has for some time analyzed the problems and the report from the Steering Committee is expected to be submitted to the Court and the Commission in the summer of 1992, with a request for their opinions.

Against the background of the rapidly changing situation in Europe today the future for the convention system is not without problems. But it is beyond doubt that the problems will somehow be solved so that the protective system under the European Convention on Human Rights will be a reality for all citizens in the whole of Europe within not too many years. This optimistic view is founded on the fundamental idea that respect for human rights originates from every individual human being, and is based on his and her respect for the life and welfare of other individuals.

[illegible]

The AIDS Pandemic and Human Rights

by

KATARINA TOMASEVSKI

Academy of European Law (ed.),
Collected Courses of the Academy of European Law, Volume II, Book 2, 99–150.

Table of Contents

Biography

Born on 8 February 1953 in Yugoslavia, Katarina Tomasevski graduated at the University of Zagreb and holds graduate degrees in International Law from Harvard Law School and University of Zagreb. She is currently Senior Research Associate at McGill Centre of Medicine, Ethics and Law (Toronto), researching the human rights aspects of the AIDS epidemic and co-teaches a graduate course entitled Human Rights for Public Health Professionals at Harvard School of Public Health. In 1989-1990 she worked on the human rights and legal issues associated with AIDS in the framework of the World Health Organization's Global Programme on AIDS. Previously, she has worked at the Danish Centre for Human Rights, at the Netherlands Human Rights Institute, and at the Institute for Social Research in Zagreb. She coordinated a number of international research projects, *inter alia* on the right to food, imprisoned children, access to information, and human rights in international development cooperation. Dr Tomasevski is a member of the Global AIDS Policy Coalition, and serves on the Board of Directors of the Human Rights and International Third World Legal Studies Association.

Principal Publications

- *Prison health* (1992) [forthcoming].
- *Development Aid and Human Rights. A Study for the Danish Centre for Human Rights* (1989) 208p.
- *Foreign Aid and Human Rights: Case Studies of Kenya and Bangladesh* (1988) 142p.
- *Right to Food: Guide through Applicable International Law* (1987) 388p.
- *Children in Adult Prisons: An International Perspective* (1986) 220p. *Des enfants en prison avec des adultes* (1986) 331p.
- *Comparative Analysis of the Draft Convention on the Rights of the Child and of the Existing International Legal Instruments*, Part 1: Comparative Study, 107p., Part 2: Documentary Supplement, 364p. (1985) [mimeographed].
- *The Right to Food* (co-editor P. Alston): International Studies in Human Rights (1985) 228p.
- *Mjerljivost ostvarivanja ljudskih prava* (Measuring the Realization of Human Rights) (1983) 181p. [mimeographed].
- *Terorizam u suvremenom svijetu* (Terrorism in the Contemporary World) (1983) 257p. [mimeographed].
- *Izazov Terorizma* (The Challenge of Terrorism) (1983) 336p.
- *Pristup istrazivanju jugoslavenske koncepcije prava covjeka* (Towards the Study of the Yugoslav Concept of Human Rights) (1981) 181p. [mimeographed].

Introduction

The first decade of the AIDS pandemic[1] ended in June 1991 with the tenth anniversary of the first cases of AIDS diagnosed in the USA.[2] The spread of AIDS, HIV infection[3] and its history[4] have been well described. Accounts of the response to AIDS by different countries, and its impact on various communities and populations are numerous, and this text does not aim to add to them. Rather it is confined to one specific and distinct aspect of AIDS: the challenge it represents to human rights and the extent to which this challenge has been met, if at all.

Infection and disease are natural phenomena and thus not human rights issues unless societal responses are inadequate or inappropriate – human rights problems are man-made. Protection against epidemics is one of the main tasks of public authorities which arises from the human right to health;[5] hence the manner in which public authorities have carried out AIDS prevention and control is a legitimate human rights concern. Moreover, the response to AIDS has created a wide range of human rights problems, and many of these difficulties have been caused by a public health heritage which recognizes individual duties and obligations rather than rights and freedoms, particularly in the case of epidemics. Public health is recognized as a legitimate ground for limiting human rights in international human rights law.[6] This limitation was, however, rarely examined before AIDS. During the AIDS pandemic many such limitations have been successfully challenged as unnecessary, illegitimate, even counterproductive, not only by human rights criteria, but also within public health. This made human rights one of the prominent issues in the professional and public debates on AIDS.

This text focuses on the legal responses to AIDS because law has been used more than ever before in responding to epidemics, and in its two mutually opposed roles: Thus traditional public health laws included coercive, compulsory, restrictive, or discriminatory AIDS control measures. This necessitated the adoption of legal protection for people targetted by such mea-

1 The term *pandemic* (*pan* and *demos*) is used in this text as it is used in AIDS literature, rather than *epidemic* to denote that HIV/AIDS affects all peoples worldwide.

2 'The HIV/AIDS Epidemic: The First 10 Years', 40 *Morbidity and Mortality Weekly Report* 22 (7 June 1991) 357.

3 Chin, 'Global Estimates of AIDS Cases and HIV Infections: 1990', 4 *AIDS 1990. Supplement 1* S277-S283.

4 M.D. Grmek, *Histoire du SIDA: Début et origine d'une pandémie actuelle* (1989).

5 The International Covenant on Economic, Social and Cultural Rights includes 'the prevention, treatment and control of epidemic ... diseases' among the steps that States Parties should undertake towards the full realization of the right to health.

6 Cf. The Siracusa Principles on the Limitation and Derogation Provisions in the International Covenant on Civil and Political Rights, Annex to UN Doc. E/CN.4/1985/4 of 28 September 1984.

sures in order to reaffirm the basic human rights and fundamental freedoms for all.

Although law is helpless with regard to the virus causing AIDS, HIV infection or development of HIV related diseases (unlike people, viruses cannot be made to observe law), two factors seem to have prompted the extensive use of law in the AIDS pandemic. Firstly, medicine has failed to provide a cure for AIDS and vaccine against HIV infection. While fear of communicable diseases had been virtually eliminated before the AIDS pandemic, at least in the so-called developed world, its resurgence was influenced by fear-inducing reports of the danger of AIDS and calls for drastic measures against AIDS and people inflicted with the disease. Secondly, further transmission of HIV infection can be prevented through changes of conduct and recourse to law; the traditional means of regulating human behaviour. HIV infection is not airborne nor can it be acquired through casual social contact; most infections are transmitted through sexual intercourse, hence prevention focused on changing individual behaviour.

The global consensus on the necessity to prevent further spread of HIV infection was not accompanied by an agreement as to how to achieve this aim. Many countries opted for the identification of HIV infected people, their deportation, detention, isolation, or segregation, and thereby for the building of physical or legal barriers between the infected and the uninfected, between 'them' and 'us'. This often entailed the denial of human rights to 'them' to protect 'us', and the consequent necessity to challenge such responses. Other countries, much fewer in number, opted for demanding responsible behaviour from all concerned, based on the following reasoning: if those who are HIV infected are expected to accept their increased responsibility not to transmit the infection to others, the public authorities should not encourage or tolerate their rejection or stigmatization. The international community, together with health and human rights bodies, reinforced this human rights rationale by explicitly affirming that human rights should apply in AIDS prevention and control.

The Human Rights Response to AIDS

Responses to AIDS are designed and implemented within public health: 'Since AIDS is a disease, it is handled within a medical model, not one of civil liberties.'[7] This medical model seldom includes human rights, while virtually every measure of disease control has human rights implications: surveillance may seek and record the personal identity of the infected per-

7 Tauer, 'AIDS and Human Rights: An Intercontinental Perspective', in C. Pierce and D. Van De Veer (eds), *AIDS, Ethics and Public Policy* (1988) 155.

sons and those persons identified as 'carriers' may be subjected to quarantine. The way in which a disease is classified may entail the application of compulsory medical examination or hospitalization envisaged in the respective disease control legislation. Because many public health measures are coercive, compulsory or restrictive, they have to be authorized by law. Public health laws thus specify what individuals ought to do (vaccination, for example),[8] and what they should not do (by defining offences against public health, including the transmission of infectious diseases);[9] hence it has not been easy to reconcile human rights and traditional public health responses to epidemics.

As always in human rights, movements to reinforce their universality emerge in response to violations. Before AIDS, such public health laws were rarely, if ever, reviewed by human rights criteria, either in individual countries or by the international human rights bodies. When the AIDS pandemic triggered off the whole gamut of public health measures, an analysis of them by human rights criteria proved that many of the public health responses were incompatible with human rights requirements,[10] and this provided an incentive for in-depth examinations of public health from the human rights viewpoint, focusing on AIDS and going beyond it.[11] In quite a few countries coercive and discriminatory AIDS control measures were carried out by the public (health) authorities (even legalized) and provoked much criticism and opposition. Discriminatory practices victimizing HIV infected people and people with AIDS by insurance companies, private employers, or medical practitioners, have been tolerated in many countries, and this prompted demands that public authorities provide protection against discrimination. Even though, information on coercive laws and on discriminatory public and private practices is fragmentary, it indicates that all human rights and fundamental freedoms have been affected.[12] Paradoxically, one of the main reasons for the paucity of information on AIDS-related human rights violations is fear of public exposure. People victimized by such violations often refrain from seeking redress because of fear of fur-

8 Cf. *Fay Godfrey* v. *United Kingdom* [No. 8542/79], 27 European Commission of Human Rights Decisions and Reports (1982) 94-99.

9 Cf. Criminal Law and Criminological Questions Raised by the Propagation of Infectious Diseases, Including AIDS. Report submitted by the Portuguese delegation, 16th Conference of European Ministers of Justice, Lisbon, 21-22 June 1988, Council of Europe, MJU-16 (88) 1 (1988).

10 P. Sieghart, *AIDS & Human Rights. A UK Perspective* (1989).

11 Tomasevski, 'Before AIDS, beyond AIDS: Human Rights of People with Communicable Diseases', in K.E. Mahoney and P.J. Mahoney (eds), *Human Rights in the Twenty-First Century: A Global Challenge* (1992).

12 Cf. AIDS Discrimination in Canada. A Study of the Scope and Extent of Unfair Discrimination in Canada Against Persons with AIDS, and those Known or Feared to be HIV Positive (1989); Report of the Working Panel on Discrimination and Other Legal Issues – HIV/AIDS (1989); *Epidemic of Fear. A Survey of AIDS Discrimination in the 1980s and Policy Recommendations for the 1990s* (1990).

ther stigmatization. Silence, as is too well known in human rights, enables human rights violations to continue unchallenged. Nevertheless, the existing information shows that all human rights and fundamental freedoms have been affected: from access to education, employment and health care, to freedom of expression, assembly and association; to freedom of movement; to the protection of the basic human rights of prisoners, children, or refugees.

No worldwide review of AIDS-related human rights problems has been made, as yet, to indicate what acts constitute human rights violations and what additional safeguards are necessary for the full application of human rights in AIDS prevention and control.[13] The United Nations appointed a Special Rapporteur in 1989 to study AIDS-related discrimination,[14] whose reports have described human rights problems as they emerge in responding to AIDS, but have not addressed the pattern of human rights violations.[15] The European Parliament called for the establishment of a unit to monitor AIDS-related discrimination in its resolution of 26 May 1989 on the fight against AIDS, but no monitoring scheme has yet been established.[16] This does not amount to saying that nothing has been done by inter-governmental bodies. The numerous international policy-documents on the human rights aspects of AIDS[17] are a good indicator of the nature and scope of the threat that responses to AIDS have created for human rights.[18]

Opposition to coercive, compulsory, restrictive, and particularly to discriminatory AIDS control measures, has been widespread and indeed worldwide, and many such measures have been successfully challenged, often by invoking human rights. The existing pattern of human rights vio-

13 Few comparative surveys of AIDS control measures have been carried out from the viewpoint of the applicable international human rights standards: R. Cohen and L.S. Wiseberg *Double Jeopardy – Threat to Life and Human Rights. Discrimination Against Persons with AIDS* (1990); *The Third Epidemic. Repercussions of the Fear of AIDS* (1990); M. Breum and A. Hendriks (eds), *AIDS and Human Rights. An International Perspective* (1988).

14 Sub-Commission on Prevention of Discrimination and Protection of Minorities, Decision 1988/111 of 1 September 1988, and Resolution 1989/19 of 31 August 1989, and Commission on Human Rights, Decision 1990/65 of 7 March 1990.

15 Concise note by Mr. Luis Varela-Quiros pursuant to Sub-Commission decision 1988/11, UN Doc. E/CN.4/Sub.2/1989/5 of 14 July 1989; Discrimination Against HIV Infected People or People with AIDS. Preliminary Report prepared by Mr. Luis Varela Quiros, Special Rapporteur, UN Doc. E/CN.4/Sub.2/1990/9 of 2 August 1990; Discrimination Against HIV Infected People or People with AIDS. Progress Report by Mr. Luis Varela Quiros, Special Rapporteur, UN Doc. E/CN.4/Sub.2/1991/10 of 24 July 1991.

16 Resolution of the European Parliament of 30 March 1989 on the fight against AIDS, OJ (1989) 158/477, 26 June 1989.

17 The most important international policy documents are listed in the *Chronology of International Policies on the Human Rights Aspects of AIDS* in the Annex.

18 Tomasevski, 'Equality and Non-discrimination: Action by the International Community Against AIDS-related Discrimination', Seventh International Colloquy on the European Convention on Human Rights, Copenhagen, Oslo, Lund, 30 May – 2 June 1990, Council of Europe, H/Coll.(90) 14 (1990).

lations has been repeated in the context of AIDS: violations have targetted those categories that are the least able to assert and protect their rights, such as prisoners, prostitutes, asylum-seekers, or drug-dependent persons, all of whom have become targets for compulsory or coercive AIDS control measures; and this has created a bridge between AIDS-related and human rights work. The merging of two distinct and historically separated areas – public health and human rights – required those involved in human rights to become familiar with public health, and for those working in public health to acquire knowledge about applicable human rights standards and procedures. In addition, some problems did not have a ready-made solution, either in public health or in human rights: fear of contagion has been used to discriminate against people who are or might be HIV positive and those associated with them, thereby creating new grounds of discrimination, the status of infectiousness,[19] and the consequent need for human rights safeguards.[20] The lack of an explicit international prohibition of discrimination on the grounds of state of health or infectiousness necessitated interpretations of the nature and scope of the prohibition of discrimination.[21] Moreover, the high costs of medical and social assistance to people with AIDS[22] reinforced discriminatory practices, particularly in employment[23] and related health insurance.[24] It is important to note that public opinion surveys often documented a relatively high level of public support for discrimination against HIV infected people,[25] while the widespread view that AIDS is a 'self-inflicted disease' further reinforced discriminatory attitudes.[26] Thus, public support for action against human rights violations could not have been taken for granted in the context of AIDS. As summarized by Kelvin Widdows:

19 Cf. State of Health in Equality in Employment and Occupation. General Survey of the Reports on the Discrimination (Employment and Occupation) Convention (No. 111) and Recommendation (No. 111), 1958, Report of the Committee of Experts on the Application of Conventions and recommendations, International Labour Conference, 75th session (1988) 69-72.

20 Conclusions of the Council and the Ministers for Health of the Member States, Meeting with the Council, on 15 December 1988 Concerning AIDS and the Place of Work, OJ 1989 C 28/2-3, 3 February 1989.

21 Trebilcock, 'AIDS and the Workplace. Some Policy Pointers from International Labour Standards', 128 *International Labour Review* 1 (1989) 29-45.

22 Vogel, 'Discrimination on the Basis of HIV Infection: An Economic Analysis', 49 *Ohio State Law Journal* (1989) 986-993.

23 Nusbaum, 'Public Health and the Law: HIV Antibody Status and Employment Discrimination', 2 *Journal of Acquired Immune Deficiency Syndromes* 2 (1989) 103-106.

24 Ohsfeldt and Gohmann, 'Societal Attitudes towards AIDS and AIDS-related Health Insurance Regulations', 4 *AIDS & Public Policy Journal* 3 (1989) 159-163.

25 Blendon and Donelan, 'Discrimination Against People with AIDS. The Public's Perspective', *The New England Journal of Medicine* (13 October 1988) 1022-1026.

26 Kegeles *et al.*, 'Perceptions of AIDS: The Continuing Saga of AIDS-related Stigma', 3 *AIDS 1989. Supplement 1* (1989) S253-258.

> Thus, in a society bent on deregulation, we see the rising tide of a new form of regulation aimed at preventing discrimination based on misunderstanding and ignorance.[27]

I. The Pandemic of AIDS Legislation[28]

The multi-layered pandemic of AIDS encompassed three distinct but related epidemics: the spread of HIV infection had been at first unnoticed. AIDS came second, starting with its recognition in 1981, with the isolation of its causative agent, HIV, in 1983, and the development of tests to detect antibodies to HIV in 1985. This was followed by an epidemic of fear, panic, and scapegoating, especially early in the pandemic. Summarizing his assessment of the responses to AIDS, the Director of the WHO Global Programme on AIDS stated:

> [B]ecause the disease is sexually transmitted, and because in many countries it occurred initially in marginalized groups, this response has been slower than we might have liked.[29]

The lack of knowledge about the transmission of HIV sometimes resulted in inappropriate legislation in the early phase of the pandemic. Laws targetting 'high-risk groups' had been adopted before it was realized that it is individual behaviour and not affiliation with a 'group' which constitutes risk;[30] in other words, it is what one does rather than who one is which determines the risk of acquiring or transmitting HIV infection. Laws criminalizing transmission of HIV have also been adopted, though it has later transpired that their enforcement has created more problems than it solved.[31]

The sheer quantity of AIDS-related laws is illustrative of the global response to AIDS: in the first decade of the AIDS pandemic, 1981-1991, 104

27 Widdows, 'AIDS and the Workplace: Some Approaches at the National Level', 4 *International Journal of Comparative Labour Law and Industrial Relations* 3 (1988) 141.

28 The results of this author's survey of the national AIDS legislation, from which the information on AIDS-related laws referred to in this text is derived, will be published in J. Mann, D. Tarantola and T.W. Netter (eds), *AIDS in the World 1992* (1992), and will include a complete list of the relevant laws and policies by country for the 104 countries encompassed by this survey. References to national AIDS laws are therefore confined to a minimum here, and only the name of the country and the date of the legislative enactment are given. Readers who wish to obtain full references or texts of specific laws are welcome to contact the author.

29 World AIDS Day 1991. Sharing the challenge of HIV/AIDS: A Health, Social and Economic Problem. An Interview with Dr Michael H. Merson, Director of the WHO's Global Programme on AIDS, Press release WHO/UN 94 (26 November 1991) 2.

30 Kirby, 'AIDS Legislation – Turning Up the Heat?', 12 *Journal of Medical Ethics* (1986) 187-194.

31 Hermann, 'Criminalizing Conduct Related to HIV Transmission', 9 *Saint Louis University Public Law Review* 35 (1990) 351-378.

countries adopted some AIDS-related legislation. As Carol Levine predicted, 'where technology is still unable to provide a solution to the spread of disease, people look to the law.'[32] An overview of AIDS legislation in the first decade, 1981-1991, is presented by two figures: the *Number of countries adopting AIDS legislation by year* provides a quantified overview, and *Chronology of AIDS legislation* includes the list of countries which adopted AIDS-related laws, by the year of their adoption.

AIDS legislation emerged as early as 1983, less than two years after AIDS had become known and more than two years before HIV was identified as its cause. The first piece of AIDS legislation, regulations of the National Board of Health and Welfare on obligatory reporting of suspected and confirmed cases of AIDS, was adopted in Sweden on 8 March 1983, and followed by similar enactments in individual European countries.[33] Legislative activity also started in Canada, Israel and the USA and most often this legislation laid down safeguards for national blood safety and introduced compulsory notification of cases of AIDS.[34] In this early period, up to 1985, no country adopted a comprehensive law on AIDS because its cause had not as yet been identified.

The period 1985-87 represented the peak of the pandemic of AIDS legislation: the cumulative number of laws on AIDS almost doubled, from 39 by the end of 1985, to 78 in 1988. In the USA alone more than 180 laws relating to HIV/AIDS were enacted in the period 1985-87,[35] and more than 840 were proposed to the states' legislatures during these two years.[36] After this peak of legislative activity in 1985-87 there has been a considerable slow-down in the adoption of AIDS legislation.

The analysis of the contents of these laws shows that the discovery of the test to detect antibodies to HIV and particularly its commercialization[37] was the strongest incentive for adopting laws: the largest number of countries adopted laws dealing with HIV testing, and many authorized the public health authorities to carry out compulsory HIV testing. Once identified, HIV infected people can be subjected to restrictions and legal authorization of their isolation, detention or compulsory hospitalization often ac-

32 Levine, 'AIDS: Public Health and Civil Liberties', *Hastings Centre Report. Special Supplement* (December 1986) 2.

33 'Summary of Legislative Situation and Policy on AIDS and HIV Infection in Europe: September 1988', in Health Legislation and Ethics in the Field of AIDS and HIV Infection. Report on an International Consultation, Oslo, 26-29 April 1988 (1989) 20-22.

34 Fluss, 'What Can Legislators do to Combat AIDS?', 9 *World Health Forum* (1988) 365-369.

35 C. Thomas, *A Synopsis of State AIDS Laws Enacted During 1983-1987 Legislative Sessions* (October 1988) preface.

36 Lewis, 'Acquired Immunodeficiency Syndrome: State Legislative Activity', 258 *Journal of American Medical Association* 17 (6 November 1987) 2410.

37 Petricciani, 'Licensed Tests for Antibody to HTLV-III', *Annals of Internal Medicine* (1985) 726-727.

companied provisions relating to compulsory testing. Only one country has made hospitalization of all HIV infected people mandatory and automatic, namely Cuba,[38] but many adopted laws giving public health authorities powers to resort to restrictive measures, including the placement of HIV infected persons under surveillance, isolation or segregation, mandatory hospitalization, or placing specific restrictions upon their behaviour.[39] This legislative pandemic was much criticized by the press. Thus the South magazine entitled its survey 'How paranoia fuels the AIDS epidemic'[40] and the New Internationalist 'AIDS witch-hunts: Legislative hysteria'.[41]

Specific factors which influenced the adoption of AIDS legislation in individual countries cannot easily be identified. As illustrated by the figure *Chronology of AIDS legislation*, the Western industrialized countries were the first and the most active in enacting AIDS legislation. Latin American and Asian countries followed soon afterwards, while AIDS legislation emerged last in Africa. The assumption that countries adopted AIDS legislation because of a high level of HIV prevalence and/or large numbers of AIDS cases is thus not confirmed by data. Countries without any cases of AIDS or of HIV infection have adopted AIDS-related laws (such as Viet Nam or Mongolia, for example), while some of those with high HIV prevalence have not (such as The Netherlands, for example). In some countries laws were adopted to prevent the 'importation of AIDS', and this is discussed below in the section dealing with aliens.

A. Human Rights Implications of AIDS Laws

Public health developed over centuries, generally relying on coercive, compulsory and restrictive measures.[42] It does not readily adjust to 20th century human rights requirements.[43] The study of the human rights implications of different public health measures has only begun with the AIDS pandemic, and criticism of the exercise of policing powers by the public health authorities has focused on ethical reasons in order to challenge coercion,

38 United Nations Commission on Human Rights, Consideration of the Report of the Mission which Took Place in Cuba in accordance with Commission decision 1988/106, UN Doc. E/CN.4/1989/46 of 21 February 1989, para. 131.

39 Fluss and Latto, 'The Coercive Element in Legislation for the Control of AIDS and HIV Infection: Some Recent Developments', 2 *AIDS & Public Policy* (1987) 11-20.

40 Hurtado, 'How Paranoia Fuels the AIDS Epidemic', *South* (June 1988) 95-96.

41 'AIDS Witch-Hunts: Legislative Hysteria', *New Internationalist* (May 1988) 27.

42 G. Rosen, *History of Public Health* (1958).

43 Jones Merritt, 'The Constitutional Balance Between Health and Liberty', 16 *Hastings Centre Report* 6 (December 1986) 2-10.

compulsion, restrictions and discrimination,[44] while seldom using human rights language.[45]

The bulk of public health measures, relating to AIDS or any other epidemic, deals with the identification of the affected categories and individuals, and with safeguards against further spread of the epidemic. The first and most important factor in determining the nature and scope of human rights problems is how AIDS was classified, because the coercive, compulsory or restrictive measures that the public health authorities apply are determined by the modes of transmission of a disease. If a disease is airborne, detection and isolation of those infected is legitimate; in the case of HIV/AIDS, because of the limited ways in which HIV infection can be transmitted, this is not necessary.

The largest number of countries adopted legislation giving the public health authorities powers to carry out surveillance (testing and notification). The exercise of such powers is often discretionary and seldom encompasses the procedural guarantees for the affected persons required by human rights standards. This prompted analyses of their compatibility with human rights guarantees in a similar way that is done for the exercise of police powers by other public authorities.[46]

1. Disease classification

Disease classification is one of the many public health measures which is considered 'technical' but it has direct consequences for the respect of human rights in disease control. Classification of a disease as contagious, communicable, transmissible, infectious, or sexually transmitted, entails the application of the corresponding law that may mandate compulsory medical examination or hospitalization, restrictions upon travel or immigration, or quarantine.

Disease classification often has stigmatizing effects, as evidenced by the frequent 'analogies' between AIDS and leprosy.[47] During the AIDS pandemic, Proposition 64, led by Lyndon LaRouche, suggested during the verbal duels concerning the response to AIDS in California in 1985, to increase the powers (in the narrowest sense of the term) of public health authorities in combating AIDS, and to base these increased powers on the

44 Manuel *et al.*, 'The Ethical Approach to AIDS: A Bibliographical Review', 16 *Journal of Medical Ethics* (1990) 14-27.

45 Gostin, 'The Politics of AIDS: Compulsory State Powers, Public Health and Civil Liberties', 49 *Ohio State Law Journal* 4 (1989) 1017-1058.

46 Gostin and Curran, 'Legal Control Measures for AIDS: Reporting Requirements, Surveillance, Quarantine, and Regulation of Public Meeting Places', 77 *American Journal of Public Health* 2 (February 1987) 214-218.

47 Volinn, 'Issues of Definitions and their Implications: AIDS and Leprosy', 29 *Social Sciences and Medicine* 10 (1989) 1157-1162.

classification of AIDS as an 'infectious, contagious and communicable disease'.[48] This shows the weight attributed to disease classification, where the accumulation of terms intended to convey the message of danger. In contrast to this, the European Parliament emphasized that 'it is impossible to accept discrimination based on a disease which is transmissible but not contagious'.[49]

The relevance of disease classification in the human rights context has been addressed fairly late in the AIDS pandemic. It suffices here to refer to two examples:

In examining the report of Finland under the International Covenant on Civil and Political Rights, the Human Rights Committee inquired why HIV infection and AIDS were not classified as contagious diseases. The representatives of Finland replied as follows:

> AIDS and HIV infection were not classified as contagious diseases dangerous to public health because the Contagious Diseases Act, which was strictly interpreted, covered only diseases whose spread could be prevented by measures directed at a person having, or suspected of having, the disease.[50]

The New York State Public Health Council refused in 1990 to classify HIV infection as sexually transmissible 'because such declaration would trigger certain statutory requirements permitting isolation and quarantine, reporting, testing and contact tracing'.[51]

Contrary to what one might expect from the scientific literature which pleads for consistency and precision in disease classification,[52] there is no uniformity in the classification of AIDS and HIV infection. Some countries classify it as a communicable disease, others as an infectious disease, yet others as a viral disease. Many countries have classified AIDS as a sexually transmitted disease (STD). The WHO seems to have endorsed this classification, based on the fact that most HIV infections are acquired and transmitted sexually.[53] More importantly from the human rights viewpoint,

48 R. Bayer, *Private Acts, Social Consequences. AIDS and the Politics of Public Health* (1989) 148-153.

49 Resolution on the VIth International Conference on AIDS (San Francisco, June 1990) OJ 1990 C 38/83, 19 February 1990.

50 Consideration of reports submitted by States Parties under Article 40 of the Covenant, UN Doc. CCPR/C/42/CRP.1/Add.4 of 17 June 1991, para. 22.

51 'Refusal to Designate AIDS Communicable Upheld by New York State Appellate Court', 5 *AIDS Policy & Law* 9 (16 May 1990) 1-2.

52 A.S. Benenson (ed.), *Control of Communicable Diseases in Man* (1985).

53 The WHO has justified the linking of AIDS and STD control as follows: 'The predominant mode of transmission of both human immunodeficiency virus (HIV) and other STD is sexual, although other routes of transmission for both include blood, blood products, donated organs or tissue, and through an infected mother to her fetus or newborn infant... Many of the measures for preventing sexual transmission of HIV and STD are the same, as are the target audiences for these interventions.'

this classification gives public health authorities wide-ranging powers under the existing STD legislation.[54] The coercive and compulsory measures envisaged in STD laws are broad, and the stigma associated with sexually transmitted diseases regularly prevents their challenge.

The main feature of legislation on STDs is the emphasis on preventing the spread of infection by denying rights and freedoms to the affected individuals to protect others and/or society:

> Criminal laws and disease control laws have the objective of protecting individuals from the threat posed by other citizens. While these laws are primarily concerned with the outward-directed behavior, they also restrict an individual's inward-directed behavior as necessary to preserve order in society. An individual may consent to be neither the victim of criminal act nor the carrier of a communicable disease. In both instances the protection of the individual is secondary to the protection of society.[55]

Despite the fact that traditional STD control measures have historically proved to be ineffective and harmful to people affected by them,[56] they have all been applied to AIDS: compulsory examination, contact tracing, restrictive measures against carriers to prevent further transmission, compulsory treatment and/or hospitalization, and extensive case finding by systematic pre-marital and pre-natal screening. The prohibitions and sanctions relating to transmission of HIV infection and/or the exposure of others to risk of HIV infection have also been taken over from STD laws.[57] Moreover, immigration regulations once enacted for STDs have been applied to AIDS in order to exclude persons who are HIV infected and thus reviving 'certificates of freedom from venereal disease'.[58]

2. HIV testing

Disease control has to be based on an assessment of its existing and likely spread in the population hence public health surveillance[59] is the first step

Consensus Statement from the Consultation on Global Strategies for Coordination of AIDS and STD Control Programmes, Geneva, 11-13 July 1990, WHO/GPA/INF/90.2 (1990) 1.

54 World Health Organization, *Social and Health Aspects of Sexually Transmitted Diseases. Principles of Control Measures* (1977).

55 Richards and Bross, 'Legal Aspects of STD Control: Public Duties and Private Rights', in K.K. Holmes *et al.* (eds), *Sexually Transmitted Diseases* (1990) 1101.

56 Brandt, 'AIDS in Historical Perspective: Four Lessons from the History of Sexually Transmitted Diseases', 78 *American Journal of Public Health* 4 (April 1988) 367-371.

57 World Health Organization, *Venereal Disease Control. A Survey of Recent Legislation* (1975).

58 C.W. Hutt, *International Hygiene* (1927) 113-149.

59 According to the WHO, 'public health surveillance is the collection of information of sufficient accuracy and completeness regarding the distribution and spread of infection to be pertinent to the design, implementation, or monitoring of prevention and control pro-

in responding to a disease. 'Surveillance' as a term is often associated with unjustified intrusions into individual privacy, and during the AIDS pandemic this has often proved to be true. People have been required to undergo HIV testing, and even subjected to it without being asked.[60] Information on those identified as HIV infected was frequently made available to the police or immigration authorities, to their employers or insurance companies, or to the mass media. The requirements that people be protected from involuntary testing therefore emerged early and forcefully in the AIDS pandemic,[61] and testing remains at the centre of controversies relating to AIDS prevention and control.

Because HIV infected persons can remain asymptomatic for a very long time and HIV infection can only be detected by blood tests, testing is important for public health surveillance. However, it is sufficient for this purpose to obtain information concerning *how many* people are infected and not *who* these people are. To identify the individuals who are HIV infected, voluntariness (free and informed consent) was advocated by WHO as indispensable pre-condition for testing, accompanied by the protection of confidentiality and counselling.[62]

Urging the adoption of these safeguards was necessary because the history of public health shows that compulsory and coercive measures were regularly applied in a discriminatory manner.[63] This was particularly transparent when an epidemic was not spread evenly but concentrated in specific populations, where the identification of 'carriers' was accompanied by the stigmatization of these populations as 'sources of infection'.[64] Whenever an epidemic was transmitted sexually, stigmatization accompanied attempts to attribute it to a specific 'source of infection', and was followed by the attribution of blame and scapegoating.[65]

grammes and activities.' *Unlinked Anonymous Screening for the Public Health Surveillance of HIV Infections. Proposed International Guidelines*, Geneva, June 1989, Annex.

60 Field, 'Testing for AIDS: Uses and Abuses', 16 *American Journal of Law and Medicine* 1-2 (1989) 34-106.

61 Hunter, 'AIDS Prevention and Civil Liberties: The False Security of Mandatory Testing', 2 *AIDS & Public Policy Journal* 3 (Summer-Fall 1987) 1-10.

62 Cf. Criteria that must be Considered in Planning and Implementing HIV Screening Programmes. Report of the WHO Meeting on Criteria for HIV Screening Programmes, Geneva, 20-21 May 1987, WHO/SPA/GLO/87.2; Screening and Testing in AIDS Prevention and Control Programmes, WHO/SPA/INF/88.1; and Unlinked Anonymous Screening for the Public Health Surveillance of HIV Infections. Proposed International Guidelines, GPA/SFI/89.3.

63 Institute of Medicine and National Academy of Sciences, *Confronting AIDS* (1986) 96.

64 Z. Gussow, *Leprosy, Racism, and Public Health. Social Policy in Chronic Disease Control* (1989).

65 Bibel, 'Santayana's Warning Unheeded: The Parallels of Syphilis and Acquired Immune Deficiency Syndrome (AIDS)', 16 *Sexually Transmitted Diseases* 4 (December 1989) 201-209.

This approach has been reflected in responses to AIDS. Since no country could have screened its whole population, because of the prohibitive cost rather than human rights considerations, HIV testing has been selective. The choice of categories to be tested have not always conformed with the epidemiological pattern of HIV/AIDS, nor to the modes of HIV transmission. Compulsory HIV testing targetted a variety of categories, such as returning nationals, resident aliens, aliens entering the country, personnel of armed forces, policemen, drug-dependent persons, prostitutes, prisoners, haemophiliacs, pregnant women, children of HIV infected mothers and hospitalized patients. Some countries mandated compulsory HIV testing of unspecified 'high-risk groups' (homosexuals, prostitutes, and drug users), although sero-prevalence studies among 'high-risk groups' shows that they are neither 'high-risk' nor indeed 'groups': HIV infection is widespread amongst some, while virtually non-existent amongst others.[66] 'Captive populations' (prisoners, refugees in closed camps, pregnant women attending ante-natal clinics, STD patients, military recruits) have been subjected to compulsory HIV testing in so many countries and in such large numbers that the only possible explanation is cynical – they are an easy target. They are within the reach of public health authorities, and often unable to refuse the HIV test, as safeguards against compulsory and/or coercive measures are unavailable or ineffective.

This quick review of the targets of compulsory screening shows that the pattern of targetting, which focuses on prisoners, aliens, prostitutes and drug-dependent persons, fits with the normal targets of human rights violations. This will be further discussed in part III of this text.

3. Notification

Notification of communicable diseases is another traditional public health measure[67] and, again, apparently 'technical' while entailing significant human rights implications. Public health laws may require physicians to report a *case* (anonymously) or *the patient* (by including his or her personal identity). In the latter case human rights problems regularly emerge but are rarely anticipated when disease notification is legislated.[68] The human rights implications of public health laws and practices, especially data protection, were the object of international protection only within the Council

66 Winkelstein and Johnson, 'Epidemiology: Overview', 4 *AIDS 1990. Supplement 1* (1990) S95-97.

67 World Health Organization, *Notification of Communicable Diseases. A Survey of Existing Legislation* (1959).

68 G.G. Griesser *et al.* (eds), *Data Protection in Health Information Systems. Considerations and Guidelines* (1980).

of Europe,[69] while the United Nations have been elaborating a set of recommended standards.[70] This became the object of professional and public debates only during the AIDS pandemic.[71]

It may be necessary to determine how many people are ill with AIDS and are HIV infected to develop AIDS prevention programmes, but not to disclose the personal identity of these people. Many countries aimed nevertheless at ascertaining the identity of the ill and the infected, by making disclosure of names part of the obligatory notification of cases of AIDS and results of HIV tests. Thus two different public health measures have been merged: epidemiological surveillance and case finding, with detrimental consequences for both, and for the protection of human rights. When notification is nominal, the protection of confidentiality is essential to prevent stigmatization and discrimination. Notification of 'carriers', persons who carry within their bodies the causal agent of communicable diseases without necessarily showing any symptoms, but are liable to infect others, is an inherently controversial issue:

> Controversies about disease reporting in the present as in the past must be understood as political conflicts; that is, conflicts about power and about values. The critical issues have never been scientific or technological.[72]

The scope of human rights problems raised by the prevailing practice of requiring physicians to disclose their HIV infected patients and those with AIDS is well illustrated by the fact that only few countries provided for purely statistical and anonymous notofication, and only a few others provided safeguards for confidentiality in the required notification of AIDS and HIV infection.[73] In many cases disclosure of the identity of HIV infected people brought about their loss of employment, housing, insurance, resi-

69 Convention for the Protection of Individuals with Regard to Automatic Processing of Personal Data, (European Treaty Series, No. 108); Regulations for Automated Medical Data Banks. Recommendation No. R (81) 1 adopted by the Committee of Ministers of the Council of Europe on 23 January 1981 and Explanatory Memorandum (1981); Protection of Personal Data Used for Scientific Research and Statistics. Recommendation No. R (83) 10 adopted by the Committee of Ministers of the Council of Europe on 23 September 1983 and Explanatory Memorandum (1984).

70 Revised version of the guidelines for the regulation of computerized personal data files prepared by Mr. Louis Joinet, Special Rapporteur, UN Doc. E/CN.4/1990/72 of 20 February 1990.

71 Edgar and Sandomire, 'Medical Privacy Issues in the Age of AIDS: Legislative Options', 16 *American Journal of Law & Medicine* 1-2 (1989) 155-210.

72 Fox, 'From TB to AIDS: Value Conflicts in Reporting Disease', 16 *Hastings Centre Report. Special Supplement* 6 (December 1989) 15.

73 Fluss and Zeegers, 'Reporting of AIDS and Human Immunodeficiency Virus (HIV) Infection: A Worldwide Review of Legislative and Regulatory Patterns and Issues', 5 *AIDS & Public Policy Journal* 1 (1989) 32-36.

dence and work permits, and often social ostracism and an increased rate of suicide followed.[74]

B. Human Rights in AIDS Prevention

1. Access to information

The main requirement of AIDS prevention is informed and responsible behaviour by all. Thus, it is essential to provide accurate information on the transmission of HIV infection and to educate the public on self-protection and protection of others. Dissemination of scientific findings on the transmission of HIV infection has contributed to the decrease of irrational responses to AIDS, but providing information is not enough. If the exclusion of HIV positive persons from society continues despite evidence that HIV is not transmitted through casual contact, trust in such evidence is undermined,[75] and conduct remains based on fear of contagion.[76]

Access to information is a universally recognized human right whose application in the context of AIDS requires a careful balancing of the rights and responsibilities of those directly involved.[77] The risk of contracting HIV infection because of ignorance favours explicit information, but because the main mode of transmission of HIV infection is sexual intercourse this is inherently conflict-prone. Human sexuality is by definition controversial, but recognizing this should not be the end of debate, but its beginning.

There are two apparently conflicting interests in providing AIDS information: public health requirements, and the protection of the existing societal, including religious, norms. The main human rights norms on access to information and the right to education provide the basic framework for balancing rights and freedoms. The International Covenant on Civil and Political Rights recognizes 'the liberty of parents to ensure the religious and moral education of their children in conformity with their own convictions'.[78] In the AIDS pandemic, this freedom has sometimes been exercised by parents to prevent their children from participating in education on the transmission of HIV infection, if deemed unacceptable by parents, and

74 D. Crimp and A. Rolston, *AIDS DemoGraphics* (1990).

75 Eisenberg, 'The Genesis of Fear: AIDS and the Public Response to Science', 16 *Law, Medicine & Health Care* (1986) 243.

76 Gerbert *et al.*, 'Why Fear Persists: Health Care Professionals and AIDS', 260 *Journal of American Medical Association* 23 (16 December 1988) 3481-3483.

77 Clark, 'AIDS Prevention: Legislative Options', 16 *American Journal of Law & Medicine* 1-2 (1990) 107-153.

78 International Covenant on Civil and Political Rights, Annex to General Assembly Resolution 2200 A (XXI) of 16 December 1966, Article 18(4).

courts have had to adjudicate whether explicit information on HIV/AIDS represents exposure to offensive information contrary to religious beliefs.[79]

The Convention on the Rights of the Child stresses that the guiding principle is the best interest of the child, not of the parents. This Convention reaffirms the freedom of the child to seek and receive information and, moreover, in defining the contents of the right to health the Convention obliges States to ensure that children are informed of and have access to education. Article 24 of the Convention, dealing with the right to health, obliges States to take appropriate measures 'to ensure that all segments of society, in particular parents and children, are informed, have access to education, and are supported in the use of basic knowledge'.[80]

2. Blood safety

The spread of HIV infection through blood transfusions and blood products has revealed the lack of protection against infection where people cannot protect themselves. While HIV infections contracted through blood transfusions and blood products are far fewer than those acquired and transmitted sexually, their prevention cannot be left to individuals. The question whether people are entitled to protection from being infected through blood transfusions and blood products was answered in those countries which legislated on the liability of the public authorities for their failure to ensure blood safety. Because many recipients of blood transfusions and a high percentage of people with haemophilia were found to be HIV infected worldwide, their compensation has been demanded in many countries.[81] Denmark was the first to adopt a regulation on the compensation of HIV infected haemophiliacs in June 1988, while issues of liability and compensation remain unresolved in many countries.[82]

The necessity of preventing transmission of HIV infection through blood transfusions and blood products (including organs, tissues, cells, breast milk, and artificial insemination) has been affirmed worldwide. The Council of Europe had adopted, as early as June 1983, before HIV was discovered as the cause of AIDS, recommendations on measures to prevent trans-

79 Cf. 'AIDS Courses Don't Infringe Freedom of Religion Rights *AIDS Policy & Law* (28 June 1989) 8.

80 Convention on the Rights of the Child, Annex to General Assembly Resolution 44/25 of 20 November 1989.

81 'Haemophilia and HIV: A Unique Condition within the Global Pandemic', *The AIDS Letter [Royal Society of Medicine]* 17 (February/March 1990) 1-2.

82 Karcher, 'Blood, HIV, and Compensation', 300 *British Medical Journal* (13 January 1990) 67-68.

mission of HIV infection through blood,[83] following its general recommendations on the prevention of transmission of infections through international transfers of blood.

Large amounts of protective legislation emerged rapidly. Different approaches have been adopted. Many countries have introduced mandatory HIV testing of all blood donors; others introduced the prohibition of donating blood, tissue, organs or breast-milk for HIV infected persons and listed those categories which are excluded from donating blood, such as 'high-risk groups', homosexuals and bisexuals, prostitutes, drug users, and persons returning from 'endemic' regions.[84] Some countries introduced obligatory control for HIV of all donated blood thus eliminating the need to rely on the self-deferral of HIV infected donors.[85] Particularly grave problems were experienced in countries where blood is sold and purchased by the need to regulate commercial blood banks,[86] and address the problem of professional blood donors.[87]

International legal regulation to ensure blood safety is lacking due to 'the reluctance of some governments to challenge the economic interests of blood trade'.[88] The WHO organized a meeting on blood safety in the context of the AIDS pandemic in 1986, and this meeting revealed that HIV contaminated blood was sold, at discount prices, to developing countries that neither had the knowledge nor the technology to determine such contamination.[89] In response the WHO has adopted some guidance on reducing the risk of HIV transmission through blood transfusions, advocating voluntary non-remunerated blood donations and safety control,[90] but not, however, specifying how these recommendations will apply internationally.

83 Council of Europe, Recommendation on Preventing the Possible Transmission of Acquired Immune Deficiency Syndrome (AIDS) from Affected Blood Donors to Patients Receiving Blood or Blood Products, No. R (83) 8 of 23 June 1983.

84 Reviron *et al*,. 'Prévention du SIDA transfusionnel. Analyse comparative des systèmes des différents pays développés', 2 *Santé Publique* 3 (1990) 37-41.

85 International Society of Blood Transfusion, *The International Experience in Anti-HIV Screening* (1986); *An Update* (1987); *A Further Update* (1988).

86 Murray, 'The Poisoned Gift: AIDS and Blood', 68 *The Milbank Quarterly. Supplement 2* (1990) 205-279.

87 'HIV Infection Among Blood Donors in India', 1 *CARC Calling [Bulletin of the Centre for AIDS Research and Control]* 2 (1988) 13-18.

88 Wallace, 'Life-saver or Blood Sucker?', *AIDS Action [Appropriate Health Resources & Technologies Action Group]* 14 (June 1991) 1.

89 J.C. Petricciani *et al.* (eds), *AIDS: The Safety of Blood and Blood Products* (1987) 330-334.

90 Global Blood Safety Initiative. Consensus Statement on Accelerated Strategies to Reduce the Risk of Transmission of HIV by Blood Transfusion, Geneva, 20-22 March 1989, WHO/GPA/INF/89.13; Minimum Targets for Blood Transfusion Services, WHO/GPA/INF/89.14.

II. International Response

The international community did not start elaborating a common global approach to AIDS until 1987. During the first years of the pandemic AIDS was seen as a 'disease of the rich' and confined to the Western industrialized countries. Indeed, one of the first internal memoranda concerning AIDS written at the WHO in 1983 stated that there was no need for the WHO to become involved because AIDS 'is being very well taken care of by some of the richest countries in the world where there is the manpower and knowhow and where most of the patients are to be found'.[91] As illustrated by the attached *Chronology of international policies on the human rights aspects of AIDS*, the common response to AIDS in (Western) Europe was elaborated as of 1983, while the global strategy emerged only in 1987. In 1985 the evidence that AIDS was a global problem started becoming available, and by the end of the 1980s the first, erroneous, image of the pandemic was corrected when it was proven that AIDS is disease of poverty rather than wealth,– as the PANOS Institute termed it 'a misery seeking missile'.[92] According to the WHO 'the developing countries are increasingly bearing the brunt of the pandemic: by the year 2000 they will have over 90% of the world's HIV infections and AIDS cases.'[93]

The global response to AIDS included, from the very beginning, an emphasis on human rights. In May 1987, at the time when the global strategy for the prevention and control of AIDS was being elaborated, Dr Jonathan Mann, the then Director of the Global Programme on AIDS, spoke about the need to counter 'the epidemic of social, economic, political and cultural reaction and response to AIDS and HIV infection.'[94] In his address to the General Assembly on 20 October 1987, the Secretary-General of the United Nations said that our fight against AIDS 'is also a fight against fear, against prejudice and against irrational action born of ignorance',[95] and added later 'that the world should make war *against AIDS*, and *not* against *people* with AIDS.'[96]

The necessity of respecting human rights in responding to HIV/AIDS was first affirmed by the Council of Europe, then by the World Health

91 Memorandum of the Director of the WHO Communicable Diseases Division to the Director-General, July 1983.

92 R. Sabatier (ed.), *Blaming Others. Prejudice, Race and Worldwide AIDS* (1988).

93 World AIDS Day 1991. World Health Organization Appeals to World Leaders to 'Share the Challenge of HIV/AIDS'. Address by Dr Hiroshi Nakajima, Director-General, Press Release WHO/UN 95 (29 November 1991) 1.

94 The Global Strategy for AIDS Prevention and Control, Doc. SPA/INF/87.1 of 5 May 1987, paras. 2-4.

95 Statement by the Secretary-General of the United Nations before the General Assembly, Press Release SG/SM/816/GA/334, 20 October 1987, 3.

96 Statement of H.E. Javier Perez de Cuellar, the Secretary-General of the United Nations on the Occasion of the World AIDS Day, 1 December 1988, 5.

Assembly, then by the United Nations Commission on Human Rights and its Sub-Commission on the Prevention of Discrimination and Protection of Minorities. These were followed by a vast number of organizations, intergovernmental and non-governmental, international and national, which adopted explicit policies or guidelines on the human rights aspects of AIDS.

A. Individual Freedom and Responsibility: Two Sides of the Same Coin

In its statement on the social aspects of AIDS prevention and control, the WHO's Global Programme on AIDS (called 'Special Programme on AIDS' at the time) said that

> AIDS prevention and control strategies can be implemented effectively and efficiently ... in a manner that respects and protects human rights', and added that 'there is no public health rationale to justify isolation, quarantine, or any discriminatory measures based solely on the fact that a person is suspected or known to be HIV infected ... [while] failure to prevent discrimination may endanger public health.[97]

The Global AIDS Strategy has thereby set a genuine precedent in the history of responding to disease by incorporating human rights. It merits emphasis that not only human rights bodies but also international organizations affirmed the application of human rights in responding to AIDS. The Global Commission on AIDS, established by the WHO, stated that no 'blanket exemption from observance of human rights obligations' may be accepted in combatting AIDS,[98] and the International Consultation on AIDS and Human Rights concluded that exemptions from observance of human rights could not be justified simply by claiming that they were required for public health reasons.[99] The Commission on Human Rights reaffirmed that the prohibition of discrimination on the grounds of health applies universally, restating that all are 'equal before the law and entitled to equal protection of the law from all discrimination and from all incitement to discrimination relating to their state of health'.[100]

When the Global AIDS Strategy was first formulated, the WHO stressed that transmission of HIV is preventable and every individual had

97 Social Aspects of AIDS Prevention and Control, WHO/SPA/GLO/87.2, Geneva, 1 December 1987.

98 Report of the Global Commission on AIDS, Geneva, 29-31 March 1989, WHO Doc. GPA/GCA(1)/89.1, para. 19.6.

99 International Consultation on AIDS and Human Rights, Geneva, 26-28 July 1989, Final Document, UN Doc. HR/AIDS/1989/3, paras. 18(d) and 13.

100 Commission on Human Rights, Non-discrimination in the Field of Health, Resolution 1989/11 of 2 March 1989, preamble.

the responsibility to prevent contracting or transmitting HIV infection.[101] This was reinforced in the resolution on the avoidance of discrimination in relation to HIV infected people and people with AIDS by emphasizing 'the responsibility of individuals not to put themselves or others at risk of infection with HIV'.[102] Detailed provisions on individual responsibilities, as a corollary to the human rights guarantees, have been elaborated by the Council of Europe. Its recommendation on the common European health policy on AIDS stated that health education should emphasize that 'the individual is responsible for the outcome of his behaviour towards himself, others and the society', and that sex education 'should encourage individuals to assume responsibility for their health by becoming aware of risks and benefits inherent in various lifestyles'.[103] Restrictive or repressive measures have not been endorsed by the WHO, and they have been explicitly rejected by the Council of Europe, because of the 'impossibility of imposing behaviour modification.'[104] For example, the Council's recommendation concerning AIDS in prison, stated that 'unless future scientific findings should indicate otherwise, HIV infected prisoners [should] not [be] isolated or segregated, provided they do not act irresponsibly.'[105] The International Consultation on AIDS and Human Rights developed a link between informed and responsible behaviour and protection against discrimination based on the notion of empowerment. It emphasized the need 'for protection of the human rights of those specially at risk for exposure to HIV so that they will be empowered to protect themselves. By so doing, they are enabled to fulfill their responsibility to protect others'.[106]

The Committee on Economic, Social and Cultural Rights added questions relating to AIDS in its consideration of States' reports on the implementation of the right to health. When discussing the report of Denmark, the Committee elicited the following description of its response to AIDS:

> [T]he official emphasis was on prevention through information. As to patients already infected by the virus, he described the efforts undertaken by his Government which, while attempting to avoid the spread of the disease, respected the

101 World Health Assembly, Global Strategy for the Prevention and Control of AIDS, Resolution WHA40.26 of 15 May 1987, preamble.

102 World Health Assembly, Avoidance of Discrimination Against HIV Infected Persons and Persons with AIDS, Resolution WHA41.24 of 13 May 1988, preamble.

103 Council of Europe, Guidelines for the Drawing Up of a Public Health Policy to Fight AIDS, Annex to Recommendation No. R (87) 25 of 26 November 1987, paras. 2.1.2 and 2.1.3.

104 Explanatory Memorandum to Recommendation No. 1116 (1989) of the Parliamentary Assembly on AIDS and Human Rights, Doc. 6104, at 13-14.

105 Council of Europe, Parliamentary Assembly, Recommendation 1080 (1988) on a Coordinated European Health Policy to Prevent the Spread of AIDS in Prisons of 30 June 1988, para. 14(iv).

106 International Consultation on AIDS and Human Rights, Final Document, Geneva, 26-28 July 1989, UN Doc. HR/AIDS/1989/3, para. 18(D).

> rights of those affected by relying on voluntary treatment, consent at all stages and anonymity.[107]

The Government of the Netherlands included AIDS in its report under the Covenant, and emphasized individual responsibility as the key to AIDS prevention:

> The legislation under preparation focuses to a large extent on reducing, where possible, the role of the State, with a view to maximizing individuals' responsibility for themselves and for their own health care. In this way it is hoped to increase the self-reliance of individuals within society.[108]

Responsibilities are the counterpart of individual freedoms. Freedom involves choice and this entails responsibility. Persons who could infect others ought to behave responsibly because there is no such thing as freedom to transmit infection. This emanates from the basic human rights principle whereby rights of any person are limited by equal rights of all others. Irresponsible behaviour on the part of those who might transmit infection jeopardizes the right of others to protect themselves from contracting infection. The importance of balancing individual rights and duties, freedoms and responsibilities, is evidenced by unacceptable results which are achieved by arguing either side of the coin in isolation. Thus arguing rights only ends up suggesting that 'potential [HIV] carriers are free not to submit to testing or not to change their behaviour after identification as carrier.'[109]

In some countries discussion of individual responsibility has been avoided by the assumption that persons who are HIV infected should not be expected to behave responsibly hence they ought to be isolated. This approach assumes that because they *may* infect others they *will* invariably do so, and is the underlying reason for adopting measures for their segregation, isolation or deportation. This assumption links two unrelated issues: the presence of antibodies to HIV in somebody's blood, and the human capacity of behaving responsibly. Such reasoning negates the essence of human rights. By analogy, one could argue against recognizing the right to vote, assuming that people cannot be trusted to cast their votes responsibly.

107 Second Periodic Reports Submitted by States Parties to the Covenant Containing Rights Covered by Articles 10 to 12, in Accordance with the Second Stage of the Programme Established by the Economic and Social Council in its Resolution 1988 (LV), Addendum 24, Denmark, UN Doc. E/C.12/1988/4 of 10 February 1988, para. 130.

108 Second Periodic Reports Submitted by States Parties to the Covenant Containing Rights Covered by Articles 10 to 12, in Accordance with the Second Stage of the Programme Established by the Economic and Social Council in its Resolution 1988 (LX), Addendum 24, The Netherlands, UN Doc. E/1986/4/Add.24, para. 330.

109 Gevers, 'AIDS: Screening of Possible Carriers and Human Rights', 7 *Health Policy* 1 (1987) 17.

B. Reconciling Human Rights and Public Health

Denial of human rights and discrimination against people with impaired health is part of the public health heritage. It is important to recall that an explicit international policy to prohibit discrimination against mentally ill persons was not adopted until 1971,[110] and such a policy did not exist with regard to disabled persons until 1975,[111] and there are still no specific provisions regarding discrimination against persons with communicable diseases.

Despite the recognition that public health officials exercise police powers,[112] courts have been reluctant to challenge them. Safeguards against abuses of power, which are the cornerstone of human rights, have yet to be applied to the public health authorities as much as they apply to other public authorities. In a typical example, a US court declared that public health measures are beyond the rule of law:

> [H]ealth regulations enacted by the state under its police powers and providing even drastic measures for the elimination of disease ... are not affected by constitutional provisions.[113]

Human rights have emerged as a much debated aspect in responding to AIDS because restrictive or coercive measures ostensibly aimed at fighting AIDS often infringe upon internationally recognized human rights and fundamental freedoms whithout public health justification and often enough do not even advance the cause of fighting AIDS. For example, the possibility of lawful detention for the purpose of preventing the spread of infectious diseases, envisaged in the European Convention on Human Rights, has not been applied to AIDS. In its resolution on human rights and AIDS, the Parliamentary Assembly of the Council of Europe urged Member States 'not to apply Article 5, paragraph 1(e) of the European Convention on Human Rights to justify automatic isolation or hospitalization solely on grounds that the applicant or holder is infected by the HIV virus'.[114]

International human rights law accepts that human rights may be limited on the grounds of public health if such limitations satisfy criteria of legitimacy, legality and proportionality and, most importantly, if they are carried out in a non-discriminatory manner. The history of societal re-

110 Declaration on the Rights of Mentally Retarded Persons, General Assembly Resolution 2856 (XXVI) of 20 December 1971.

111 Declaration on the Rights of Disabled Persons, General Assembly Resolution 3447 (XXX) of 9 December 1975.

112 M. Turshen, *The Politics of Public Health* (1986) 41-57.

113 Merrit, 'Communicable Disease and Constitutional Law: Controlling AIDS', *New York University Law Review* (November 1986) 754.

114 Recommendation 1116 (1989) on AIDS and Human Rights of 29 September 1989, para. D(ii).

sponses to epidemics, however, has developed the notion of *individual obligations* rather than rights. The WHO's submission on the limitations on human rights in 1975 stated the following:

> The individual is obliged to notify the health authorities when he is suffering from communicable diseases (including venereal diseases) or has been exposed to infection, and must undergo examination, treatment, surveillance, isolation or hospitalization. In particular, obligatory isolation or hospitalization in such cases constitutes a limitation on freedom of movement and the right to liberty and security of person.[115]

Nevertheless, a decade later the WHO explicitly included human rights in its Global AIDS Strategy, and thus a precedent has been set by the global health authority in responding to epidemics. The basis for merging public health and human rights has been the assertion that they are not mutually incompatible, but complement and reinforce each other. This was strengthened by the evidence that AIDS prevention can only be effective and sustainable if the rights of all are protected.

It has been documented in a number of countries that the lack of safeguards for confidentiality in HIV testing and for the avoidance of discrimination against persons who test positive, caused decreased participation in testing. Suffice it here to mention a few examples. A study of patients consenting to and declining HIV testing at a clinic for sexually transmitted diseases in New Mexico, carried out in 1986-88, revealed that those declining to be tested were five to eight times more likely to be HIV infected.[116] Reasons had not been inquired into nor systematically recorded, but researchers subsequently established that the main reason was concern about confidentiality and fear of stigmatization if knowledge of HIV infection became known. A study in New York City showed that only 22% of the patients of an STD clinic would have been willing to take the HIV test if this entailed disclosure of their personal identity.[117] In a survey carried out in March 1989 in San Francisco, 'the vast majority of men said they would consent to required testing if anti-discrimination laws were in place'.[118] In 1987, the publicity for the then-forthcoming legislation on HIV/AIDS of Japan, which included provisions for disclosing the personal identity of those testing positive, caused a decreased attendance at STD clinics.

115 E.-I. Daes, *The Individual's Duty to the Community and the Limitations on Human Rights and Freedoms under Article 20 of the Universal Declaration of Human Rights* (1983) 100.

116 Hull *et al.*, 'Comparison of HIV Antibody Prevalence in Patients Consenting to and Declining HIV Antibody Testing in an STD Clinic', 260 *Journal of American Medical Association* 19 (August 1988) 935-938.

117 Fordyce, 'Mandatory Reporting of Human Immunodeficiency Virus Testing Would Deter Blacks and Hispanics from being Tested', 262 *Journal of American Medical Association* 3 (21 July 1989) 349.

118 'Mandatory HIV Reporting Testing Deterrent?', *CDC AIDS Weekly* (27 March 1989) 8.

Attitudes towards HIV testing were further examined in 1988 to determine whether notification of personal identity to the authorities would deter people from HIV testing. More than 30% of respondents indicated their preference for HIV testing without such notification.[119] In Bavaria the announcement in 1987[120] of forthcoming restrictive measures led to a decrease in participation in educational programmes, and prompted some people to leave Bavaria to avoid compulsory HIV testing.

A good example of the ineffectiveness of compulsory HIV testing was the introduction and the subsequent abolition of compulsory pre-marital testing for HIV. On 18 July 1989 the requirement of obtaining a medical certificate confirming that applicants for marriage licenses were free of HIV antibodies was revoked in Louisiana. It had been adopted on 20 July 1987. At the time of adoption a legislative task force had been formed to review its application and its findings upon the completion of the first year of the application of compulsory pre-marital screening confirmed that it was wasteful and ineffective. In the case of Illinois such wastefulness was well documented. Mandatory premarital testing had been introduced through law in 1987 and took effect on 1 January 1988.[121] During 1988, the number of applicants for marriage licenses declined by 22%. Out of the 155,000 applicants which were tested for HIV twenty-six were found HIV positive. The cost was $208,000 per every HIV positive result.[122] This was broadly publicized and the requirement was revoked on 11 September 1989.[123]

The beginning of democratization in Central and Eastern Europe brought about a change in responding to AIDS, but also information on the previous policies and practices. Dr Valentin Pokrovsky, the President of the Academy of Medical Sciences of the USSR, publicly declared that the screening of 18 million people in 1988 was not cost-effective. He illustrated this by comparing the compulsory screening of 4 million pregnant women where 6 were found HIV positive, and voluntary anonymous testing of 19,000 people where 4 were found HIV positive. Hence the voluntary testing programme proved 1400 times more effective than compulsory screening.[124]

The empirical evidence thus confirmed the link between participation in HIV testing and protection of HIV positive people against stigmatization and discrimination. This was reaffirmed by the Council of Europe:

119 Ohi *et al.*, 'Notification of HIV Carriers: Possible Effect on Uptake of HIV Testing', *The Lancet* (22 October 1988) 947-949.

120 Gorgens, The Third Epidemic. Special Report, *World AIDS* (May 1989) 11.

121 Illinois Public Health Act 85-925, House Bill No. 936 (1987).

122 Data for the first 12 months of mandatory pre-marital HIV testing, Illinois Department of Public Health, undated, [mimeographed].

123 Illinois Public Act 86-884, House Bill No. 18 (1989).

124 Connor, 'Eastern Europe Faces a Western Epidemic', *New Scientist* (8 April 1989) 25-26.

> Society ... has an obligation to alleviate the possible negative consequences of such detection by preventing discrimination which may act as a disincentive to the detection of infection, ... [therefore, an explicit policy] should state unequivocally that HIV infected individuals have the right to enjoy the same civil and social rights as the non-infected, while bearing ethical, civil and legal responsibilities to contain transmission.[125]

C. The Primacy of Non-Discrimination

It is significant that both in public health and in human rights non-discrimination was addressed as the key to integrating human rights into AIDS prevention and control. This reinforced the prohibition on discrimination under international human rights law, but also provided an incentive for its broadening, particularly by urging that it be extended to cover the grounds for discrimination which were – and continue – to be used in the context of AIDS. These are in particular, discrimination on the grounds of sexual orientation,[126] and the state of health, especially disability.[127]

This text does not include a discussion of AIDS-related discrimination nor does it review the existing pattern of discrimination and available remedies, because the literature in this area is vast.[128] Instead, it addresses fairly unexplored facets of AIDS-related discrimination by presenting a cursory review of prohibitions on discrimination in national laws, focusing on non-Western countries, and analyses gender discrimination which has been neglected in both research and policies on the human rights aspects of AIDS.

As mentioned above, law has been used in two mutually contradictory roles: it legalized coercive and discriminatory approaches to AIDS prevention and control, but it also embodied safeguards for individual rights and freedoms. As always in human rights, legislation to protect individual rights and freedoms has been a reaction to their violations. Thus the first pieces of anti-discrimination legislation appeared in the USA, the Los An-

125 Explanatory Memorandum to the Recommendation (89)14 on the Ethical Issues of HIV Infection in Health Care and Social Settings, Council of Europe, Strasbourg, 24 October 1989, paras. 154 and 163(iv).

126 Ashman, 'Homosexuality and Human Rights', *Second ILGA Pink Book. A Global View of Lesbian and Gay Liberation and Oppression* (1988) 45-54.

127 Human Rights and Disability. Progress Report Prepared by Mr. Leandro Despouy, Special Rapporteur, UN Doc. E/CN.4/Sub.2/1988/11 of 13 June 1988.

128 Cf. Stoddard and Reiman, 'AIDS and the Rights of the Individual: Toward a More Sophisticated Understanding of Discrimination', 68 *The Milbank Quarterly. Supplement 1* (1990) 143-174; O'Brien, 'Discrimination: The Difference with AIDS', 6 *Journal of Contemporary Health Law and Policy* (1990) 93-125.

geles AIDS Discrimination Ordinance of June 1985,[129] and many States in the USA had adopted anti-discrimination laws by 1988.[130]

As with human rights legislation in any other area, the mere adoption of an AIDS-specific anti-discrimination provision does not necessarily signify a commitment to human rights protection nor should it be presumed that non-discrimination is applied and enforced. It is too well known in human rights that words are not necessarily matched by deeds. It is, however, important to stress that prohibitions on AIDS-related discrimination were adopted as a result of pressure, and this is symbolic but indicative of the advance in human rights protection.

Comores adopted its first AIDS law in November 1988. This legislation stresses that one of the main functions of the National AIDS Control Committee was to ensure the protection of citizens' rights, and conformity of the national AIDS programme to the Global AIDS Strategy. The AIDS legislation of Argentina, the Law on AIDS No. 23 of 16 August 1990, states in Article 2 that no AIDS-related regulations may be adopted if they would infringe upon personal dignity or result in discriminatory or marginalizing effects for those affected or likely to be affected. It requires respect for individual dignity, medical secrets and privacy, and prohibits marginalization, degradation and humiliation of persons affected by HIV/AIDS. In the USSR the Law on Prevention of AIDS of 23 April 1990, states in Article 8(4):

> Dismissal from work, refusal of work, refusal of admission to medical and educational establishments, refusal to admit children to pre-school establishments, the restriction of other rights, and limitation of the legitimate interests of such individuals solely on the grounds that they are carriers of the virus or are suffering from AIDS, as well as restrictions of the right to accommodation and other rights and legitimate interests of relatives and close associates of an infected person, shall be prohibited.

The Japanese AIDS Prevention Law of 23 December 1988 stipulates in Article 2(3) that the authorities 'shall give consideration to protecting the human rights of AIDS patients', and continues in Article 3 by saying that 'the public shall ensure that the human rights of AIDS patients' shall not be endangered. In Kuwait, the Committee to Combat AIDS has been asked to 'propose the arrangements and procedures to ensure safeguarding the rights and personal liberties of victims in the framework of social values and conventions'.[131]

129 Roden, 'Educating Through the Law: The Los Angeles AIDS Discrimination Ordinance', 33 *U.C.L.A. Law Review* (June 1986) 1410.

130 Anti-Discrimination Statutes in the States. State AIDS Reports, *Intergovernmental Health Policy Project* 5 (October-November 1988).

131 Ministerial Decision No. 291 for 1988 of 20 July 1988, para. 5. Cf. note 28.

The need to respect human rights, even if not included in national AIDS legislation, has been articulated in national debates on AIDS laws and policies. Contrary to the frequent remark that human rights are 'Western', the following examples from Asia demonstrate that the universal scope of human rights has been matched by worldwide calls for their observance.

In September 1989 the Ministry of Public Health of Thailand proposed a draft law on AIDS which included provisions for compulsory screening of 'high-risk groups' and registration and detention of HIV positive people. This draft also contained a prohibition of discrimination against people with AIDS.[132] Public hearings on this draft law were held on 23 November 1989 and the Bangkok Post reported that all those who took part in the hearings stressed that the rights of people with HIV/AIDS must be protected.[133]

In December 1989 the Bombay High Court rejected the petition by two mothers to release their HIV positive sons from detention in Goa (India), based on public health law.[134] The Court noted that 'isolation results in social ostracism and encroaches on the individual's liberty', but added that isolation was necessary because of fear of AIDS amongst the public: 'an error on the safer side may be more agreeable since the dimension of AIDS created a fear psychosis'.[135] Less than two years later, detention of a large number of prostitutes, forcibly tested for antibodies to HIV, was overruled, thus signifying a change in the interpretation of law.[136]

AIDS literature has been, and remains, dominated by the focus on male homosexuals,[137] because among the categories targetted by coercive and discriminatory AIDS control measures, they have been the only one able to generate information and influence policy-making. Gender discrimination has been relatively neglected in the context of AIDS, and moreover, there have been instances in the Western industrialized countries where preference was given to women as part of screening out possible male homosexuals from employment. Such rare examples of reverse gender discrimination in the context of AIDS have not changed the main trend in responding to AIDS, which is characterized by the neglect of women. An important reason for this neglect was the dominance of the industrialized Western countries

132 'Anti-AIDS Legislation Defended', *The Nation* (Bangkok), 22 September 1989.

133 'Hearing Draws Strong Support for AIDS Bill', Bangkok Post (24 November 1989).

134 The Goa Public Health (Amendment) Act of 5 June 1989 gave health officers powers to 'remove or cause to be removed' to hospital or 'other place' any person suffering from an infectious disease or any person who appears to the health officer to be suffering from an infectious disease.

135 'High Court Upholds Isolation of HIV Carriers', The Herald [Pajim Goa] (9 December 1989) 1.

136 A. Bhandari *et al.*, *Women and AIDS. Denial and Blame* (1990).

137 Tindall and Tillet, 'HIV-related Discrimination', *AIDS 1990. A Year in Review* (1991) S251-S256.

(North America and Western Europe) in responding to AIDS during the first decade of the pandemic. As AIDS was first diagnosed in the USA, and its transmission assumed to be confined to male homosexuals, women were neglected. The male-female ratio at the beginning of the pandemic was 20:1. A similar ratio was assumed for other regions. The dominant view was – and still is – that the AIDS pandemic affected women later and less than men, despite the fact that women constitute the *majority* of HIV infected people in Africa. Epidemiological data for sub-Saharan Africa demonstrate that the male-female ratio was probably 1:1 from the very beginning of the AIDS pandemic and recent studies now reveal a higher incidence of HIV infection in women.[138] The low level of HIV infection in women in the industrialized Western countries, particularly in Western Europe, is probably indicative of the status of women and their corresponding possibilities for self-protection, much as the high sero-prevalence rates in Africa point to their proverbially low status.

Just a few examples are included here to illustrate the multitude of human rights dimensions relating to women and AIDS. Access to information, taken for granted in the industrialized Western countries, is not a reality for many women in developing countries. For example, a study of the rural population in India demonstrated that only 8,7% of women, compared with 77% of men, knew what AIDS was and how HIV infection was transmitted.[139] Blood transfusions represent a risk for women in many parts of the world. A Mexican research team showed that 61,8% of HIV infected women were infected through blood transfusions.[140] The scope of discrimination against women is unknown. Evidence is rare, but indicative: the New York City Anti-Discrimination Unit revealed that women were more often victims of discrimination than men.[141] The formal equality in rights has not yet been attained for women and legalized discrimination against women, widespread in many parts of the world, constitutes an obstacle to effective AIDS prevention.

Most internationally adopted policies on women and AIDS do not, however, address the status of women in society in responding to AIDS, nor, indeed do they relate to *all* women, but group women and children together, thus reinforcing that attention is paid to women only in their childbearing role. The research and policies on women and AIDS show that HIV

138 Berkley *et al.*, 'AIDS and HIV Infection in Women in Uganda – Are More Women Infected Than Men?', 4 *AIDS 1991* 12.

139 Chuttani *et al.*, 'Awareness and Knowledge about AIDS Among a Rural Population in India', in Second International Conference on AIDS Education, Yaounde, 1989, Panel 1.1, Abstract 3.

140 Villareal *et al.*, 'Mexican Women Infected with HIV', in International Conference on the Implications of AIDS for Mothers and Children, Paris, 1989, Abstract F.22.

141 *Falling Between the Cracks: AIDS and Discrimination Against Women*, [mimeographed] (1988).

transmission *from* rather than *to* women was their focus, and, specifically, perinatal transmission and prostitution were the most frequent topics. The United Nations General Assembly stated that 'women and children may be at a higher risk of [HIV] infection than previously and may otherwise suffer deprivation as a consequence of the indirect impact of AIDS on their families and communities'.[142] The Paris Declaration on Women, Children and AIDS, adopted by the International Conference on the Implications of AIDS for Mothers and Children in 1989, discussed women and AIDS in the context of 'the health of women, children and families', and focused on drug abuse as a principal concern, despite the fact that this problem is not relevant for many developing regions.[143] The World Health Assembly adopted its Resolution WHA43.10 on 16 May 1990, in which it endorsed the Paris Declaration and repeated many provisions therefrom.

Calls to address the human rights dimensions of responses to AIDS relating to women came from human rights bodies. The Committee on the Elimination of All Forms of Discrimination against Women [CEDAW] adopted a general recommendation relating to avoidance of gender discrimination in responding to AIDS. The incentive was found in the need to reach beyond the impact of AIDS on women and consider how the existing national responses to AIDS affect women.[144] The basis for this Recommendation was the Convention itself, which specifies in its Article 12 the obligation of States to eliminate discrimination against women in the field of health, and to secure equal access to health care services for men and women. The Declaration of Buenos Aires, adopted on 17 November by the First Latin American and Caribbean Symposium on Women and AIDS, stressed that it was 'necessary for Governments to enforce international conventions on women and on AIDS through effective and concrete mecha-

142 Prevention and Control of Acquired Immunodeficiency Syndrome (AIDS), Resolution 44/233 of the General Assembly of 22 December 1989, preamble and para. 7(b)(i).

143 International Conference on the Implications of AIDS for Mothers and Children: Technical Statements and Selected Presentations, Paris, 27-30 November 1989, WHO/GPA/DIR/89.12, 2-5.

144 CEDAW recommended, *inter alia*: 'That programmes to combat AIDS should give special attention to the rights and needs of women and children, and to the factors relating to the reproductive role of women and their subordinate position in some societies which make them especially vulnerable to HIV infection' and 'That all States parties include in their reports under article 12 of the Convention information on the effects of AIDS on the situation of women and on the action taken to cater to the needs of those women who are infected and to prevent specific discrimination against women in response to AIDS.'
General Recommendation No. 15 (ninth session, 1990), Report of the Committee on Elimination of Discrimination Against Women, UN Doc. A/45/38 of 8 February 1990, para. 438.

nisms that enable women to make decisions regarding their health, their sexual and reproductive rights, and the health of their children'.[145]

III. Protecting Groups Vulnerable to Human Rights Violations

A recurrent theme of this text is the concordance between the targets of 'conventional' and AIDS-related human rights violations. This has exposed the *lacunae* in the international human rights system, where the protection of basic rights of some marginalized categories – such as drug-dependent persons or prostitutes – is generally insufficient, and the protection of prisoners, although representing a large proportion of human rights litigation, nationally and internationally, still too often leaves prisoners without effective protection. The reasons for insufficient human rights protection are the same as those for AIDS-related human rights violations: in countries where human rights protection is not assured in other areas, its lack has been proven regarding AIDS as well. Even in countries where national human rights protection is fairly effective in 'conventional' areas, it was not always immediately and fully extended to AIDS-related issues:

> Democratically elected governments, under the pressure to be seen to be doing something effective in the face of a major epidemic, may be tempted to legislate against particular groups. Migrants, prisoners, drug users and prostitutes, in particular, lack an effective voice to dissuade lawmakers from provision of laws discriminating against them.[146]

A. Prisoners

As mentioned above, data on compulsory HIV testing shows that 'captive populations', such as prisoners, have been subjected to compulsory testing more often than persons at liberty. This conforms with the general pattern of human rights violations: human rights of prisoners are denied, jeopardized and violated more often than those of persons at liberty. Jeopardy of the basic human rights of prisoners has not stopped at compulsory testing and segregation of HIV infected inmates:

145 Declaration of Buenos Aires by the Latin American and Caribbean Women Regarding AIDS in Women, the First Latin American and Caribbean Symposium on Women and AIDS, organized by PAHO/WHO and the Latin American and Caribbean Women's Health Network of ISIS International, Buenos Aires 16-17 November 1990, [mimeographed].

146 Kirby, 'AIDS – Legal Issues', 2 *AIDS 1988. Supplement 1* (1989) S212.

All women inmates who require hospital care, and male inmates who are too ill to be treated in prison ward hospitals are outposted to civilian wards. Although under constant supervision of armed correction officers, they are manacled to their beds by their legs being cuffed to an eight-inch chain. They are so manacled twenty-four hours a day, without regard to their medical condition or their security level.[147]

Earlier in the AIDS epidemic prisoners were deemed to constitute a 'bridge' between 'high-risk groups' and the 'general population',[148] and the idea of containment found expression in suggestions that prisoners be tested for HIV before their release to protect the 'general population'. Only later was attention paid to the transmission of HIV infection *within* prison, and in particular to the protection of prisoners from contracting HIV infection. Denial of self-protection may amount to 'denying inmates access to preventive health care services such as condoms [and] subjecting them to disease and death'.[149] To enable prisoners to protect themselves the prison authorities need to accept that behaviour which is likely to transmit HIV infection takes place in prison, despite the fact that virtually any activity that may transmit infection is prohibited and constitutes a disciplinary offence. Thus, not surprisingly, the prison authorities have been reluctant to undertake preventive measures. In the court cases in the USA, for example, where prisoners argued that HIV infection acquired in prison was a consequence of the failure of prison authorities to put in practice effective programmes to prevent HIV transmission, the courts have not declared the prison authorities liable but affirmed their discretion in responding to AIDS.[150]

In response to the severity and urgency of problems created by AIDS in prisons, the WHO developed recommendations for AIDS prevention and control in prison in 1987.[151] Most importantly, the WHO affirmed the principle of equivalence, namely that the same AIDS prevention and control strategy should be applied in prisons as in other parts of society. This means, in particular, that prisoners should have the same right of access to information and to educational programmes designed to minimize the

147 Association of the Bar of the New York City, AIDS and the Criminal Justice System: A Preliminary Report and Recommendations, Part II: Discrimination Against Prisoners with AIDS within the Criminal Justice System, Joint Subcommittee on AIDS in the Criminal Justice System of the Committee on Corrections and Committee on Criminal Justice Operations and Budget of the Association of the Bar of the City of New York, November 1989.

148 Report on a Coordinated European Health Policy to Prevent the Spread of AIDS in Prisons, Council of Europe, Doc. 5897 of 10 May 1988, para. 25.

149 American Public Health Association 'HIV Education and Condoms in Correctional Facilities', Resolution 9017, 81 *American Journal of Public Health,* 1991 2 (February 1990) 252.

150 Takas and Hammet, 'Legal Issues Affecting Offenders and Staff', *AIDS Bulletin* (May 1989) 2.

151 Consensus Statement of WHO Consultation on Prevention and Control of AIDS in Prisons, Geneva, 16-18 November 1987, WHO/SPA/INF/87.14.

spread of HIV infection. Moreover, the WHO suggested that careful consideration should be given to making condoms available to prisoners to prevent further spread of HIV infection in prison. The testing of prisoners for HIV infection should comply with the same conditions that apply to persons at liberty, namely consent, confidentiality, and pre- and post-test counselling. In addition, the WHO urged that medical, nursing, in-patient and out-patient services be made available to prisoners with AIDS, and that prisoners with AIDS should be considered for compassionate early release to die in dignity and freedom.

A common policy on AIDS in prison has been developed by the Council of Europe, and although it is confined to the industrialized European countries, its recommendations can be applied worldwide. These call upon the national authorities 'to ensure that compulsory screening is not introduced ... for any given population group such as 'captive' populations, e.g. prisoners.'[152] The recommendations go on to call for measures to ensure that HIV infected prisoners are not isolated or segregated, provided they do not act irresponsibly, and to make condoms available to prisoners. The public health authorities had been first asked 'to consider seriously ... the provision of instructions on the method of cleaning needles and the availability of condoms in prison', and were later invited 'to allow clean, one-way syringes and clean needles in prison', with the following explanation: 'Considering that the occurrence of homosexual activities and intravenous drug abuse in prison, both of which entail a considerable risk of spreading HIV infection amongst the prison population and eventually outside prison, must be accepted as realities.'[153] But there is a vast gulf between the practices recommended by international organizations and those prevailing in prisons.

The Inter-regional Preparatory Meeting for the Eighth United Nations Congress on the Prevention of Crime and the Treatment of Offenders stressed the urgency of addressing HIV/AIDS in prison, which exacerbated the difficult conditions prevailing in many penitentiary systems:

> At the most general level, humiliating or dehumanizing conditions could be equated with denying the inmates their basic human rights and with endangering their lives by exposing them, more so than in regular prison conditions, to AIDS and other communicable diseases. During the Eighth Congress the international community should do its utmost to emphasize that aspect of overcrowding.[154]

152 Recommendation No. R (89) 14 of the Committee of Ministers to Member States on the Ethical Issues of HIV Infection in Health Care and Social Settings of 24 October 1989, Article 24.

153 Recommendation 1080 (1988) on a Coordinated European Health Policy to Prevent the Spread of AIDS in Prisons of 30 June 1988, paras. 14A(viii) and 11.

154 Report of the Interregional Meeting for the Eighth United Nations Congress on the Prevention of Crime and the Treatment of Offenders, Vienna, 30 May – 3 June 1988, UN Doc. A/CONF.144/IPM/4 of 9 June 1988, para. 50.

In response, the Eighth United Nations Congress on the Prevention of Crime and the Treatment of Offenders adopted a resolution on HIV/AIDS in prison, stressing the necessity of introducing and/or strengthening the provision of information on HIV/AIDS to the penitentiary staff and prisoners.[155]

The most difficult problem has been the association between HIV/AIDS and drug use. AIDS was diagnosed among prisoners early in the epidemic and immediately linked to injecting drug use.[156] This link was confirmed by a survey carried out for the Council of Europe: 'The proportion of HIV seropositive prisoners ... reflects directly the proportion of drug addicts in the prison population'.[157] These results have been proven in most industrialized countries. The problem is exacerbated by the continued use of injected drugs within prisons.[158]

B. Drug-Dependent Persons

Drug use, abuse, addiction and dependence is a controversial topic, even without its association with AIDS. While human rights should apply in drug control as in any other part of governmental activity, little is known about the human rights problems that emerge in this area.[159] It is known that drug-dependent persons are typically found in prisons rather than in treatment centres, and this indicates the dominant societal and legal response. Legal norms relating to drug (ab)use were added in the international narcotic control treaties and thus follow the same legal approach: 'A system of administrative controls and penal sanctions established for the purpose of keeping narcotic drugs from actual and potential victims ... continues to be the essence of the Single Convention.'[160] This was considered to bring about the prevention of drug abuse. The WHO has concluded, however, that criminalization of drug consumption does not have a preventive impact: 'the criminalization of drug use as currently applied should probably be seen mainly as a punitive measure without noticeable preven-

155 Infection with Human Immunodeficiency Virus (HIV) and Acquired Immunodeficiency Syndrome (AIDS) in Prison, Resolution 18, in Report of the Eighth United Nations Congress on the Prevention of Crime and the Treatment of Offenders, Havana, Cuba, 27 August – 7 September 1990, UN Doc. A/CONF.144/28 of 5 October 1990, 167.

156 Wormser *et al.*, 'Acquired Immunodeficiency Syndrome in Male Prisoners. New Insights into an Emerging Syndrome', 98 *Annals of Internal Medicine* 3 (1983) 297-303.

157 Control of Communicable Diseases in Prisons. Conclusions Adopted by the Eighth Conference of Directors of Prison Administrations, *8th Conference of Directors of Prison Administrations*, Strasbourg, 2-5 June 1987, (1988) 43.

158 Kennedy *et al.*, 'Drug Misuse and Sharing of Needles in Scottish Prisons' 302 *British Medical Journal* (22 June 1991) 1507; Dye and Isaacs 'Intravenous Drug Misuse Among Prison Inmates: Implications for Spread of HIV', 302 *British Medical Journal* (22 June 1991) 1506.

159 'Individual Rights and the Drug Epidemic. A Special Report', 17 *Human Rights* 2 (Summer 1990) 14-29.

160 *Commentary on the Convention on Psychotropic Substances* (1976) 330.

tive effects,'[161] while its survey of national laws found that 'the international conventions on drug control have had a somewhat mixed effect on the development and implementation of national legislation *authorizing* the treatment of drug-dependent persons' [emphasis added].[162] This wording is indicative of the prevailing attitude: treatment could be provided at the discretion of law enforcement agencies.

In an increasing number of countries, treatment of drug addicts pertains to both law enforcement and health authorities, creating controversial situations where 'drug addicts all too often find themselves in the position where they are pursued by the law but at the same time are encouraged to register as addicts.'[163] The WHO has advocated stronger links between health and law enforcement, and argued that 'avoidance of very severe criminal penalties for clearly dependent, sick persons, can help to encourage such persons to seek early treatment and rehabilitation'.[164]

There is a slowly emerging recognition of the need to separate health from law enforcement in legislating on drug abuse. This has been recommended to the Council of Europe where 'the introduction of legislation that distinguishes between traffickers and users – though without invariably regarding users as innocent victims' has been proposed, to be accompanied with 'the prescribing of socio-medical treatment as an alternative to punishment' for drug dependent persons.[165] The Eighth United Nations Congress for the Prevention of Crime and the Treatment of Offenders followed a similar approach by adopting a separate resolution on measures against drug addiction, which recognizes that 'the addict is most often a sick person', and argues for facilitation of access to detoxification programmes, development of alternatives to punishment, and assistance to drug addicts 'in the medical, educational and social areas'.[166]

The AIDS pandemic has increased attention on drug use, but discussions of changes in law and practice have been confined to needle-exchange programmes. This reductionism sidelines causes and effects by addressing just one ramification of the prevalent societal response to drug abuse: the

161 M. Gossop and M. Grant (eds), *Preventing and Controlling Drug Abuse* (1990) 63.

162 L. Porter *et al.*, *The Law and the Treatment of Drug- and Alcohol-Dependent Persons* (1986) 83.

163 Report drawn up on behalf of the Committee of Inquiry into the Drug Problem in the Member States of the Community on the Results of the Inquiry, European Parliament, Doc. A-2-114/86/Corr.1 of 2 October 1986, para. 107.

164 Curran *et al.*, 'Guidelines for Assessing and Revising National Legislation on Treatment of Drug- and Alcohol-Dependent Persons', 38 *International Digest of Health Legislation. Supplement 1* (1987) 5.

165 Parliamentary Assembly of the Council of Europe, Recommendation 1085 (1988) on the fight against drugs of 4 October 1988, para. 15(i).

166 Measures against drug addiction, Resolution 13, Report of the Eighth United Nations Congress on the Prevention of Crime and the Treatment of Offenders, Havana, Cuba, 27 August – 7 September 1990, UN Doc. A/CONF.144/28 of 5 October 1990, 156-157.

fact that self-injecting drug users share their injecting equipment and this contributes to the spread of HIV infection. The interplay between preserving the health of drug-dependent persons and enforcing the prohibition of drug abuse has attained publicity with the controversial introduction of needle-exchange programmes to reduce the transmission of HIV infection. The WHO Consultation on HIV infection and self-injecting drug users recommended 'programmes to facilitate access to sterile needles and syringes, including needle and syringe exchange programmes',[167] and the Council of Europe suggested that States 'consider arranging for the distribution of syringes and study the expediency of allowing the sale of disposable syringes only, so as to limit the effects of AIDS and reduce the number of deaths from infection'.[168] There has been, not surprisingly, much opposition to needle-exchange programmes: they were accused of promoting drug abuse. The government's supply of needles has been said to supplement the traffickers' supply of drugs. However, it has also been recognized that the legal prohibition of the possession of drug-injecting equipment has contributed to the spread of HIV infection by necessitating its sharing. Controversies continue, but some reconciliation seems forthcoming. The International Narcotics Control Board recognized that 'measures that may decrease the sharing of hypodermic needles among intravenous drug abusers are necessary to reduce the spread of AIDS', and announced that 'the legal aspects related to the controlled distribution of hypodermic needles and syringes' were under study, but reiterated that 'any prophylactic measures which are urgently needed should neither promote nor facilitate drug abuse.'[169]

C. Prostitutes

The prevalence of HIV infection in female prostitutes, particularly in Africa, has been one of the frequent topics of AIDS research.[170] Immense amounts of data have been published, and coercive and repressive measures against prostitutes have followed. The stigmatizing impact of such research has escaped attention.[171] While stigmatization of individuals was acknowledged early in the pandemic, and safeguards provided through anonymity

167 Report of the Meeting on HIV Infection and Drug Injecting Intervention Strategies, Geneva, 18-20 January 1988, Doc. WHO/GPA/SBR/89.1, 8.

168 Recommendation 1085 (1988) on the Fight Against Drugs of 4 October 1988, para. 14(ix).

169 Summary of the Report of the International Narcotic Control Board for 1989, UN Doc. E/1990/16 of 1 February 1990, para. 11.

170 P. Lamptey and P. Pio, *The Handbook for AIDS Prevention in Africa* (1990) 144-180.

171 Cohen *et al.*, 'Prostitutes and AIDS: Public Policy Issues', 3 *AIDS & Public Policy* 2 (1988) 16-22.

and/or confidentiality, the stigmatizing effects on frequently targetted categories have only recently been addressed.[172]

Prostitution has been made a scapegoat for AIDS and often treated as a risk *factor* rather than *people* at risk.[173] Coercive measures have been applied even in countries where HIV prevalence among prostitutes is low. Such measures included compulsory HIV testing, deprivation of liberty of HIV infected prostitutes and prohibition of continuing prostitution for those infected. Such prohibitions appear to be inherently ineffective: if no alternative livelihood is available, an HIV infected prostitute does not have an option to discontinue prostitution.[174]

The WHO Consultation on HIV Epidemiology and Prostitution recommended that increased attention be paid to the protection of human rights of prostitutes: 'A meeting with appropriate representation from the international legal and civil rights communities should be organized to address issues such as laws which impinge on social, economic, and legal rights of prostitutes and therefore impede HIV prevention efforts.'[175]

D. Aliens

Earlier in the AIDS pandemic, every country claimed that AIDS had come from the outside. In Asia, where the virus arrived last and where the AIDS caseload is still considerably lower than in other regions, responses to HIV/AIDS were influenced by the fact that as late as 1987 there were no cases of 'indigenously transmitted' AIDS.[176] The general assumption was that aliens are *the* potential source of HIV and entry restrictions have been imposed ostensibly to prevent the 'importation of AIDS'. The then Swedish Ombudsman on Ethnic Discrimination pointed out that opposition to immigration is sometimes based on the prejudice that immigrants may be afflicted by unknown, terrible diseases which they would spread into the domestic population.[177]

As usual in the case of epidemics, one country blamed another, 'scientific' proof that AIDS originated somewhere else mushroomed, and

172 'Ethics and Epidemiology. XXVth CIOMS Conference', 66 *Weekly Epidemiological Record* 4 (1991) 17-19.

173 'Interventions for Female Prostitutes in AIDS', *The Second Decade* (1990) 253-288.

174 Effects of the Acquired Immunodeficiency Syndrome (AIDS) on the Advancement of Women, UN Doc. E/CN.6/1989/6/Add.1 of 17 February 1989, paras. 43-48.

175 Consensus Statement of WHO Consultation on HIV Epidemiology and Prostitution, Geneva, 3-6 July 1989, WHO/GPA/INF/89.11.

176 AIDS: Situation in South-East Asia and Prevention and Control. Report of an Inter-country Consultation, New Delhi, 5-7 August 1987, SEA/CD/105 (2 November 1987).

177 Nobel, 'The Role of Ombudsmen', Paper presented at the International Consultation on Health Legislation and Ethics in the Field of AIDS and HIV Infection, Oslo, 26-29 April, 1989.

many countries carried out epidemiological surveys to show that the first cases of AIDS came from abroad. Consequently, aliens have been a particularly frequent target of compulsory HIV screening. Haiti was the first target because all immigrants from Haiti were determined to constitute a 'high-risk group' in the USA. In March 1983 the American Red Cross included 'Haitian immigrants' among categories excluded from blood donation because of their 'high risk of carrying AIDS'. A year later, in April 1984, the US Centre for Disease Control (CDC) deleted 'recent Haitian immigrants' from the list of categories at greatest risk.[178] Africa and Africans were often blamed for the origin of AIDS.[179] Africans living in other regions, or travelling to them, have borne a heavy burden of discrimination, leading the former Director-General of the WHO, Dr Halfdan Mahler, to note 'the ugly head of racism' in such practices.[180] Amongst aliens, some were considered more likely than others to introduce and/or spread HIV infection. Thus foreign students have been targetted more often than foreign diplomats, and students from Africa more often than those from other regions.[181]

The protection of human rights of aliens, insufficient as it is, is further exacerbated by the fact that there is no human right to enter a foreign country for an alien. This, however, does not imply that entry restrictions imposed by requiring HIV testing for aliens and prohibiting the entry to those infected, are beyond the reach of international human rights law. In interpreting provisions of the International Covenant on Civil and Political Rights applicable to aliens, the Human Rights Committee stated that:

> The Covenant does not recognize the right of aliens to enter or reside in the territory of a State party. It is in principle a matter for the State to decide who it will admit to its territory. However, in certain circumstances an alien may enjoy the protection of the Covenant even in relation to entry or residence, for example, when considerations of non-discrimination, prohibition of inhuman treatment and respect for family life arise.[182]

Aliens, by virtue of being human beings, are entitled to all human rights and fundamental freedoms and thereby to equal protection against discrimination. This requires that human rights be guaranteed to all, citizens and aliens, while any differences must be justified and consistent with interna-

178 H.R. Malinowsky *et al.*, '*AIDS Information Sourcebook 1989-90*' (1989) Annex 1, Chronology, 3-4.

179 R.C. Chirimuuta and R.J. Chirimuuta, *Aids, Africa and Racism* (1987).

180 'WHO Can Help to Fight AIDS: Interview with Halfdan Mahler', *Newsweek* (13 July 1987) 48.

181 Tomasevski, 'AIDS, Travel and Migration: Legal and Human Rights Aspects', 29 *International Migration* 1 (1990) 33-50.

182 Human Rights Committee, General Comment 15 (27), The Position of Aliens Under the Covenant, Report of the Human Rights Committee, UN Doc. A/41/40, Annex VI, at 117-119.

tionally recognized human rights. The Council of Europe recommended that no health control at borders or restrictions of movement be applied, and urged its Member States 'not to refuse the right of asylum on the sole ground that the asylum-seeker is contaminated by the HIV virus or suffers from AIDS'.[183]

Moreover, HIV/AIDS-related entry restrictions were denied any public health rationale,[184] and declared contrary to the International Health Regulations.[185] These Regulations are the sole international legal instrument providing safeguards against excessive restrictions upon international movement imposed under the pretext of fighting AIDS. The imposition of HIV/AIDS-related restrictions by more than 50 countries,[186] in defiance of explicit provisions of International Health Regulations, has prompted criticism of their lack of enforcement.[187] The first prohibition of entry for HIV infected people, introduced by Saudi Arabia early in 1986, was reported together with the protest of the United Kingdom to the WHO, which urged that the International Health Regulations be applied.[188] The WHO stated later that 'no country bound by the Regulations may refuse entry into its territory to a person who fails to provide a medical certificate stating that he or she is not carrying the AIDS virus',[189] and yet later added: 'It must be vigorously stressed that to require such certificates, let alone to insist on blood tests on arrival, would be totally contrary to the International Health Regulations.'[190] Nevertheless, practices in breach of the Regulations have continued and no action has been undertaken to identify instances of non-compliance and promote compliance with the sole binding international instrument prohibiting unnecessary restrictions.

183 Recommendation 1116 (1989) on AIDS and Human Rights of 29 September 1989, para. D(iii).

184 World Health Organization, *Vaccination Certificate Requirements and Health Advice for International Travel* (1988).

185 World Health Organization, *International Health Regulations [1969]* (1971).

186 Duckett and Orkin, 'AIDS-Related Migration and Travel Policies and Restrictions: A Global Survey', 3 *AIDS. Supplement 1* (1989) S231-S252.

187 Cf. Nelson, 'International Travel Restrictions and the AIDS Epidemic', 81 *AJIL* (1987) 230-236; Allin, 'The AIDS Pandemic: International Travel and Immigration Restrictions and the World Health Organization's Response', 28 *Va.J.Int'l.L.* (1988) 1043-1064.

188 In March 1986 Saudi Arabia introduced the requirement for all foreign visitors to present 'certificates showing that visitors are free of AIDS', and the Government of United Kingdom lodged a complaint with the WHO, stating that this requirement was a breach of the International Health Regulations. 'Saudi Arabian Visa Regulation – UK Protest', 1 *AIDS Newsletter 3* (7 March 1986) 1.

189 60 *Weekly Epidemiological Record* 40 (4 October 1985) 311.

190 Functioning of the International Health Regulations for the period 1 January to 31 December 1985 (Part I), 61 *Weekly Epidemiological Record* 50 (12 December 1986) 389.

AIDS-related entry restrictions have disproportionately affected asylum-seekers and refugees.[191] In the case of refugees, the internationally accepted principle of burden-sharing urges admission of refugees on humanitarian grounds. UNHCR has therefore stressed that national measures 'taken to combat AIDS and to prevent the spread of HIV infection must be related to the overall objectives of the international system, namely, protection', because 'screening, for example, may result in refoulement, refusal to grant protection or denial of refugees' right to return voluntarily to their country of origin'. Burden-sharing is the only feasible means of coping with the refugee problem hence it should apply to AIDS:

> The economic cost of admission and care must be seen as essential to overall international efforts, as has long been the case for physically and mentally disabled refugees.[192]

The rationale for entry restrictions has followed the pattern described at the beginning of this section: aliens, and in particular all asylum-seekers or refugees, do not have a political voice. The enactment of restrictions in the USA, which have attained much publicity, has been described as follows:

> As in the case with most legislation which costs nothing to pass, even those senators who were at first opposed to the amendment ultimately voted for it. Indeed, at first glance, the amendment seemed a simple way to conserve medical, and more importantly financial resources for use by American citizens rather than aliens.[193]

Concluding Remarks

The lesson from the first decade of AIDS is that merging public health and human rights is difficult but not impossible. The period of panic and the resulting irrational responses to AIDS is over. We have learned, yet again, how strong fear is in motivating human behaviour, fear of the unknown, of death, of stigmatization.

We have also learned that respect of human rights does not just happen: commitment is needed at all levels, from global to local. However, we have also recognized that human rights have influenced our response to the AIDS pandemic more than ever before in the history of epidemic control.

The AIDS pandemic has revealed gaps in human rights protection. While AIDS-related human rights violations have conformed with the pat-

191 International Organization for Migration, *Report of the Seminar on Migration Medicine, Geneva, 6-9 February 1990* (1990).

192 Refugees and AIDS, Doc. UNHCR/IOM/70-FOM/63/88 of 6 May 1988, para. 12.

193 Morrow, 'AIDS and Immigration: The United States Attempts to Deport a Disease', 20 *University of Miami Inter-American Law Review* (1988) 131.

tern of 'conventional' violations and thus demonstrated that human rights protection is least effective for those most vulnerable to abuses, they have also highlighted the lack of protection, particularly for prostitutes and drug-dependent persons.

Moreover, most literature on the human rights aspects of AIDS, which has reflected and also influenced the public debates, has focused on protection of the individual from coercive or compulsory measures by the public authorities. Demands that governments undertake measures to meet individual entitlements to information or health care have been relatively infrequent. Moreover, while access to health care constitutes one of the most important AIDS-related human rights issues, the lack of an authoritative international interpretation of the nature and scope of this human right[194] has precluded demands for its consistent application in responding to AIDS.[195]

194 Tomasevski, 'The Role of International Law in Promoting and Protecting Human Health', in O. Scachter and C. Joyner (eds), *The United Nations and the International Legal Order* (1992).

195 Mariner, 'Access to Health Care and Equal Protection of the Law: The Need for a New Heightened Scrutiny',12 *American Journal of Law & Medicine* 3&4 (1986) 345-380.

Annex

Human Rights in AIDS Prevention and Control: Chronology

23 June 1983	Recommendation No. R (83) 8 of the Committee of Ministers to Member States on Preventing the Possible Transmission of Acquired Immune Deficiency Syndrome (AIDS) from Affected Blood Donors to Patients Receiving Blood [Council of Europe]
23 November 1983	Resolution 812 (1983) on the Acquired Immune Deficiency Syndrome (AIDS) [Council of Europe, Parliamentary Assembly]
13 September 1985	Recommendation No. R (85) 12 of the Committee of Ministers to Member States on the Screening of Blood Donors for the Presence of AIDS Markers [Council of Europe]
29 May 1986	Resolution of the Representatives of the Governments of Member States Meeting within the Council on AIDS [OJ 1986 C 184]
3 March 1987	WHO Consultation on International Travel and HIV Infection (Doc. WHO/SPA/GLO/87.1)
15 May 1987	Global Strategy for the Prevention and Control of AIDS (Res. WHA40.26)
15 May 1987	Conclusions of the Council and of the Governments of the Member States Meeting within the Council concerning AIDS [OJ 1987 C 178]
21 May 1987	WHO Meeting on Criteria that Must be Considered in Planning and Implementing HIV Screening Programmes (Doc. WHO/SPA/GLO/87.2)
6 June 1987	HIV Infection and Health Workers (Doc. SPA/INF/87.6)
27 July 1988	Conclusions of the Council and of the Representatives of the Governments of the Member States Meeting with the Council concerning AIDS [OJ 1988 C 197]
30 July 1987	UNFPA Guidelines on AIDS (Doc. UNFPA/CM/87/38)
17 September 1987	*Note verbale* from the WHO Director-General on the Prevention of HIV Transmission Through Skin-piercing Procedures (Doc. C.L.30.1987)
27 October 1987	Prevention and Control of AIDS (UNGA Res. 42/8)

18 November 1987	Consensus Statement of WHO Consultation on Prevention and Control of AIDS in Prisons (Doc. WHO/SPA/INF/87.14)
26 November 1987	Recommendation No. R (87) 25 of the Committee of Ministers to Member States on a Common European Health Policy to Fight the Acquired Immunodeficiency Syndrome (AIDS) [Council of Europe]
1 December 1987	Social Aspects of AIDS Prevention and Control Programmes (Doc. WHO/SPA/GLO/87.2)
1988	WHO Statement on Screening of International Travellers for Infection with Human Immunodeficiency Virus (Doc. WHO/GPA/INF/88.3)
January 1988	WHO Meeting on HIV Infection and Drug Injecting Intervention Strategies (Doc. WHO/GPA/SBR/89.1)
28 January 1988	London Declaration on AIDS Prevention of the World Summit of Ministers of Health
15 February 1988	UNHCR Health Policy on AIDS (Doc. UNHCR/IOM/21/88)
13 May 1988	Avoidance of Discrimination in Relation to HIV Infected People and People with AIDS (Res. WHA41.24)
17 May 1988	WHO Global Blood Safety Initiative Meeting (Doc. WHO/GPA/DIR/88.9)
31 May 1988	Conclusions of the Council of the European Communities concerning AIDS
29 June 1988	Consensus Statement of WHO/ILO Consultation on AIDS and the Workplace (Doc. WHO/GPA/INF/88.7)
30 June 1988	Recommendation 1080 (1988) on a Coordinated European Health Policy to Prevent the Spread of AIDS in Prisons [Council of Europe, Parliamentary Assembly]
1 September 1988	Discrimination Against Persons with the HIV Virus or Suffering from AIDS [Decision 1988/111 of the Sub-Commission for Prevention of Discrimination and Protection of Minorities]
27 October 1988	Prevention and Control of Acquired Immunodeficiency Syndrome (AIDS) [UNGA Res. 43/15]
23 November 1988	Resolution of the Council and of the Ministers of Education Meeting within the Council concerning Health Education in Schools [OJ 1989 C 3]

15 December 1988	Conclusions of the Council and the Ministers for Health of the Member States Meeting with the Council concerning AIDS [OJ 1989 C 28]
15 December 1988	Conclusions of the Council and the Ministers for Health of the Member States Meeting with the Council concerning AIDS and the Place of Work [OJ 1989 C 28]
January 1989	Heterosexual Transmission of HIV and Certain Common Social Situations [Doc. WHO/GPA/INF/89.5]
January 1989	Consensus Statement of WHO Consultation on Partner Notification for Preventing HIV Transmission [Doc. WHO/GPA/INF/89]
2 March 1989	Consensus Statement of WHO Consultation on Criteria for International Testing of Candidate HIV Vaccines [Doc. GPA/INF/89.8]
2 March 1989	Non-discrimination in the Field of Health [United Nations Commission on Human Rights, Res. 1989/11]
30 March 1989	Resolution of the European Parliament on the Fight Against AIDS [OJ 1989 C 158]
31 March 1989	Attention to Applicable International Law. [WHO Global Commission on AIDS, Doc. GPA/GCA(1)/89.1]
16 May 1989	Conclusions of the Council and the Ministers for Health of the Member States Meeting with the Council Regarding the Prevention of AIDS in Intravenous Drug Users [OJ 1989 C 185]
26 May 1989	Resolution of the European Parliament on the Fight Against AIDS [Doc. A2-35/89]
6 July 1989	Consensus Statement of WHO Consultation on HIV Epidemiology and Prostitution [Doc. WHO/GPA/INF/89.11]
28 July 1989	Final Document of the International Consultation on AIDS and Human Rights [UN Doc. HR/AIDS/1989/3]
31 August 1989	Discrimination Against HIV Infected People or People with AIDS [Sub-Commission on the Prevention of Discrimination and Protection of Minorities, Res. 1989/18]
29 September 1989	Recommendation 1116 (1989) on AIDS and Human Rights [Council of Europe, Parliamentary Assembly]
24 October 1989	Recommendation No. R (89) 14 of the Committee of Ministers to Member States on the Ethical Issues of HIV Infection in the Health Care and Social Settings [Council of Europe]

30 November 1989	Paris Declaration on Women, Children and AIDS
22 December 1989	Prevention and Control of Acquired Immunodeficiency Syndrome (AIDS) [UNGA Res. 44/233]
22 December 1989	Resolution of the Council and the Ministers for Health of the Member States Meeting within the Council on the Fight Against AIDS [OJ 1990 C 10]
1 February 1990	Avoidance of Discrimination Against Women in National Strategies for the Prevention and Control of AIDS [CEDAW, General Recommendation No. 15]
7 March 1990	Discrimination Against HIV Infected People or People with AIDS [United Nations Commission on Human Rights, Decision 1990/65]
11 May 1990	*Note verbale* of the WHO Director-General Referring to Avoidance of Discrimination in National AIDS Programmes Worldwide [WHO Doc. C.L.7.1990]
31 August 1990	Infection with Human Immunodeficiency Virus (HIV) and Acquired Immunodeficiency Syndrome (AIDS) in Prison [Resolution 18 of the Eighth United Nations Congress on the Prevention of Crime and the Treatment of Offenders]

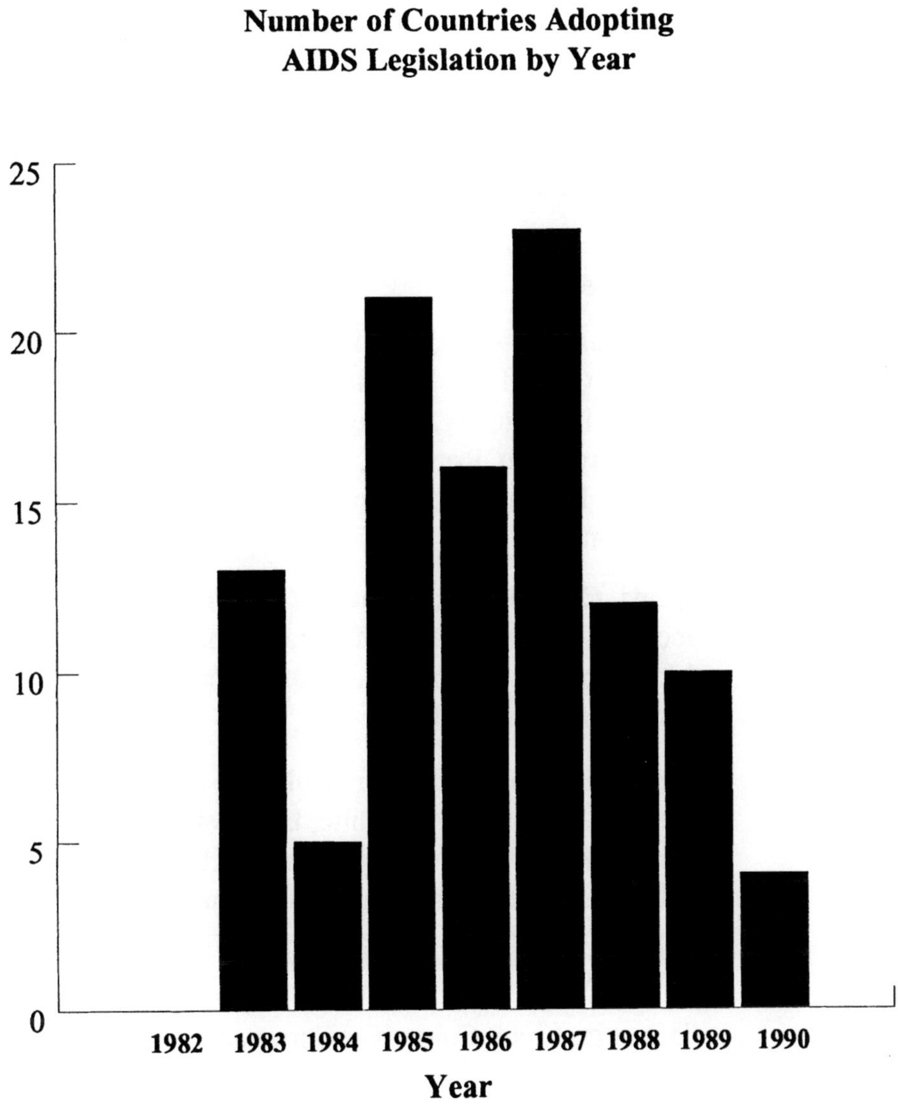
Number of Countries Adopting
AIDS Legislation by Year
25
20
15
10
5
0
1982 1983 1984 1985 1986 1987 1988 1989 1990
Year

Chronology of AIDS Legislation

1983	Austria, Canada, Denmark, France, Germany, Greece, Israel, Italy, New Zealand, Norway, Sweden, Turkey, USA
1984	Australia, Chile, Luxembourg, Uruguay, Venezuela
1985	Bahamas, Barbados, Belgium, Bermuda, Brazil, Congo, Costa Rica, Ecuador, Finland, French Polynesia, Hungary, Malaysia, Panama, Paraguay, Peru, Romania, Singapore, Spain, Thailand, United Arab Emirates, United Kingdom
1986	China, Cuba, Egypt, Grenada, Guatemala, Iceland, Kuwait, Malta, Mexico, Monaco, Mozambique, Philippines, Poland, Portugal, Switzerland, Yugoslavia
1987	Belize, Brunei Darussalam, Bulgaria, Burundi, Cyprus, Dominican Republic, El Salvador, Iraq, Jordan, Kenya, Republic of Korea, Liberia, Libya, Liechtenstein, Mauritius, Netherlands, Niger, Papua New Guinea, South Africa, Sudan, Syria, Togo, USSR
1988	Bulgaria, Chad, Colombia, Comores, Czech and Slovak Republic, Equatorial Guinea, Guinea, Hong Kong, Japan, Mali, Sri Lanka, Suriname
1989	Algeria, Bolivia, Guinea-Bissau, India, Mongoli, Nicaragua, Rwanda, Tunesia, Viet Nam, Yemen
1990	Argentina, Bahrain, Madagascar, Senegal

The International Protection against Torture and Inhuman or Degrading Treatment or Punishment

by

HANS DANELIUS

Academy of European Law (ed.),
Collected Courses of the Academy of European Law, Volume II, Book 2, 151–198.

Table of Contents

Biography

Mr Hans Danelius, a Swedish national, was born on 2 April 1934 and obtained his law degree at the University of Stockholm in 1955. In 1988, he received a doctor of law honoris causa from the same University.

After serving at various courts in Sweden, Mr Danelius was a member of the secretariat of the European Commission of Human Rights at Strasbourg from 1964 to 1967. He was an associate judge at the Svea Court of Appeal in Stockholm from 1967 to 1968, and then served at the Swedish Ministry of Justice as a legal adviser and, from 1971, at the Swedish Ministry of Foreign Affairs as Deputy Director of the Legal Department. At the same Ministry he was, from 1974 to 1984, Under-Secretary for Legal and Consular Affairs, and in 1977 he attained the rank of Ambassador. He was Ambassador of Sweden to the Netherlands from 1984 to 1988. Since 1988 he has been a Justice of the Supreme Court of Sweden.

Mr Danelius was the Chief Editor of the law journal *Svensk Juristtidning* from 1973 to 1984. He was Chairman of the Baltic Sea Fishery Commission from 1982 to 1984 and Chairman of the Board of Trustees of the United Nations Voluntary Fund for Victims of Torture from 1983 to 1989. Since 1982 he has been a member of the Permanent Court of Arbitration in The Hague, and since 1983 he has been serving as a member of the European Commission of Human Rights.

Principal Publications

- *Mänskliga rättigheter* (4th ed., 1989);
- *The United Nations Convention against Torture* (1988) (co-author);
- numerous articles on human rights and international law in Swedish and foreign journals.

I. Introductory Remarks

A provision prohibiting torture and other kinds of cruel treatment is a natural part of any comprehensive human rights instrument, and it is no coincidence that this right occupies a very prominent place in most human rights agreements. It generally appears immediately after the most fundamental of all human rights, i.e. the right to life.[1] Moreover, in the basic human rights conventions, the prohibition against torture is absolute and unconditional, which means that it allows no exceptions in special cases or in order to satisfy weighty public needs. Indeed, it is one of the few rights from which no derogation may be made in time of war or other emergency.

Further, no other human right has been dealt with in so many different international instruments, although the means by which the problem is addressed in them differ. Some instruments are legally binding and some recommendatory, some are intended to have worldwide application, while other instruments are regional. Some provide for examination of reports or complaints, while others may emphasize the duties and responsibilities of special professional groups, or establish a system of visits to prisons and other places of detention. Besides the adoption of treaties and recommendations, other methods have also been employed, such as the appointment of a Special Rapporteur and the setting up of a fund to assist victims of torture.

II. Historical Background

At present, torture is not officially accepted by any State as a proper method of interrogation or punishment. Where it occurs, the facts are often denied or, alternatively, said to be the result of misbehaviour by individual police officers or other public officials having acted in contravention of their duties and without any approval or acquiescence by the responsible authorities. In this respect, torture is different from, for instance, capital punishment which is still accepted in many countries as being a legitimate penal sanction.

However, a few centuries ago torture was viewed differently. Torture was then considered to be a normal part of the system of criminal justice in most, if not all, parts of Europe. Gradually, some opposition developed against the use of torture. The first strong movement in this direction developed in the 18th century. It was closely linked with the philosophy of the

1 See Article 7 of the International Covenant on Civil and Political Rights, Article 3 of the European Convention on Human Rights and Article 5 of the American Convention on Human Rights.

Enlightenment and was part of a more general endeavour to increase the fairness of criminal justice and to protect the fundamental rights of the individual.

Of great importance were Cesare Beccaria's ideas as reflected in his work *Dei delitti e delle pene* (On Crimes and Punishments), first published in 1764. The book contains a chapter, entitled *Della tortura,* in which Beccaria strongly condemns torture and presents moral as well as rational arguments to demonstrate why it should not be used.

Beccaria states that torture is widely used in most nations in the investigation of crime. The purposes are to force the suspect to confess, to remove contradictions in statements and to make guilty persons reveal the identity of other alleged offenders.

Beccaria deals with these purposes one by one and argues that torture is an ineffective means of achieving them. He points out that torture can make even an innocent person confess and it can add new contradictions rather than remove existing ones. Instead of denouncing other offenders, the suspect may well denounce innocent persons in order to escape further torture; and it may also be possible for a guilty person, if he has sufficient strength, to resist torture and thereby obtain his acquittal. Consequently, torture does not in any way guarantee that the information which is given by the tortured person corresponds to the truth. Finally, using an argument which is quite consistent with modern legal thinking, Beccaria emphasizes that any person is entitled to the protection of society until he has been proven guilty by a judge according to the law and that, consequently, when torture is used during a criminal investigation, it is to be regarded as being used against an innocent person, for which there can be no moral justification.

Beccaria's book was widely read and translated into many languages. Its impact was considerable. Beccaria's ideas supported an already ongoing humanitarian development in many European countries. Fredrik the Great of Prussia – who was much influenced by the philosophers of the Enlightenment and a friend of Voltaire – had already prohibited torture by introducing certain legal reforms in the 1740s and the 1750s. In Sweden, the new General Code of 1734 had restricted the use of torture, and these restrictions were followed up in 1772 by a Royal Decree in which the King Gustavus III ordered the destruction of all torture instruments and torture chambers.

At the end of the 18th century and the beginning of the 19th century, legislative measures were taken in virtually all European countries to eradicate torture. The statutory abolition of torture in criminal law was so widespread that Victor Hugo found it justified to announce in 1874 that 'torture has ceased to exist'.

Maybe Victor Hugo's statement was to some extent an exaggeration. The fact that torture was no longer to be found on the statute books as an accepted method of interrogation did not necessarily mean that it was not used in practice. Moreover, it is well-known that prison conditions in 19th century Europe were often so deplorable that, at least by modern standards, they would have constituted inhuman or degrading treatment. It is also clear that Victor Hugo's favourable assessment of the situation only applied to Europe, whereas in many colonial territories methods were practised against the indigenous population which in some cases undoubtedly amounted to torture. After all, this was a period when slavery still existed in many places and indigenous people in colonial territories were in no way recognized as equals and as persons whose human integrity deserved respect.

Nevertheless, it was an important step forward that, as a result of the reforms of the 18th and 19th centuries, torture was outlawed and no longer accepted as legitimate. Insofar as it was still practised, it was a violation of the law and contrary to the predominant views of the civilized world.

But unfortunately, a serious relapse occurred during the first half of the 20th century. In the wake of the First World War, totalitarian regimes seized power in several European countries. The Russian Bolsheviks, the Italian Fascists and the German Nazis were all ready to use harsh methods to quell any opposition. Human rights were also disregarded by the Franco regime in Spain. The methods used by these regimes undoubtedly included torture and inhuman or degrading treatment, and their use was tolerated and often encouraged by the leaders. The concentration camps in Germany and in countries dominated by it were a particularly horrid example of the consequences of an ideology which totally disregarded the human value of those who, on racial or political grounds, were seen as inferior, undesirable or hostile elements. The Second World War added to the sufferings, and torture was then widely used as a means of terror in countries under German occupation or domination.

The very grave large-scale violations of human rights which had characterized much of the first half of the 20th century in Europe and elsewhere made it an urgent task in the aftermath of the Second World War to create international guarantees for human rights. Protection against torture was considered an essential part of such guarantees.

Thus, the general human rights conventions and declarations which have been adopted during the post-war period all contain provisions prohibiting torture. In addition, a number of special instruments have been adopted which deal more specifically with torture and contain more detailed rules about measures which States must take in order to combat it.

III. United Nations Instruments

Article 5 of the *Universal Declaration of Human Rights*, adopted by the United Nations General Assembly in 1948, contains a prohibition against torture. However, the prohibition goes on to include 'cruel, inhuman or degrading treatment or punishment',[2] and this prohibition is also generally found in subsequent human rights instruments. It is a vague concept which is difficult to define but whose content has to some extent been clarified in international practice and, in particular, in the case-law relating to the relevant provisions of the basic human rights conventions.

The provision in Article 5 of the Universal Declaration is repeated verbatim in Article 7 of the 1966 *International Covenant on Civil and Political Rights*. However, one sentence is added which prohibits medical or scientific experiments without the free consent of the person concerned.[3]

According to Article 4 of the Covenant, the Contracting States may take measures derogating from some of their obligations under the Covenant in time of public emergency which threatens the life of the nation. However, the same Article refers to Article 7 as one of the few provisions from which no derogation may be made. This emphasizes the absolute character of the prohibition and the special importance attributed to it.

But torture has remained a serious international human rights problem. On many occasions, there have been alarming reports about events in various countries which have aroused public opinion and given rise to a call for new and effective measures to combat this evil.

In 1972, Amnesty International launched a one year campaign for the abolition of torture. As part of this campaign, a report was published which investigated the problem,[4] and its conclusions were far from optimistic. A second campaign against torture was launched by Amnesty International in 1984, and a new report was then published which assessed the global situation.[5] It stated that, 'while governments universally and collectively condemn torture, more than a third of the world's governments have used or tolerated torture or ill-treatment of prisoners in the 1980s'. It would seem that people are tortured, in particular, in times of political unrest, mostly by authoritarian regimes and often as a means of repressing political opposition. But even regimes that are generally democratic have in times of

2 Article 5 of the Universal Declaration of Human Rights reads as follows: 'No one shall be subjected to torture or to cruel, inhuman or degrading treatment or punishment.'

3 Article 7 of the Covenant on Civil and Political Rights reads as follows: 'No one shall be subjected to torture or to cruel, inhuman or degrading treatment or punishment. In particular, no one shall be subjected without his free consent to medical or scientific experimentation.'

4 Report on Torture, London 1973.

5 Torture in the Eighties, London 1984.

French in Algeria during the Algerian struggle for independence, by the United States during the Vietnam war, and by the British during certain periods of tension in Northern Ireland.

The campaign of Amnesty International in 1972-1973, together with the overthrow of the Allende regime in Chile in September 1973 and the severe repression, including the use of torture, which followed upon the coup, created pressure on a number of democratic Governments to take action within the United Nations. In 1973, the General Assembly of the United Nations adopted a procedural resolution proposed by Sweden, according to which the question of torture would be considered later on the basis of a note which was to be prepared by the Secretary General. During the following session of the General Assembly in 1974, another resolution was adopted, based on a Dutch-Swedish proposal. According to this resolution, the Fifth United Nations Congress on the Prevention of Crime and the Treatment of Offenders, which was to be held in 1975, was asked to consider rules for the protection against torture and a code of ethics for police and other law enforcement agencies. Moreover, the World Health Organization was requested to draft principles on medical ethics.

The Congress referred to in this resolution met in September 1975. It had before it a Dutch-Swedish proposal for a Declaration against torture and other cruel, inhuman or degrading treatment or punishment. On the basis of this draft, a text was approved and forwarded to the General Assembly for final adoption. On 9 December 1975, the *Declaration on the Protection of All Persons from Being Subjected to Torture and Other Cruel, Inhuman or Degrading Treatment or Punishment* was adopted by the General Assembly. The Declaration consists of 12 Articles, in which the measures States should take to eliminate and prevent torture are defined. Although not legally binding, the Declaration is a valuable supplement to, and a further elaboration of, the laconic prohibition against torture which appears in previous human rights instruments.

After the Declaration had been adopted, the work continued on the special instruments which had been envisaged in regard to the particular obligations of law enforcement officials (police officers, prison warders etc.) and medical personnel. The *Code of Conduct for Law Enforcement Officials* was adopted by the General Assembly on 17 December 1979 and the *Principles of Medical Ethics relevant to the Role of Health Personnel, particularly Physicians, in the Protection of Prisoners and Detainees against Torture and Other Cruel, Inhuman or Degrading Treatment or Punishment* on 18 December 1982. Like the 1975 Torture Declaration, these two instruments are merely recommendatory in character.

The 1975 Torture Declaration had been drafted and adopted in a short time. Encouraged by this success, some States considered that the situation was favourable for taking another, and more important, step, namely to transform the rules of the Declaration into a binding treaty. Other States had doubts about this approach. They felt that it might even weaken the authority of the Declaration, if it was followed up by a Convention to which only a limited number of well-behaved States might become parties.

Nevertheless at the United Nations General Assembly in 1977 Sweden took the initiative and proposed that work should be undertaken on a new Convention against torture. The matter was referred to the Commission on Human Rights, where it was dealt with for several years.

While the adoption of the 1975 Declaration had been a comparatively easy task, the same could not be said about the work on the Convention. States were much more cautious when they were to agree on treaty provisions which would be binding upon them, and the drafts which were presented by Sweden to the Working Group of the Commission on Human Rights contained certain elements which proved to be controversial. One such element was the proposed so-called universal jurisdiction, namely the idea that it should be possible to bring a suspected torturer to justice in any Convention State. Another controversial point concerned the international supervision machinery which was to be set up as an essential part of the Convention.

After negotiations which went on for almost a decade, the Convention against Torture and Other Cruel, Inhuman or Degrading Treatment or Punishment was finally adopted by the General Assembly on 10 December 1984. A binding international instrument had been created, which laid specific obligations on States with regard to the elimination of torture and which also provided for international supervision, although it was not as far-reaching and effective as some of the supporters of the Convention had hoped.

The international control system in the 1984 Torture Convention is, generally speaking, of a rather traditional character insofar as it includes examination of national reports and complaints lodged by States or individuals. During the work on the Convention, a different control system had been proposed by Costa Rica. According to the Costa Rican proposal, there would be an Optional Protocol to the Convention which would provide for a system of regular visits to places of detention in the States parties to the Protocol. This was an idea which had originally been advocated with vigour by a former Swiss banker, Jean-Jacques Gautier, and had been further developed and supported by the Swiss Committee against Torture and the International Commission of Jurists. They believed that during visits to places of detention any use of torture or other forms of cruel treatment as well as any conditions creating risks of such treatment would be likely to be disclosed, and the system would therefore have a strong preventive effect. However, it was not an easy task to have a system of this kind accepted on a worldwide level, and Costa Rica decided not to insist on its proposal being adopted at the same time as the Convention itself, but agreed to defer consideration of it until a later time. However, the Costa Rican proposal has not been abandoned, and it will be discussed again at the 1992 session of the Commission on Human Rights. Moreover, a similar system has in the meantime been adopted at the regional level in the European Convention for the Prevention of Torture and Inhuman or Degrading Treatment or Punishment (see below under IX).

On 9 December 1988, the General Assembly adopted the *Body of Principles for the Protection of All Persons under Any Form of Detention or Imprisonment*. Some of these principles are aimed at providing protection against torture. They contain few new elements in comparison with previous instruments. The most interesting provision in this connection would seem to be Principle 33, where the right of a detained person to complain of his treatment is been dealt with in detail.

In addition to the standard-setting work described above, the United Nations has also attempted in other ways to deal with the problem of torture. In the Commission on Human Rights, a practice has developed to appoint Special Rapporteurs to investigate serious human rights problems and such an appointment was made in 1985 with regard to torture. The original one year mandate of the Rapporteur has been extended and annual reports have been submitted containing conclusions and recommendations. In a number of cases 'urgent action' has been taken which means that the Rapporteur has addressed appeals to Governments regarding persons alleged to be subjected to torture or who are in danger of being so subjected. There has been extensive correspondence with Governments and visits to various countries upon invitation resulting in special recommendations. The general recommendations which have appeared in the Special Rapporteur's annual reports have concerned matters such as the abolition of *incommunicado* detention, the importance of giving detainees quick access to a lawyer and of having them medically examined.

In 1981, the General Assembly also set up a *Voluntary Fund for Victims of Torture*. The Fund collects money in the form of voluntary contributions, mainly from Governments, and it distributes the money as support for various projects in favour of victims of torture. The projects which have received money from the Fund have generally concerned medical treatment and rehabilitation of such victims.

IV. Regional Instruments

The first regional human rights convention was the *European Convention on Human Rights*, adopted in the framework of the Council of Europe in 1950. Its Article 3 prohibits torture and inhuman or degrading treatment or punishment. No further details are given in the text of the Convention.[6] The importance of the prohibition, however, is emphasized by the fact that the derogations allowed by Article 15 of the Convention which apply in time of war or other public emergency threatening the life of the nation cannot be used in relation to the prohibition against torture and inhuman or degrading treatment or punishment in Article 3.

The case-law which has developed in regard to the European Convention on Human Rights is more extensive and detailed than the case-law in regard to any other human rights treaty. A number of the cases dealt with by the European Court and Commission of Human Rights have concerned Article 3, and there are judgments, reports and decisions which in various ways clarify the interpretation of that Article.

The *American Convention on Human Rights* dates from 1969 and contains in Article 5 a prohibition against torture as well as cruel, inhuman or degrading punishment or treatment.[7] In the *African Charter on Human and Peoples' Rights* of 1981, the prohibition is worded differently. Article 5 provides that all forms of exploitation and degradation of man, particularly slavery, slave trade, torture, cruel, inhuman or degrading punishment and treatment, shall be prohibited.[8]

In 1985, an *Inter-American Convention to Prevent and Punish Torture* was adopted. This is a regional convention based very much on the principles already developed in the 1984 United Nations Convention against Torture.

As explained above under III, there was a proposal by Costa Rica for an Optional Protocol to be attached to the United Nations Convention against Torture. This Protocol would provide for a system of regular visits to prisons by an international committee, the purpose being to operate in a pre-

6 Article 3 of the European Convention on Human Rights reads as follows: 'No one shall be subjected to torture or to inhuman or degrading treatment or punishment.'

7 Article 5 paragraphs 1 and 2 of the American Convention on Human Rights read as follows: '1. Every person has the right to have his physical, mental, and moral integrity respected. 2. No one shall be subjected to torture or to cruel, inhuman, or degrading punishment or treatment. All persons deprived of their liberty shall be treated with respect for the inherent dignity of the human person.'

8 Article 5 of the African Charter on Human and Peoples' Rights reads as follows: 'Every individual shall have the right to the respect of the dignity inherent in a human being and to the recognition of his legal status. All forms of exploitation and degradation of man particularly slavery, slave trade, torture, cruel, inhuman or degrading punishment and treatment shall be prohibited.'

ventive manner. After it had proved impossible, for the time being, to adopt the proposal within the United Nations, the Swiss Government decided to explore the possibilities of establishing this kind of scheme at the regional level within the Council of Europe. This led to the adoption in 1987 of the *European Convention for the Prevention of Torture and Inhuman or Degrading Treatment or Punishment*. The idea of checking torture and inhuman or degrading treatment by means of preventive international visits to places of detention has been adopted for the first time in this document, and it is hoped that it will become a model for other regional or worldwide conventions.

V. The Covenant on Civil and Political Rights

The scope of the protection provided by Article 7 of the International Covenant on Civil and Political Rights has been clarified in some respects by the Human Rights Committee, the body set up under the Covenant which is responsible for the international supervision of the Covenant.

The Human Rights Committee has adopted a 'general comment' which explains the scope of the obligation created by Article 7. In this comment, the Committee emphasizes that it is not sufficient for a State to prohibit torture or cruel, inhuman or degrading treatment or punishment or to make it a crime, but it is also required that States should ensure an effective protection through some machinery of control. The Committee adds in this respect:

> Complaints about ill-treatment must be investigated effectively by competent authorities. Those found guilty must be held responsible, and the alleged victims must themselves have effective remedies at their disposal, including the right to obtain compensation. Among the safeguards which may make control effective are provisions against detention *incommunicado*, granting, without prejudice to the investigation, persons such as doctors, lawyers and family members access to the detainees; provisions requiring that detainees should be held in places that are publicly recognized and that their names and places of detention should be entered in a central register available to persons concerned, such as relatives; provisions making confessions or other evidence obtained through torture or other treatment contrary to article 7 inadmissible in court; and measures of training and instruction of law enforcement officials not to apply such treatment.[9]

The Committee also dealt with the concept of 'cruel, inhuman or degrading treatment or punishment' and stated in this regard that it might not be necessary to draw sharp distinctions between the various prohibited forms of

9 General comment adopted by the Human Rights Committee at its 378th meeting on 27 July 1982.

treatment or punishment, the distinguishing criteria being the kind, purpose and severity of the particular treatment. The Committee noted, however, that the prohibition in Article 7 'must extend to corporal punishment, including excessive chastisement as an educational or disciplinary measure' and that 'even such a measure as solitary confinement may, according to the circumstances, and especially when the person concerned is kept *incommunicado*, be contrary to this article'. The Committee further pointed out that Article 7 protects not only persons arrested or imprisoned, but also pupils and patients in educational and medical institutions and that it is the duty of public authorities to ensure protection by the law against such treatment even when committed by persons acting outside or without any official authority.

The Human Rights Committee has received and examined many individual complaints regarding violations of Article 7. Most of the cases dealt with were directed against Uruguay and concerned serious allegations of torture and deplorable conditions of detention. In most of these cases violations were found of Article 7 (sometimes together with Article 10 of the Covenant, which provides that all persons deprived of their liberty shall be treated with humanity and with respect for the inherent dignity of the human person).

A problem in many of the cases against Uruguay was that the Government simply denied the accusations and gave very scarce information of what had really happened. A primary question therefore was the burden of proof. The Human Rights Committee stated its position on this question in the following way:

> With regard to the burden of proof, this cannot rest alone on the author of the communication, especially considering that the author and the State party do not always have equal access to the evidence and that frequently the State party alone has access to relevant information. It is implicit in article 4(2) of the Optional Protocol that the State party has the duty to investigate in good faith all allegations of violation of the Covenant made against it and its authorities, especially when such allegations are corroborated by evidence submitted by the author of the communication, and to furnish to the Committee the information available to it. In cases where the author has submitted to the Committee allegations supported by substantial witness testimony, ..., and where further clarification of the case depends on information exclusively in the hands of the State party, the Committee may consider such allegations as substantiated in the absence of satisfactory evidence and explanations to the contrary submitted by the State party.[10]

10 Communication No. 30/1978 *Irene Bleier Lewenhoff et al.* v. *Uruguay*, views adopted on 29 March 1982.

One case against Madagascar concerned incommunicado detention in a small cell for several years.[11] The treatment was clearly in breach of Article 7.

There have also been a number of cases against Zaire. In one of them the Human Rights Committee found that deprivation of food and drink for four days after arrest, and unacceptable sanitary conditions, amounted to inhuman treatment.[12]

Many cases have concerned poor conditions of detention. One such case was about the arrest of a lawyer and human rights activist in the Dominican Republic. The circumstances were described by the Human Rights Committee as follows:

> On 14 June 1984 at 6 a.m., he was arrested at his home, according to the author, because of his activities as a leader of a human rights association, and taken to a cell at the secret service police headquarters, from where he was transferred to another cell measuring 20 by 5 metres, where approximately 125 persons accused of common crimes were being held, and where, owing to lack of space, some detainees had to sit on excrement. He received no food or water until the following day.[13]

Not surprisingly, the Human Rights Committee considered this to constitute inhuman and degrading treatment.

One case against Jamaica is of a different character. The applicants had been sentenced to death and had appealed against their sentences. After the appeals had been heard by the Court of Appeal, nearly four years went by before there was a written judgment rejecting the appeals. In the meantime, the applicants were on death row. A warrant had been issued for their execution on 24 February 1987. On the day before, 23 February 1987, a stay of execution was granted, but the applicants were not informed of this decision until 45 minutes before the time of the planned execution.

The Human Rights Committee considered that the case raised two issues with regard to Article 7. The first one was whether the excessive delays in the judicial proceedings constituted 'cruel, inhuman and degrading treatment'. The Committee stated that, in principle, prolonged judicial proceedings do not *per se* constitute cruel, inhuman or degrading treatment even if they can be a source of mental strain for the convicted prisoners. However, the situation may be different in cases involving capital punishment and an assessment of the circumstances of each case would be neces-

11 Communication No. 49/1979 *Dave Marais Jr* v. *Madagascar*, views adopted on 24 March 1983.

12 Communications Nos. 241/1987 and 242/1987 *Birindwa ci Birhashwirwa et al.* v. *Zaire*, views adopted on 2 November 1989.

13 Communication No. 188/1984 *Martinez Portorreal* v. *Dominican Republic*, views adopted on 5 November 1987.

sary. In the present case the Committee did not find that the applicants had sufficiently substantiated their claim that delay in judicial proceedings constituted for them cruel, inhuman and degrading treatment under Article 7. The second problem under that Article concerned the issue of warrants for execution and the notification of the stay of execution. On this point the Committee stated as follows:

> The issue of a warrant for execution necessarily causes intense anguish to the individual concerned... It is uncontested that the decision to grant a first stay of execution, taken at noon on 23 February 1987, was not notified to the authors until 45 minutes before the scheduled time of the execution on 24 February 1987. The Committee considers that a delay of close to 20 hours from the time the stay of execution was granted to the time the authors were removed from their death cell constitutes cruel and inhuman treatment within the meaning of article 7.[14]

Although the case-law of the Human Rights Committee relating to Article 7 is rather extensive, it is difficult, when reading most of the Committee's decisions, to draw from them any clear legal conclusions. This is because the Committee scarcely provides detailed reasons. It normally indicates the facts of each case, as they have been established, and then, without much further discourse, reaches the conclusion that Article 7 has been breached. In many cases, the breach found relates to both Article 7 and Article 10, and it is difficult in those cases to draw a separate conclusion regarding Article 7. Moreover, it must be admitted that in very many cases submitted to the Human Rights Committee, the circumstances have been so serious that there could hardly be any doubt that Article 7 had been violated. Decisions in such cases do not really add much knowledge about the scope and the limits of the protection afforded by Article 7.

VI. The 1975 Declaration against Torture

The Declaration on the Protection of All Persons from Being Subjected to Torture and Other Cruel, Inhuman or Degrading Treatment or Punishment represented a first attempt at the international level to specify the measures that States ought to take in order to combat torture; thus it was necessary to define more precisely the type of conduct which falls within its ambit.

A definition of torture was proposed in the draft presented by the Netherlands and Sweden; the model had to some extent been the definition used by the European Commission of Human Rights in its Report in the *Greek* case (see below under VIII). However, the proposed text was much discussed

14 Communications Nos. 210/1986 and 225/1987 *Pratt et al.* v. *Jamaica*, views adopted on 6 April 1989.

and further developed, and the definition which appears in Article 1 of the Declaration is long and rather complicated. It reads as follows:

> For the purpose of this Declaration, torture means any act by which severe pain or suffering, whether physical or mental, is intentionally inflicted by or at the instigation of a public official on a person for such purposes as obtaining from him or a third person information or confession, punishing him for an act he has committed or is suspected of having committed, or intimidating him or other persons. It does not include pain or suffering arising only from, inherent in or incidental to, lawful sanctions to the extent consistent with the Standard Minimum Rules for the Treatment of Prisoners.

The crucial concept in the definition is that of infliction of severe pain or suffering, and the determination of the point at which pain or suffering has the required severity remains of course to some extent a subjective matter. It further appears from the definition that the act must have a specific purpose, although the purposes indicated in the definition are not exhaustive.

The question whether certain types of punishments are so cruel as to constitute torture proved to be controversial, and the exception which has been added in the second sentence of the definition is a compromise. Lawful sanctions normally fall outside the definition, but it is a condition that they are consistent with the Standard Minimum Rules for the Treatment of Prisoners, adopted in 1955 by the First United Nations Congress on the Prevention of Crime and the Treatment of Offenders. This is an indication that not every sanction is acceptable just because it has a basis in domestic criminal law.

As both the Universal Declaration of Human Rights and the Covenant on Civil and Political Rights refer not only to torture but also to cruel, inhuman or degrading treatment or punishment, it was considered desirable that the Declaration on Torture should also include protection against such treatment or punishment. However, the authors of the Declaration on Torture did not find it possible to define the notion of 'cruel, inhuman or degrading treatment or punishment'. They simply gave a general indication of the relationship between torture and such treatment or punishment: in paragraph 2 of Article 1 there is a provision stating that torture constitutes an aggravated and deliberate form of cruel, inhuman or degrading treatment or punishment.

Article 2 of the Declaration is basically of a declaratory nature. It makes it clear that torture and other cruel, inhuman or degrading treatment or punishment are to be condemned as contrary to the principles of the United Nations and the Universal Declaration of Human Rights.

From Article 3 it appears that the obligation of a State is not limited to a duty not to inflict torture. It is also part of the obligation that the State shall not permit or tolerate torture or other cruel, inhuman or degrading treatment or punishment. It is added that no exceptional circumstances, including a war, can ever justify the use of such methods.

But the obligation of the State goes further: it appears from Article 4 that the State must take positive action – the Article refers to 'effective measures' – to prevent torture and other cruel, inhuman or degrading treatment or punishment from being practised within its jurisdiction.

Article 5 indicates that certain practical measures are also required. The prohibition against the use of such methods must be given weight in the training of police officers, prison staff and other officials responsible for detainees, and it should also, where appropriate, be included in rules and instructions for such personnel. According to Article 6, attention must also be given to interrogation methods and arrangements for custody and the like.

Article 7 provides that torture must be punishable under criminal law. According to Article 8, there shall be a right to obtain an impartial examination of complaints regarding torture or other cruel, inhuman or degrading treatment or punishment. It follows from Article 9 that an impartial investigation shall also be made ex officio when there is reasonable ground to believe that an act of torture has been committed. Where the suspicion is sufficiently confirmed, proceedings shall be instituted against the offender. This appears from Article 10.

According to Article 11, the victim of torture or other cruel, inhuman or degrading treatment or punishment shall have a right to obtain compensation. Finally, Article 12 provides that a statement made as a result of torture or other cruel, inhuman or degrading treatment or punishment shall not be invoked as evidence in court proceedings.

The Declaration on Torture is not legally binding, and its direct practical effect can be expected to be limited. Nevertheless, it indicates for the first time in some detail how States are expected to act in this area, and it certainly gives human rights groups and other non-governmental organizations a basis for proceeding against States in whose territories torture occurs. Moreover, the Declaration gave a rather firm foundation for the further work which finally resulted in the adoption in 1984 of the Convention against Torture.

VII. The 1984 Convention against Torture

The Convention against Torture and Other Cruel, Inhuman or Degrading Treatment or Punishment, adopted in 1984, is undoubtedly the central international instrument regarding the issue of torture. The negotiations regarding the Convention started not long after the 1975 Declaration had been adopted, and the latter served as a model. The draft Convention, which was proposed by Sweden, formed the basis of the negotiations and was almost identical to the text of the Declaration, but provisions which had not given rise to any problems in the Declaration created difficulties in the context of the Convention. It was obvious that many States considered the drafting of a Convention to be a much more serious matter than the drafting of a non-binding Declaration.

Not even the definition of torture which appeared in Article 1 of the Declaration was quite acceptable as far as the Convention was concerned. Thus, this definition was further elaborated and refined, and in its final form it reads as follows:

> For the purposes of this Convention, the term 'torture' means any act by which severe pain or suffering, whether physical or mental, is intentionally inflicted on a person for such purposes as obtaining from him or a third person information or a confession, punishing him for an act he or a third person has committed or is suspected of having committed, or intimidating or coercing him or a third person, or for any reason based on discrimination of any kind, when such pain or suffering is inflicted by or at the instigation of or with the consent or acquiescence of a public official or other person acting in an official capacity. It does not include pain or suffering arising only from, inherent in or incidental to lawful sanctions.

As in the Declaration, the crucial element in torture is the infliction of severe pain or suffering. Consequently, the act must be of a certain gravity. While the typical methods of torture consist of infliction of physical pain, infliction of mental suffering can also constitute torture. Such suffering may consist, for instance, of threats of execution or of reprisals against family members. Forcing a person to witness ill-treatment of his wife or children may also cause such severe suffering as to constitute torture. Although the definition refers to an 'act', an omission – for instance failure to provide a prisoner with food, water or elementary sanitary facilities – could probably also be regarded, in certain circumstances, as torture.

It is emphasized in the definition that torture must be an intentional act. The infliction of pain by negligence or by accident will therefore not constitute torture, even if the pain is severe.

The definition also indicates that, in order to constitute torture, the act shall be performed for a certain purpose, although the purposes mentioned in the definition are merely examples, and not exhaustive. Where the motive is exclusively sadistic or where the act is an act of personal revenge, it is at least doubtful whether the act falls within the definition. Where the purpose is a good one, for instance to save a person's life or to improve his health, there can be no question of torture; a medical operation is a typical example.

Another important requirement is that the public authorities must somehow be responsible for the act, at least in the sense that they have tolerated it or not tried to prevent it. If, on the other hand, the act is committed by one private person against another without any official involvement, then it is outside the scope of the Convention. Such an act constitutes an ordinary crime under penal law, and it can be expected that the police and the prosecuting authorities take appropriate action against the offender, without any international control being necessary.

Although this is not specifically stated in the definition, it would seem that torture presupposes that the person on whom pain or suffering is inflicted is detained or at least under the factual control of the person inflicting the pain or suffering. The soldier or the policeman who shoots at a demonstrator or at a suspected criminal would hardly be considered to have committed an act of torture to which the Torture Convention applies.

As in the 1975 Declaration, the second sentence of the definition, which makes an exception for lawful sanctions, is a highly controversial provision. While the corresponding provision of the Declaration requires, as a condition, that the sanctions shall be consistent with the Standard Minimum Rules for the Treatment of Prisoners, there is no similar condition in the Convention, the reason being that it was considered inappropriate in a binding treaty to base an exception on provisions in a text which is merely recommendatory in character. Consequently, the provision in the Convention could be read as allowing a State to include in its legal system any sort of cruel punishment without any risk of conflict with the prohibition against torture in the Convention, and some Convention States undoubtedly consider this to be the correct interpretation of the Convention. However, this is by no means the only way of reading Article 1. It is in fact well-known that other Convention States consider that, for a sanction to be lawful, it must be consistent not only with domestic law but also with international law, and those States would argue that corporal punishments and other forms of cruel punishments are prohibited under the rule which appears in several human rights instruments and prohibits cruel, inhuman or degrading punishment. Consequently, in their opinion, such punishments are not, if they cause severe pain or suffering, excluded from the definition of torture in Article 1 of the Convention.

Like the 1975 Declaration, the Convention contains no definition of the concept of cruel, inhuman or degrading treatment or punishment.

Article 2 paragraph 1 of the Convention makes it clear that a State must take effective measures to prevent torture. A mere prohibition is not sufficient, but the State must see to it that the prohibition is also respected. A State may not be able to guarantee that no act constituting torture is ever committed on its territory, but it must do what can reasonably be expected to prevent it from happening. If it nevertheless occurs, the State must take further measures to avoid a repetition. Such measures might include a change of personnel, a stricter supervision or the like.

The responsibility of the State extends to any territory under its jurisdiction. This includes the territorial sea, ships flying the flag of that State, the continental shelf etc. It also includes occupied territories, and the prohibition of torture may in fact often have a particular importance in cases of military occupation.

Article 2 paragraph 2 indicates that no exception from the prohibition against torture may be made under any circumstances, including time of war or other public emergency. It may be recalled that the 1977 Additional Protocols to the 1949 Geneva Conventions on Humanitarian Law in Armed Conflicts already contain a prohibition against torture being used against civilians and prisoners of war.

The principle established at the Nuremberg trial, according to which a superior order is no excuse for serious crimes under international law, is the underlying principle of the provision in paragraph 3 of Article 2, which states that an order from a superior officer or a public authority may not be invoked as a justification for torture.

However, it is not sufficient that a State ensures that torture does not take place in its own territory. It must also refrain from handing a person over to another State in whose territory he runs a substantial risk of being tortured. This appears from Article 3 paragraph 1 of the Convention which contains a prohibition against expulsion or extradition in situations where such a risk exists. A source of inspiration has been Article 33 of the 1951 Geneva Convention Relating to the Status of Refugees, which provides that no Contracting State shall expel or return a refugee to a territory where his life or freedom would be threatened on discriminatory grounds. Another model was found in the case-law of the European Commission of Human Rights, which had for a long time taken the view that the prohibition against torture and inhuman treatment in the European Convention on Human Rights should be understood also to prevent expulsion or extradition to countries where there is a serious risk that the prisoner will be subjected to torture or ill-treatment.

According to paragraph 2 of Article 3, a consistent pattern of gross, flagrant or mass violations of human rights in a certain country shall be of particular relevance when assessing whether expulsion or extradition should be refused. It was the Soviet Union which insisted on the inclusion of a provision of this kind. However, the provision also indicates that all relevant circumstances shall be taken into account, which means that, on the one hand, expulsion or extradition to a country where there is no pattern of gross violations of human rights may well be unacceptable in a specific case, and that, on the other hand, the circumstances in the concrete case may show that there is no risk of torture, although human rights are in fact massively violated in the country concerned.

According to Article 4, torture must be an offence under criminal law, and the penalties must be fixed in view of the gravity of the offence. This means that the punishment must be severe, but what is severe should be assessed in relation to other penalties in the criminal law of the country concerned. It would be reasonable to consider that the punishment for acts of torture should be close to the punishments for the most severe offences under criminal law.

Article 4 does not require that torture should be included in the penal code as a separate and specific offence. Some States have in fact found it difficult to make torture a separate offence, since the definition in Article 1 of the Convention may not be considered precise enough to form the basis of a provision in a penal code. What is required is that acts of torture are punishable and that the penalties are severe. The technical manner of achieving this aim is to be determined by each Contracting State.

One of the most controversial issues during the negotiations regarding the Convention was the proposal of Sweden to introduce into the Convention, as a basic element, a system of so-called universal jurisdiction. A system of this kind was finally adopted and is reflected in Articles 5-8 of the Convention. The background was as follows.

The rules of jurisdiction in criminal cases differ between different States. In Anglo-Saxon countries, criminal jurisdiction is mainly territorial, which means that only offences committed within the country are made the subject of prosecution. In continental Europe, criminal jurisdiction is both territorial and based on nationality. This means that not only offences committed within the country are prosecuted but also offences committed abroad by a national of the State concerned. Moreover, both the Anglo-Saxon countries who are parties to the Convention and most other countries have accepted the idea that there are certain crimes in respect of which, because of their serious nature, prosecution should be possible everywhere. In regard to such crimes, the principle of universal jurisdiction is thus applied.

The crimes which were prosecuted at the Nuremberg trial – war crimes, crimes against peace, crimes against humanity – are regarded as international crimes, and it is generally accepted that they are subject to universal jurisdiction. The 1949 Geneva Conventions also provide that certain crimes shall be prosecuted on the basis of universality of jurisdiction. Perpetrators shall be prosecuted regardless of their nationality, unless they are handed over to another Contracting State which has made out a prima facie case for jurisdiction.

The same principle was applied in a number of subsequent treaties dealing with various kinds of terrorist offences: the Convention for the Suppression of Unlawful Seizure of Aircraft, the Convention for the Suppression of Unlawful Acts against the Safety of Civil Aviation, the Convention on the

Prevention and Punishment of Crimes against Internationally Protected Persons, including Diplomatic Agents, and the Convention against the Taking of Hostages. All these conventions are based on the principle of universal jurisdiction in the form of ***aut dedere aut punire***. In other words, a State where a suspected offender is found shall either extradite him to another State for the purpose of prosecution or – provided that sufficient evidence is available – prosecute him in its own territory. Each State must therefore have jurisdiction over the offence in the sense that prosecution must be legally possible in its territory, but if it chooses to extradite a suspected offender to another country, it does not have to exercise its own jurisdiction over the offence. The principle which lies behind this system is that a person who has committed a serious crime of the kinds dealt with in these conventions shall not be allowed to escape the consequences of his act by fleeing to another country which will not take any measures against him.

This was the background against which the system of universal jurisdiction was introduced into the Torture Convention, and the provisions of the various terrorist conventions formed the model for Articles 5-8 of the Torture Convention.

Article 5 first makes it clear in paragraph 1 that a Contracting State must have jurisdiction over a crime of torture both when the crime was committed in its territory and when the perpetrator was one of its nationals. The Article also refers to a third criterion of jurisdiction, the nationality of the victim, but does not oblige the Contracting States to use that element as a criterion for jurisdiction. What makes it justified to speak about universal jurisdiction is the provision in paragraph 2, according to which a State must have jurisdiction when the alleged offender is present in its territory and it does not extradite him to another State which has jurisdiction.

Article 6 contains certain subsidiary rules aimed at making the system work efficiently. It provides for the taking of the suspected offender into custody and for the preliminary inquiry which should be made into the facts.

Article 7 is a central provision. It deals with the exercise of jurisdiction. Where a person alleged to have committed torture is found in the territory of a Contracting State, it is the duty of that State either to extradite him or to submit the case to its own prosecuting authorities, which shall decide, as with any other serious offence, whether or not to institute criminal proceedings.

Extradition normally presupposes a request from another State, and it is not clear how long a State is justified in waiting for a possible extradition request before the alternative obligation arises to submit the case to its own prosecuting authorities. No answer is found in the Convention, and the question must be determined in light of the facts of each case. The opinion that the obligation to submit the case to the local prosecuting authorities only applies if there has been an extradition request which has been rejected, is not convincing, because it would result in many offenders escaping prosecution and thus contradict the central idea behind the system of universal jurisdiction, which insists that there should be no safe-haven for perpetrators of torture.

It appears from the text of Article 7 that the alternative obligation is not to prosecute but to examine whether prosecution is justified on the basis of the usual principles applied in regard to serious crimes. This will mean, generally speaking, that criminal proceedings will only be instituted when the evidence is sufficiently strong to make a conviction foreseeable. And when the alleged offender is found in a country other than that where the crime was committed, it will often be difficult to gather sufficient evidence, especially in cases where the authorities of the latter country are not willing to co-operate in the investigation. Lack of evidence can therefore often be expected to bar prosecution in cases of this kind.

Article 8 is intended to ensure that the crime of torture is always an extraditable offence.

Although the system of universal jurisdiction is a system which in theory deprives the alleged offender of a safe-haven, it is not certain that it will be very effective in practice. In any case, the practical importance of the system should not be exaggerated. However, there might well be occasions when the system will work. Before the Convention was adopted, there have indeed been a few cases where the question of legal proceedings for torture committed abroad has arisen.[15] The Argentinian officer Astiz was suspected of having been involved in torture and murder of a Swedish girl and two French nuns. It so happened that he was taken a prisoner of war by the British forces during the Falkland war and taken to the United Kingdom. The question of his extradition to Sweden or France was discussed but not pursued, since it would no doubt have raised difficult problems in connection with his status as a prisoner of war. Another case, which is more important as a precedent, is the *Filártiga* case. It concerned a young boy who had been tortured to death in Paraguay. When the suspected torturer was in the USA, the family Filártiga brought tort proceedings against him before the American courts. The US Federal Court of Appeals stated in regard to the question of jurisdiction as follows:

> ... deliberate torture ... violates universally accepted norms of the international law of human rights, regardless of the nationality of the parties. Thus whenever an alleged torturer is found and served with process by an alien within our borders, section 1350 of the Alien Tort Statute provides federal jurisdiction.

15 About these cases, see N.S. Rodley, *The Treatment of Prisoners under International Law* (1987) 102-106.

It is likely that this judgment made it easier for the US Government to accept the idea of a system of universal jurisdiction as one of the key elements in the Torture Convention.

Article 9 of the Convention imposes an obligation of mutual assistance upon States. According to Article 10, education and information regarding the prohibition against torture shall be included in the training of various groups of officials and in the rules or instructions issued in regard to their activities. Article 11 provides that interrogation rules, instructions, methods and practices as well as custody arrangements shall be kept under review in order to prevent torture. According to Article 12, cases of suspected torture shall be investigated promptly and impartially, and according to Article 13, a prompt and impartial examination shall also take place when there is a complaint by a person who claims to have been subjected to torture.

Article 14 provides for compensation to the victim of torture. The compensation shall be fair and adequate, but it is inevitable that States must enjoy a great deal of discretion in determining the level of the compensation to be paid. What should be compensated, however, should be not only costs incurred for medical or psychological treatment but also non-material damage which the victim has suffered.

A prohibition against using a statement obtained through torture as evidence in judicial or other proceedings is included in Article 15 of the Convention.

Like the 1975 Declaration, the Torture Convention deals not only with torture but also with other cruel, inhuman or degrading treatment or punishment. In the Declaration, almost the same provisions apply both to torture and to these other kinds of treatment and punishment. In the Convention, this is not the case, the reason being that it was not considered appropriate, in a binding treaty, to attach precise and specific obligations to such a vague and imprecise concept as cruel, inhuman or degrading treatment or punishment. In particular, this concept could not be a suitable basis for an obligation to punish, to prosecute or to extradite. As a result, the undertaking of the Contracting States insofar as cruel, inhuman or degrading treatment or punishment is concerned is much more general in character. It is included in Article 16 of the Convention and amounts to a general obligation to prevent acts of cruel, inhuman or degrading treatment or punishment and to a more specific obligation to observe Articles 10 (education of certain officials), 11 (review of interrogation methods), 12 (investigations of suspected cases) and 13 (investigations based on complaints) of the Convention.

The following part of the Torture Convention – Articles 17-24 – contain the implementation provisions. The responsible body is a Committee against Torture, composed of ten independent experts elected by the Contracting States. The main tasks are those which also appear in other human rights treaties, namely examination of reports submitted by the Contracting States, examination of inter-state complaints (provided that the competence of the Committee in this regard has been recognized by the States concerned) and examination of complaints by individuals (provided that the competence of the Committee in this regard has been recognized by the respondent State).

However, besides these traditional functions Article 20 adds a new element insofar as it authorizes the Committee to make an inquiry when it 'receives reliable information which appears to it to contain well-founded indications that torture is being systematically practised in the territory of a State Party'. In the Swedish draft Convention which was the basis of the negotiations, Article 20 was proposed to be a mandatory provision applicable to all Contracting States. To some extent, the source of inspiration had been the procedure instituted under ECOSOC resolution 1503, which authorizes the UN Commission on Human Rights, in connection with communications from non-governmental sources, to examine particular situations which appear to reveal a consistent pattern of gross and reliably attested violations of human rights. However, as a method of implementation of a human rights treaty, this innovation was not acceptable to all States. This was therefore one of the most controversial parts of the Convention, and in the end, those who favoured the system felt obliged to agree to a compromise making it possible for a Contracting State to opt out of the system provided for in Article 20 by making a special declaration to this effect.

Although the Committee against Torture has met a number of times, it has not yet had many occasions to examine individual cases of alleged torture and to develop a real case-law in regard to the Convention. In the report which the Committee submitted to the United Nations General Assembly in 1990, it is stated that three communications had been considered, all submitted by Argentinian citizens on behalf of their deceased relatives, who had allegedly been tortured to death by Argentine military authorities in 1976. The applicants also complained of an Argentinian Act of 8 June 1987, which presumed, without admitting proof to the contrary, that those persons who held lower military ranks at the time the crimes were committed were acting under superior orders, and the Act therefore exempted them from punishment. The immunity also covered, to a large extent, superior military officers. The Committee against Torture declared the communications inadmissible *ratione temporis*, because the Convention could not be applied retroactively and it only had effect from 26 June 1987. However, the Committee observed, in an *obiter dictum*, that the law in question was 'incompatible with the spirit and purpose of the Convention' and urged Argentina not to leave the victims of torture and their dependants wholly without a remedy. It added: 'If civil action for compensation is no longer possible because the period of limitations for lodging such an action has run, the Committee would welcome, in the spirit of Article 14 of the Convention, the adoption of appropriate measures to enable adequate compensation.'

VIII. The European Convention on Human Rights

The most extensive and detailed international case-law in regard to the prohibition against torture and other cruel treatment is based on Article 3 of the European Convention on Human Rights and has been developed by the European Court and the European Commission of Human Rights. The judgments of the Court and the reports and decisions of the Commission often contain a great deal of legal reasoning and they have given some substance to the convention provision which is only phrased in very general terms.

Article 3 has been raised in many different kinds of cases. The following categories may be mentioned as being of particular importance:

1. A number of cases have concerned physical ill-treatment. Some of them have raised the question of the limit between torture and inhuman or degrading treatment. It may be argued that this limit is of minor importance, since Article 3 prohibits all these kinds of treatment. Nevertheless, many Governments would consider it to be a much more serious stigma if they are found guilty of torture than if the finding is one of inhuman or degrading treatment.

2. Another category of cases relating to Article 3 concerns conditions of detention. In some cases, the complaints have concerned generally unsatisfactory conditions (small cells, inadequate sanitary facilities, insufficient food or medical attention). In other cases, the treatment in the particular case has been harsh (prolonged solitary confinement, disciplinary punishments). Of course, bad conditions of detention may also sometimes be combined with physical assault of some kind.

3. A special group of cases concerns corporal punishment, either as a penal sanction or as disciplinary punishment at schools.

4. Finally, Article 3 has often been invoked in cases of expulsion or extradition to a country where the expelled or extradited person may be exposed to certain risks.

A. Physical Ill-Treatment

While questions of torture in the form of physical ill-treatment of detained persons had been already raised in the 1950s before the European Commission in one of the cases regarding Cyprus brought by Greece against the United Kingdom, it was in the inter-state case brought by *Denmark, Norway and Sweden* v. *Greece*[16] in the 1960s that questions of torture were first dealt with extensively on the basis of the European Convention. The general statement which the Commission made in the *Greek* case regarding the interpretation of Article 3 of the Convention is of considerable interest and has influenced, or at least served as a point of departure for, the drafting of the definition in the United Nations Declaration of 1975 and Convention of 1984. The Commission, after referring to the three concepts of 'torture', 'inhuman treatment' and 'degrading treatment', stated as follows:

> It is plain that there may be treatment to which all these descriptions apply, for all torture must be inhuman and degrading treatment and inhuman treatment also degrading. The notion of inhuman treatment covers at least such treatment as deliberately causes severe suffering, mental or physical, which, in the particular situation, is unjustifiable.
> The word 'torture' is often used to describe inhuman treatment, which has a purpose, such as the obtaining of information or confessions, or the infliction of punishment, and it is generally an aggravated form of inhuman treatment. Treatment or punishment of an individual may be said to be degrading if it grossly humiliates him before others or drives him to act against his will or conscience.[17]

The Commission further dealt with the questions of evidence, which are of particular importance in this context and which also cause particular difficulties in cases where a person alleges that, while being detained, he was tortured or ill-treated in private by his interrogators or by the police or prison officers assisting in the interrogation. The Commission insisted that the allegations must be proved beyond reasonable doubt. It added that 'a reasonable doubt means not a doubt based on a merely theoretical possibility or raised in order to avoid a disagreeable conclusion, but a doubt for which reasons can be given drawn from the facts presented'.[18]

The Commission went on to detail the problems with regard to evidence in this area:

16 The case against Greece was also brought by the Netherlands, but as regards the allegations of torture and ill-treatment the three Scandinavian Governments were the only applicants.

17 Report adopted on 5 November 1969, Chapter IV, Introduction, paragraph 2.

18 Report, Chapter IV, Introduction, paragraph 30.

> There are certain inherent difficulties in the proof of allegations of torture or ill-treatment. First, a victim or a witness able to corroborate his story might hesitate to describe or reveal all that has happened to him for fear of reprisals upon himself or his family. Secondly, acts of torture or ill-treatment by agents of the police or armed services would be carried out as far as possible without witnesses and perhaps without the knowledge of higher authority. Thirdly, where allegations of torture or ill-treatment are made, the authorities, whether the police or armed forces or the Ministries concerned, must inevitably feel that they have a collective reputation to defend, a feeling which would be all the stronger in those authorities that had no knowledge of the activities of the agents against whom the allegations are made. In consequence there may be reluctance of higher authority to admit, or allow inquiries to be made into, facts which might show that the allegations are true. Lastly, physical traces of torture or ill-treatment may with lapse of time become unrecognisable, even by medical experts, particularly where the form of torture itself leaves little external marks.[19]

One statement by the Commission in the *Greek* case is difficult to accept. In fact, the Commission seemed to say that less serious forms of physical violence against detainees could more or less be accepted, at least in a society where such treatment is regarded as normal. The Commission expressed itself in the following way:

> It appears from the testimony of a number of witnesses that a certain roughness of treatment of detainees by both police and military authorities is tolerated by most detainees and even taken for granted. Such roughness may take the form of slaps or blows of the hand on the head or face. This underlines the fact that the point up to which prisoners and the public may accept physical violence as being neither cruel nor excessive, varies between different societies and even between different sections of them. However, the allegations raised in the proceedings generally concern much more serious forms of treatment which, if established, clearly constitute torture or ill-treatment.[20]

It does indeed seem difficult to accept that a slap or a blow of the hand on the head or face of an arrested or detained person would not be considered a violation of Article 3. It also seems difficult to accept that the conclusion should vary depending on the society or sector of society at issue. It would rather seem that the physical integrity, particularly of a person in a dependent position such as a detainee, is something which should be effectively protected by Article 3, irrespective of the country or area in which the person is detained.

Against the background of its general considerations, the Commission then examined 30 concrete cases. It found that torture or ill-treatment had been proved in 11 cases and that in 17 other cases further investigations were needed; the evidence varied from indications or establishment of prima facie cases to strong indications.

19 Report, Chapter IV, Introduction, paragraph 31.
20 Report, Chapter IV, Opinion of the Commission, paragraph 11.

Questions of violations of Article 3 were again at issue in the Northern Ireland case, brought by *Ireland* v. *United Kingdom* and finally adjudicated by the European Court of Human Rights in 1978. The case concerned primarily five techniques which had been used in connection with the interrogation of suspected terrorists in Northern Ireland. These techniques were described in the Court's judgment as follows:

> (a) *wall-standing:* forcing the detainees to remain for periods of some hours in a 'stress position', described by those who underwent it as being 'spreadeagled against the wall, with their fingers put high above the head against the wall, the legs spread apart and the feet back, causing them to stand on their toes with the weight of the body mainly on the fingers';
> (b) *hooding:* putting a black or navy coloured bag over the detainees' heads and, at least initially, keeping it there all the time except during interrogation;
> (c) *subjection to noise:* pending their interrogations, holding the detainees in a room where there was a continuous loud and hissing noise;
> (d) *deprivation of sleep:* pending their interrogations, depriving the detainees of sleep;
> (e) *deprivation of food and drink:* subjecting the detainees to a reduced diet during their stay at the centre and pending interrogations.[21]

The Commission considered that the use of these methods constituted torture, but the Court did not agree.

The Court first pointed out that ill-treatment must attain a minimum level of severity if it is to fall within the scope of Article 3. The Court added that the assessment of this minimum is, in the nature of things, relative; it depends on all the circumstances of the case, such as the duration of the treatment, its physical or mental effects and, in some cases, the sex, age and state of health of the victim, etc. The Court considered that the premeditated five techniques, which had lasted for hours at a stretch, had caused, if not actual bodily injury, at least intense physical and mental suffering to the persons subjected thereto and had also led to acute psychiatric disturbances during interrogation. They accordingly fell into the category of inhuman treatment within the meaning of Article 3. The techniques were also degrading since they were such as to arouse in their victims feelings of fear, anguish and inferiority capable of humiliating and debasing them and possibly breaking their physical or moral resistance.

The Court then noted that the distinction, embodied in Article 3, between the notion of torture and that of inhuman or degrading treatment derives principally from a difference in the intensity of the suffering inflicted. The intention behind the distinction was, in the Court's opinion, that torture should be deliberate inhuman treatment causing very serious and cruel suffering and that a special stigma should be attached to torture.

21 ECHR (1978) Series A, No. 25; paragraph 96 of judgment.

And when applying this general reasoning to the specific case, the Court made the following statement:

> Although the five techniques, as applied in combination, undoubtedly amounted to inhuman and degrading treatment, although their object was the extraction of confessions, the naming of others and/or information and although they were used systematically, they did not occasion suffering of the particular intensity and cruelty implied by the word torture as so understood.[22]

Needless to say, this conclusion has not remained uncontested. Many observers, not least in humanitarian organizations, have criticized the Court for taking a too restrictive view on the kind of acts which should be regarded as torture. They have felt that the five techniques were in fact characterized by such cruelty as to deserve the special stigma to which the Court referred in its general reasoning.

The case brought by *Cyprus* v. *Turkey* and dealt with by the Commission in a report of 1976 concerned a number of allegations of violations of Article 3, including rapes, ill-treatment of prisoners causing considerable injuries and in one case the death of a prisoner as well as withholding of adequate supply of food and drinking water and of adequate medical treatment. The Commission found that the acts complained of amounted to inhuman treatment under Article 3. As regards the responsibility of Turkey for acts of rape committed by Turkish soldiers and officers, the Commission noted that it had not been shown that the Turkish authorities had taken adequate measures to prevent such acts from happening or that they had generally taken any disciplinary measures following such incidents. The Commission therefore considered that the non-prevention of the said acts was imputable to Turkey under the Convention.

In the case brought by *Denmark, France, the Netherlands, Norway and Sweden* v. *Turkey*, Article 3 was also at issue, but the proceedings were discontinued after a friendly settlement had been reached between the parties.

One important case, namely the case of *Tomasi* v. *France*, is at present pending before the European Court of Human Rights. It is an interesting case, in particular as regards the problems of evidence. The applicant was suspected of having been involved in an attack on a military installation in Corsica. He was held for 48 hours (*garde à vue*) at a police station and was then brought before an investigating judge (*juge d'instruction*). At that stage, he complained of having been ill-treated. He was examined by a doctor who found various injuries on his body. It was established that there had been no injuries when he was arrested. The French Government argued that there was no evidence showing the origin of the injuries. The Commission considered that, in a situation of this kind when a person is injured

22 Judgment, paragraph 167.

while he is being detained and thus in the hands of the authorities, it is for the authorities to explain how the injuries came about. In the absence of any such explanation in the present case, the Commission found that the applicant's allegation of having been ill-treated should be accepted and that Article 3 had therefore been violated.[23]

B. Conditions of Detention

There have been numerous cases before the European Commission of Human Rights, in which it has been alleged that the general conditions of detention were such as to constitute inhuman or degrading treatment contrary to Article 3. This is an area where it may be doubtful whether the notion of inhuman or degrading treatment can be given a uniform application. Conditions of detention must presumably, at least to some extent, be assessed against the background of the general standard of living in a given society, and in this respect there are still considerable differences even between the States which are parties to the European Convention on Human Rights. This is also an area where there has been a relatively quick development. What was considered in the beginning of this century as normal conditions of detention may appear as shocking today.

Generally speaking, the Commission has been reluctant to interfere in matters relating to the conditions of detention. The usual finding of the Commission has been that the circumstances complained of did not reach the level of severity necessary to bring them within the scope of Article 3 of the Convention.

The length of the imprisonment is in principle not a matter which raises an issue under Article 3 of the Convention. However, it is conceivable that it could do so in exceptional cases, for example, when the term of imprisonment is clearly disproportionate to the gravity of the offence. It is also possible that life imprisonment without any hope of release could raise a problem under Article 3.[24] On the other hand, the Commission had no objection when a war criminal, whose death sentence had been commuted to life imprisonment, had spent 30 years in detention in a Dutch prison.[25]

A leading case as regards solitary confinement in a prison is the case of *Ensslin, Baader and Raspe* v. *Federal Republic of Germany*, which concerned the conditions of detention of members of the Baader-Meinhof group. The Commission noted that these prisoners had been subjected to exceptional detention arrangements, characterized by their exclusion from the prison community and their confinement to a security area. However, the

23 Commission's Report of 11 December 1990, paragraphs 99-100.
24 Commission's decisions regarding applications Nos. 14289/88 and 15776/89.
25 Application No. 7994/77 *Kotälla* v. *Netherlands*.

Commission was convinced that there were pressing reasons for subjecting them to arrangements more directly based on security measures. The Commission went on to state:

> The segregation of a prisoner from the prison community does not in itself constitute a form of inhuman treatment. In many States Parties to the Convention, more stringent security arrangements exist for dangerous prisoners. These arrangements (strict isolation, removal of association, dispersal in special, very small units etc.), which are intended to prevent the risk of escape, attack or disturbance of the prison community, or even to protect a prisoner from his fellow-prisoners, are based on separation from the prison community together with tighter controls.
>
> The Commission has already been confronted with a number of such cases of isolation... However, in assessing whether such a measure may fall within the ambit of Article 3 of the Convention in a given case, regard must be had to the objective pursued and its effects on the person concerned. Complete sensory isolation coupled with complete social isolation can no doubt ultimately destroy the personality; thus it constitutes a form of inhuman treatment which cannot be justified by the requirements of security, the prohibition on torture and inhuman treatment contained in Article 3 of the Convention being absolute in character...[26]

However, in the concrete case the Commission found no evidence to suggest that the applicants had been subjected to sensory isolation brought about by a substantial reduction in stimulation of the sensory organs. The cells had been well-lit, the walls had been largely covered with books and posters, the cells had not been sound-proofed, the applicants had had the use of a radio and later of a television-set and a record-player, and they had been able to take daily walks in the open air and to do physical exercises. On the other hand, they had been subjected to a degree of social isolation by being excluded from the social activities of the prison and by having no contact with other prisoners, but they had been able to receive many visits from their defence lawyers and their families. Having regard to the overall circumstances of the case, the Commission considered that the applicants could not be deemed to have been deliberately subjected to a range of physical or mental suffering designed to punish them, to destroy their personality or to break down their resistance. Consequently, there had been no inhuman or degrading treatment.

In the *McFeeley* case, the Commission reached a similar conclusion. It considered that the form of segregation the applicants were subjected to did not amount to solitary confinement or to total social isolation. It was more correctly characterized as a form of removal from association with other prisoners. Each of the applicants shared a cell with another prisoner. Moreover, it was still open to the applicants to leave their cells for certain pur-

26 Applications Nos. 7572/76, 7586/76 and 7587/76, decision of 7 July 1978, The Law, A, paragraph 5.

poses, e.g. to take one hour's exercise every day in the open air, to receive visits from lawyers, to attend religious services or to visit the medical or welfare officer, to visit the toilet facilities, to take a shower twice weekly, to visit the library and to collect meals from the dining room.[27]

In the case of a dangerous prisoner – *X.* v. *United Kingdom* – the Commission stated that, while the applicant appeared to have been segregated for an unusual and undesirable length of time, this could neither be described as arbitrary nor of such severity as to fall within the scope of Article 3.[28]

In the case of *B.* v. *United Kingdom*, the applicant had been in Broadmoor Mental Hospital for three and a half years. The hospital had been overcrowded and the sanitary conditions as well as medical treatment had been inadequate. The Commission described the conditions as 'extremely unsatisfactory' but found nevertheless, in all the circumstances of the case, that they did not amount to inhuman or degrading treatment contrary to Article 3.[29]

There have been more cases concerning conditions in British prisons and other places of detention, but the Commission's conclusion has always been the same. Some cases have concerned other countries, and the following among them warrant particular mention.

In the case of *Kröcher and Möller* v. *Switzerland*, two German terrorists had been subjected to very harsh measures, particularly during the first month of their detention. The Commission nevertheless found that the applicants had not been subjected to a form of physical or moral suffering designed to punish them, destroy their personality or break their resistance and that the special conditions imposed on them could therefore not be construed as inhuman or degrading treatment within the meaning of Article 3. However, a rather strong minority of the Commission disagreed and considered that there was no proportionality between the security requirements and the restrictions imposed on the applicants and that Article 3 had therefore been breached.[30]

The case of *E.* v. *Norway* concerned an aggressive prisoner who had spent five years in solitary confinement and 118 days in security cells, but he had had access to reading material and had had contacts with prison staff. The Commission concluded as follows:

> The Commission has not overlooked the statements of the Norwegian courts ... from which it appears that the applicant should have received treatment for his mental deficiencies in a hospital rather than being placed in preventive detention

27 Application No. 8317/78.
28 Application No. 8158/78.
29 Application No. 6870/75.
30 Commission's Report of 16 December 1982, paragraphs 75-76.

> where he obviously could not receive any such treatment. The Commission can only support these views. Furthermore, the Commission has noted with concern that the authorities, under the court authorisation given to them, obviously failed for a regrettable period of time to implement the measures appropriate to the applicant's needs. Nevertheless, having regard to the case-law of the Commission and the Court of Human Rights and to the circumstances of the applicant's detention, in particular in the light of his distinct dangerousness, the Commission must conclude that the stringency of the measures, when compared to the objective pursued and the effects on the applicant, did not attain the level of seriousness which would make the treatment inhuman or degrading within the meaning of Article 3 of the Convention.[31]

In one recent case which is now pending before the European Court of Human Rights – the case of *Herczegfalvy* v. *Austria* – a different conclusion was reached. The applicant was a mental health patient who had been treated with sedatives in a mental hospital. This was in itself considered necessary in view of his aggressiveness. On one occasion, there had been a fight in which the applicant had been involved, and he had then been tied to a bed for several weeks. He had also been subjected to compulsory feeding and isolation. Taken together, these measures were considered to constitute a violation of Article 3 of the Convention.[32]

The Commission has sometimes been criticized for its cautious attitude in cases regarding conditions of detention. The normal conclusion has been, even in serious cases, that the treatment to which an applicant had been subjected did not reach the severity necessary to make it a violation of Article 3. This has been the conclusion even in some cases where the Commission found it justified to express regrets at what had happened or to describe conditions as unsatisfactory. The Commission has itself established a criterion to which it has frequently reverted, namely that complete sensory isolation during detention could constitute a violation of Article 3. However, real sensory isolation would hardly occur in practice except in most unusual circumstances, and as long as the Commission bases itself on such a criterion, the conclusion will almost invariably be that the Convention has not been breached. Other criteria used, for instance whether the intention has been to destroy the personality of the detainee, will also in practically all cases lead to the conclusion that Article 3 has not been violated.

It has sometimes been said that this is an area where the Commission – and the Court insofar as the cases are in the end referred to the Court – could play an important part in promoting a development towards a more humane prison regime in some countries. If this should be achieved, more flexible criteria would have to be used. However, it may be more natural for the new European Committee for the Prevention of Torture, set up under the

31 Application No. 11701/85.

32 Commission's Report of 1 March 1991, paragraph 254.

1987 European Convention for the Prevention of Torture and Inhuman or Degrading Treatment or Punishment, to make suggestions for improvements in this area.

C. Corporal Punishment

Another group of cases are those which concern corporal punishment. There is only one case about judicial corporal punishment, namely the *Tyrer* case, but a number of other cases have concerned corporal punishment as a disciplinary sanction within the school system.

In the *Tyrer* case, a young man was accused before a juvenile court in the Isle of Man of assault on a senior pupil at his school. He was sentenced for this offence to three strokes of the birch in accordance with the relevant legislation in force in the Isle of Man. The sentence was executed some time later.

The European Court of Human Rights considered that the execution of the sentence did not constitute torture or inhuman punishment, but the question was whether it was degrading punishment. The Court noted that in judicial punishment there is usually and almost inevitably an element of humiliation but that Article 3, insofar as it refers to degrading punishment, must be understood to mean something more. The Court went on:

> In the Court's view, in order for a punishment to be 'degrading' and in breach of Article 3, the humiliation or debasement must attain a particular level and must in any event be other than that usual element of humiliation referred to in the preceding sub-paragraph. The assessment is, in the nature of things, relative: it depends on all the circumstances of the case and, in particular, on the nature and context of the punishment itself and the manner and method of its execution.[33]

The Court further pointed out that the Convention is a living instrument which must be interpreted in the light of present-day conditions and that the Court had to be influenced by the developments and commonly accepted standards in the penal policy of the member States of the Council of Europe in this field. As regards the concrete case, the Court stated as follows:

> The very nature of judicial corporal punishment is that it involves one human being inflicting physical violence on another human being. Furthermore, it is institutionalised violence, that is in the present case violence permitted by the law, ordered by the judicial authorities of the State and carried out by the police authorities of the State... Thus, although the applicant did not suffer any severe or long-lasting physical effects, his punishment – whereby he was treated as an object in the power of the authorities – constituted an assault on precisely that which it is one of the main purposes of Article 3 to protect, namely a person's

33 ECHR (1978) Series A, No. 26; paragraph 30 of judgment.

> dignity and physical integrity. Neither can it be excluded that the punishment may have had adverse psychological effects.
> The institutionalised character of the violence is further compounded by the whole aura of official procedure attending the punishment and by the fact that those inflicting it were total strangers to the offender.
> Admittedly, the relevant legislation provides that in any event birching shall not take place later than six months after the passing of sentence. However, this does not alter the fact that there had been an interval of several weeks since the applicant's conviction by the juvenile court and a considerable delay in the police station where the punishment was carried out. Accordingly, in addition to the physical pain he experienced, Mr. Tyrer was subjected to the mental anguish of anticipating the violence he was to have inflicted on him.[34]

The conclusion was therefore that the judicial corporal punishment inflicted on the applicant amounted to degrading punishment within the meaning of Article 3 of the Convention.

The cases regarding corporal punishment at schools all come from the United Kingdom. One basic principle which can be derived from the *Tyrer* case is that a punishment is degrading only when the humiliation caused by it reaches a certain level of severity. In the case of disciplinary punishments at schools, it is reasonable to say that in many cases that level of severity has not been reached, but the conclusion on this point must be based on a consideration of the circumstances of each case.

The only case of this kind which has been decided so far by the European Court of Human Rights is the *Campbell and Cosans* case. In that case the applicants were parents whose children had been going to a school where corporal punishment was practised, but their own children had not been exposed to it. The Court stated that a mere threat of corporal punishment could in certain circumstances amount to inhuman treatment, but that was not the situation in the present case. Nor was there any indication that the threat constituted degrading treatment. As corporal punishment was frequently practised in Scottish schools, the threat of it was not degrading, and there was nothing to suggest that the applicants' children had been debased in their own eyes. Consequently, there was no violation of Article 3.[35]

In the case of *Warwick* v. *United Kingdom*, a 16 year old girl had been corporally punished at school. The Commission considered the circumstances to be such as to warrant the conclusion that Article 3 had been breached. It attached importance to the fact that the punishment had resulted in some injury, that the injury had been inflicted by a man, in the presence of another man, on a girl of 16, who was a woman of marriageable age. Moreover, the effects had been visible for more than a week and it

34 Judgment, paragraph 33.
35 ECHR (1982) Series A, No. 48; paragraphs 29-30 of judgment.

could not be excluded that the event had caused negative psychological consequences.[36]

The cases now referred to – *Campbell and Cosans* and *Warwick* – both related to schools for which the State was directly responsible. However, a similar problem could also arise in regard to private schools, and the question will then be whether the State is obliged to interfere by legislation or otherwise in order to ensure that corporal punishment in such schools does not occur, or occurs only on special conditions. Two cases of this kind – *Costello-Roberts* v. *United Kingdom* and *Y* v. *United Kingdom* – are at present pending before the European Court. In the first case, the Commission found that Article 3 had not been violated, whereas it found a violation of that Article in the second case.

As regards the situation in private schools, the Commission considered in these two cases that the United Kingdom has a duty under the Convention to ensure that all pupils, including pupils at private schools, are not exposed to treatment contrary to Article 3. The different conclusions reached in the two cases were based on differences as regards the severity of the two punishments at issue. In the first case, it was a seven year old boy who had received three smacks, through shorts, with a soft-soled shoe. In the second case, it was a teenage boy who had been hit with a cane with such force that four weals appeared on his buttocks, with swelling and bruising, causing considerable pain for some time after thc act itself.[37]

D. Expulsion and Extradition

Although the European Convention on Human Rights does not prohibit a person's expulsion or extradition to another country, the Commission has frequently stated in its case-law that a measure of expulsion or extradition may in specific circumstances give rise to an issue under Article 3 of the Convention. According to this case-law, there could be a violation of Article 3 if the expelled or extradited person would risk exposure in the country of destination to torture or other ill-treatment. This case-law has on the whole been confirmed during the last years by the European Court of Human Rights.

The issue which in such cases arises under the Convention is unusual in two respects. First, when the Commission or the Court examines a case of this kind, the expulsion or the extradition has normally not yet taken place, and the Commission or the Court is asked to establish that the transfer of the person to a specific country would violate Article 3. Consequently, the

36 Commission's Report of 18 July 1986, paragraphs 86-88.
37 Commission's Report of 8 October 1991 in the *Costello-Roberts* case, paragraph 42, and its Report of the same date in the *Y.* v. *United Kingdom* case, paragraphs 43-45.

Convention organs are asked to rule about an event which has not yet taken place and which may never take place. Secondly, it is not the State against which the complaint is directed that is accused of torturing the applicant or exposing him to similar treatment, but what is at issue is the risk that this might be done in a different country and hereby the expulsion or the extradition would become inhuman treatment contrary to Article 3. However, both these unusual features have been accepted by the Convention organs, the reason being that the expulsion or the extradition would generally create an irreversible situation which would make any subsequent control by the Commission and the Court ineffective. And it is a fundamental principle that the guarantees of the Convention should be so applied that they become effective and not only formal guarantees.

Before the Commission, there have been very many cases over the years where it has been argued that the applicant would be exposed to serious risks if he were to be expelled. However, in the large majority of cases, the Commission has found such allegations to be insufficiently supported by the facts of the case. The *Amekrane* case was the first case of this kind to be declared admissible by the Commission. It concerned a Moroccan officer, who had fled from Morocco to Gibraltar after an aborted coup and who was returned by the British authorities. Back in Morocco, he was executed, allegedly after having been tortured. The case was brought by his widow but ended in a friendly settlement in which the United Kingdom Government agreed to pay to the widow a sum of £ 37.500.

The first case belonging to this category referred to the European Court of Human Rights was the *Soering* case. The circumstances were as follows. Together with his American girl-friend, the applicant, who was a German citizen, had killed his girl-friend's parents in the USA. The applicant and his girl-friend had both escaped to the United Kingdom where they were arrested. The US Government asked for their extradition. The girl-friend agreed and returned to the USA. The applicant opposed the extradition request. According to the law of the State of Virginia, he could be sentenced to death for the two murders and, if so, he would probably be detained on so-called death row for several years pending decisions on appeals and other petitions. He alleged that his extradition would be contrary to Article 3 in view of the treatment to which he would be exposed in the USA. He invoked in particular the inhuman character of the life of a prisoner on death row. It should be observed that the death sentence as such is not prohibited by the Convention but only by Protocol No. 6 to the Convention, which had not been ratified by the United Kingdom.

The Court noted that the death penalty could not be considered to be prohibited by the Convention. However, this did not mean that circumstances relating to a death sentence could never give rise to an issue under Article 3. The manner in which the death penalty is imposed or executed, the personal circumstances of the condemned person and a disproportionality to the gravity of the crime committed, as well as the conditions of detention awaiting execution, were examples of factors capable of bringing the treatment or punishment received by the condemned person within the proscription under Article 3. The Court added that present-day attitudes in the Contracting States to capital punishment were relevant for the assessment whether the acceptable threshold of suffering or degradation had been exceeded.[38]

The Court further stated that it would not be compatible with the underlying values of the Convention if a State were knowingly to surrender a fugitive to another State where there were substantial grounds for believing that he would be in danger of being subjected to torture, however heinous the crime allegedly committed. The same would apply when there is a real risk of exposure to inhuman or degrading treatment or punishment.[39]

Moreover, the Court noted that it is not normally the task of the Convention institutions to pronounce on potential violations of the Convention. However, a departure is necessary in regard to extradition in view of the serious and irreparable nature of the alleged suffering risked. In the present case, the likelihood of the applicant being exposed to the death row phenomenon was such as to bring Article 3 into play.[40]

The Court then went on to examine the special circumstances of the case. It noted that a prisoner who has been sentenced to death in Virginia can normally expect to spend between six and eight years on death row under a very stringent custodial regime. It took into account the applicant's age – he had only been 18 years old when he committed the crimes – and his disturbed mental health. Some importance was also attached to the fact that the United Kingdom Government had the alternative possibility of extraditing the applicant to the Federal Republic of Germany whose Government had also asked for his extradition. All in all, the Court considered that the applicant's extradition to the USA would expose him to a real risk of treatment going beyond the threshold set by Article 3.[41]

While the *Soering* judgment is important in some respects, its value as a precedent is somewhat reduced by the fact that the Court bases its conclusions on a large number of different elements and that it is not possible to know whether all or only some of these elements were necessary to reach the conclusion. One argument seems to be rather doubtful, namely the reference to the possibility of extraditing the applicant to Germany. If the treatment to be expected is of sufficient gravity, the assessment under Article 3 should

38 ECHR (1989) Series A, No. 161; paragraph 104 of judgment.
39 Judgment, paragraph 88.
40 Judgment, paragraphs 90 and 99.
41 Judgment, paragraph 111.

not depend upon whether alternatives might be open to the Government concerned if it should decide not to extradite.

One further difficulty resides in the fact that the death penalty is not prohibited under the Convention (but only under a Protocol which was not applicable in the *Soering* case). It follows that sending a person to a country where he will be sentenced to death and executed would not in itself be contrary to Article 3, and therefore it could be viewed as inconsistent to hold that sending a person to a country where the execution of the death sentence will be postponed pending the outcome of various legal remedies is in violation of Article 3. It is a different matter that there were special circumstances in the present case, in particular the applicant's young age and disturbed mental state, which could justify the conclusion that his extradition, exposure to death row and possible execution constituted inhuman treatment.

In the *Cruz Varas* case, the European Court of Human Rights made it clear that the general approach of the Court in the *Soering* case was applicable not only in extradition cases but also in expulsion cases. The *Cruz Varas* case concerned the expulsion of a person from Sweden to Chile. Although the expulsion had in fact taken place, the Court stated that the assessment of a risk of torture or inhuman treatment should be made on the basis of those facts which were known or ought to have been known to the Contracting State concerned at the time of the expulsion. What in reality happened after the expulsion was therefore not decisive, but could serve as a confirmation of the assessment made before the expulsion. In the present case, there was evidence that the applicant had been ill-treated in the past, but there was no evidence that the Chilean Government had been responsible for that ill-treatment. Moreover, the applicant's silence about past events and the fact that he had changed the story he had first told cast doubts on his credibility. Finally, the democratic process in Chile had proceeded to such a degree that any risks which might have existed in the past must be considered to have been reduced. The Court's conclusion was that no substantial grounds for a risk of treatment contrary to Article 3 had been shown to exist.[42]

Another case decided by the Court – *Vilvarajah and Others* v. *United Kingdom* – concerned a decision to remove five Sri Lankan asylum seekers from the United Kingdom to Sri Lanka. The applicants were Tamils and they could be considered to be subjected to certain risks upon return to their home country. The Court considered, however, that substantial grounds had not been established for believing that they would be exposed to a real risk of treatment contrary to Article 3. There had, at the time of the expulsion, been a certain improvement in the general situation in Sri Lanka, and it

42 ECHR (1991) Series A, No. 201; paragraphs 77-82 of judgment.

had not been established that the applicants' personal situation was any worse than that of most other Tamils returning to Sri Lanka. A mere possibility of ill-treatment in such circumstances was not, in the Court's opinion, sufficient to give rise to a breach of Article 3.[43]

It is difficult to draw any general conclusions from the judgments in these cases. In the *Soering* case the circumstances were very unusual. In the *Cruz Varas* and *Vilvarajah* cases, on the other hand, the facts were similar to those which exist in a very large number of cases of expulsion. In such cases, the person concerned has normally left his home country which is struck by political instability and unrest and where political opponents of the regime may also be persecuted. It cannot be excluded that in extreme cases any expulsion to such a country would constitute inhuman treatment, but this will only rarely be the case. Normally the person concerned will have to show that he runs a special risk because of his personal circumstances. Full evidence is often difficult to produce, and proving the probability of such a risk must frequently be considered to suffice. The evidence may be based on medical opinion showing signs of ill-treatment in the past or on documents indicating participation in political activities or the like. However, such evidence must of course be assessed against developments in the country concerned, where the political situation may well have improved and the risks for former opponents may, as a consequence, have been reduced or eliminated.

IX. The European Convention against Torture

The 1987 European Convention for the Prevention of Torture and Inhuman or Degrading Treatment or Punishment represents a new way of combating torture and other ill-treatment in prisons and other places of detention. The novel approach establishes a system of international inspections of places of detention in the Contracting States. A European Committee for the Prevention of Torture and Inhuman or Degrading Treatment or Punishment (CPT) has been set up, and members of that Committee, if necessary assisted by experts, make visits to institutions where people are detained. The Committee itself has described the new system in the following way:

> The making of the Convention and the establishment of the CPT were revolutionary steps for the international community. For the first time a group of States has set up an international body of independent experts endowed with broad monitoring powers in the area of human rights. This body has been granted the unprecedented right to enter the territory of sovereign States and visit, free from

43 ECHR (1992) Series A, No. 215; paragraph 111 of judgment.

any impediment, all places where persons are deprived of their liberty by a public authority.[44]

From Article 7 paragraph 1 of the Convention it appears that the Committee shall organize periodic visits to the Contracting States. Moreover, it may also make other visits – so-called *ad hoc* visits – when circumstances so require.[45] A visiting delegation consists of three to five members of the Committee, assisted by one or two experts and members of the Secretariat.[46] During their visit, the delegation examines the general conditions in the institutions concerned. The delegation observes the attitudes of law enforcement officials and other staff towards the detainees, some of whom they interview in private in order to understand the general situation and hear any grievances they may have. It is also the task of the delegation to examine the general legal and administrative framework on which the deprivation of liberty is based.

Each visit to a country is followed by a report to the Contracting State concerned. In this report the Committee sets out the facts found during the visit and makes such recommendations as appear to it to be necessary. The system of visits, while differing from the normal implementation rules in human rights treaties, has similarities with the activities of the International Committee of the Red Cross (ICRC), but in order to avoid duplication of work a provision has been included in Article 17 paragraph 3 of the Convention, according to which the CPT shall not visit places which the ICRC visits regularly under the relevant conventions on humanitarian law in armed conflicts.

The CPT is not a judicial body and its task is not to determine whether a State has violated its international obligations by allowing, tolerating or even encouraging torture on its territory or by failing to take adequate measures when incidents involving such treatment occur. The main function of the Committee is rather to prevent such abuses from occurring in the future, and for such purpose the Committee shall examine the general situation in places of detention, draw the attention of Governments to any deficiencies which it discovers and recommend improvements. In view of the special character of its functions, the Committee is not composed exclusively of lawyers, but its membership also includes doctors, experts in penitentiary

44 The Committee's First General Report, paragraph 97.

45 During the first fourteen months of its existence (from November 1989 to December 1990), the Committee carried out four periodic visits (to Austria, Denmark, Malta and the United Kingdom) and one *ad hoc* visit (to Turkey).

46 According to Article 7 paragraph 2 of the Convention, visits shall be carried out by at least two members of the Committee. However, the Committee has decided that delegations going to large countries should consist of five Committee members, plus one or two experts and two members of the Secretariat, whereas delegations going to small countries should be composed of three to four Committee members, plus one expert and one or two members of the Secretariat. See First General Report, paragraph 55.

questions and criminologists. The Committee has even recommended that a greater number of its members should belong to such non-legal professions.[47]

Much of the Committee's work is of a confidential nature, this having apparently been a condition for the readiness of many States to accept this kind of international supervision. Article 11 paragraph 1 of the Convention thus provides that the information gathered by the Committee in relation to a visit, its report and its consultations with the State concerned shall be confidential. Consequently, it is difficult for outside observers to get a full picture of the activities of the Committee. However, some important data are available. First, Article 11 paragraph 2 of the Convention provides that the Committee shall publish, upon request by the State concerned, its report concerning a visit to that State together with any comments which that State has made. In accordance herewith, the reports regarding two visits made in 1990, namely to Austria and Denmark, have been published. Secondly, Article 12 of the Convention provides that the Committee shall every year submit to the Committee of Ministers of the Council of Europe a general report on its activities, which shall be made public. The first general report, which covers the period from November 1989 to December 1990, is in fact an interesting document which gives substantial information about the Committee's work and working methods.

It may be assumed that, in most of the countries where the European Convention for the Prevention of Torture is in force, torture in the proper sense of that term only exceptionally occurs. However, the Convention also covers inhuman or degrading treatment or punishment, which is a much wider concept. From the reports on visits which have been published it can be seen that rather detailed examinations have been made of the conditions in prisons and other institutions and that the Committee has made suggestions which have not necessarily been limited to problems of inhuman or degrading treatment, at least as this concept has been interpreted by the European Court and Commission of Human Rights. Indeed, the Committee has taken the view that, in order to accomplish its preventive function effectively, it must aim at a degree of protection which is greater than that upheld by the Court and the Commission when adjudging cases of ill-treatment of detainees and conditions of detention.[48] As stated above (see under VIII), the European Commission has been very cautious in applying Article 3 of the European Convention of Human Rights to prison conditions and has therefore hardly played any significant part in contributing to the improvement of such conditions. It can well be imagined that the CPT, in the light of its eye witness observations and in view of its less juridical ap-

47 First General Report, paragraph 88.
48 First General Report, paragraph 51.

proach, will find it possible to point at various shortcomings and deficiencies in the operation of prisons, houses of detention and other institutions and to bring about improvements.

It would seem – at least from the reports on visits published so far – that the Committee has mainly visited prisons, police stations and certain other establishments under the responsibility of the police. It would no doubt be useful if the Committee would in the future extend its visits to psychiatric institutions where mentally disturbed persons are kept and treated on a non-voluntary basis. Such deprivation of liberty gives rise to special, very difficult humanitarian problems and the fact that several of the members of the Committee are medical experts could make the Committee well equipped to deal with those problems.

It remains to be seen how effective the Committee's work will be in practice. Its report to a Contracting State following a visit cannot under the Convention for the Prevention of Torture contain any binding decisions but only recommendations and suggestions. Consequently, the State is not legally bound to take any measures on the basis of such a report. The effectiveness will therefore to a very large extent depend on the willingness of the States to co-operate with the Committee. This willingness may in its turn depend on the way the Committee carries out its work and on the moral authority with which it speaks. In any event, the Committee's report should not, as the Committee itself has pointed out,[49] be seen as the end of the procedure but as the beginning of a dialogue with the State concerned. The Committee expects the State to react on the report by giving information about measures taken, and the Committee is of course free to follow up by making new visits or in other ways. The ultimate remedy against a State which refuses to co-operate is on the other hand not very strong: Article 10 paragraph 2 of the Convention merely provides that in such a situation the Committee can make a public statement on the matter.

The European Convention for the Prevention of Torture and Inhuman or Degrading Treatment or Punishment can be seen as an experiment. The idea of an inspection system of this kind was first launched within the United Nations, where it would, if widely accepted, have become applicable to States with much more serious problems of inhuman detention than those which exist within most European Convention States. But if the European system proves effective and convincing, it may at some time provide a model for other parts of the world, and in this respect its novel approach also deserves special attention.

49 First General Report, paragraphs 32-33.

X. Concluding Remarks

Torture is a particularly serious violation of human rights. This is clearly demonstrated by the attention which has been given to it in the international work for the protection of human rights. The result has been a large number of international treaties and other instruments which outlaw torture and establish machinery aimed at eliminating it. It is difficult, however, to assess the practical results of all these efforts. Unfortunately, there are reasons to believe that torture still occurs in a large number of countries and often regularly and systematically.

The real improvements which have been achieved are usually the result of political changes in the countries concerned. Where there is a well-functioning democratic system, it becomes unlikely that opponents of the regime will be exposed to repressive measures. International support of a democratic development may therefore also be an effective way of eradicating torture.

This is not to say that the effect of international norm-setting and international supervision should be underestimated. Governments are usually anxious to maintain a respectable international reputation and they know that the use of torture, when it becomes known to the world, is fatal to their good name. It is therefore important that torture, where it occurs, also becomes widely known, and it is in this area that the work of several non-governmental organizations is of particular importance.

Legal Responses to Gender Discrimination in Europe and the USA

by

FRANCES OLSEN

Academy of European Law (ed.),
Collected Courses of the Academy of European Law, Volume II, Book 2, 199–268.

Table of Contents

Biography

Frances Olsen, Studied at Roskilde, Denmark 1966-67, B.A. 1968, Goddard College; J.D. 1971, University of Colorado; S.J.D. 1984, Harvard University; Member, Colorado State Bar and Federal Bar for the District of Colorado since 1972. Law Clerk, Chief Judge Alfred A. Arraj, US Federal District Court, Denver, Colorado, 1971-72; Lawyer, American Indian Movement, Wounded Knee, South Dakota (Throughout 1973 Uprising).

Professor of Law, UCLA. Previously Senior Fulbright Professor, Germany (University of Frankfurt) 1991-92; Visiting Professor, Harvard Law School 1990-91; Visiting Professor of Law, University of Michigan 1988; Visiting Fellow, Oxford University (New College) 1987.

Member, Board of Editors, *Contention* (founding Board); Member, Board of Advisors, *Yale Journal of Law and Feminism* (since 1989); Member, Board of Advisors, *Queens Law Journal*, 1991-94; Member, Board of Editors, *University of Colorado Law Review* 1969-71.

Co-Chair, Women's Rights Committee, Washington State ACLU 1977-79; Member, Conference on Critical Legal Studies (since 1977); Member, European Conference on Critical Legal Studies (since 1985); Chair 1987-88, Executive Committee 1987-90, Association of American Law Schools Section on Jurisprudence; Executive Committee 1986-89, Association of American Law Schools Section on Women in Law Teaching.

Parsons Fellow, Sydney University, Sydney, Australia, 1991; Outstanding Alumni Award, University of Colorado School of Law, 1989; Honorary Fellow, Institute for Legal Studies, and Senior Fellow, Legal History Colloquium, Wisconsin, Summer 1985; Visiting Scholar, Harvard Law School 1981-82; National Endowment for the Humanities Summer in Humanities (and Classics) for Law Professors, University of Chicago, Summer, 1979; Member, Order of the Coif (Law Honorary).

Principal Publications

'The Family and the Market: A Study of Ideology and Legal Reform', 96 *Harvard Law Review* (1983) 1497.

Reprinted: *Critical Legal Studies* (*Harvard Law Review* 1986) *American Legal Scholarship* (ZERP, Bremen, West Germany, 1986); major excerpts, A. Hutchinson (ed.), *Critical Legal Studies* (1989).

'Statutory Rape: A Feminist Critique of Rights Analysis', 63 *Texas Law Review* (1984) 387.

Reprinted: K. Bartlett, R. Kennedy (eds), *Feminist Legal Theory* (1991).

'The Politics of Family Law', 2 *Journal of Law and Inequality* (1984) 1.

Reprinted: H. Kraus (ed.), *Family Law* (1992).

Translated: 'De politieke dimensies van het familierecht', 2 *Nemesis* (Amsterdam, The Netherlands, 1986) 144.

'Socrates on Legal Obligation: Legitimation Theory and Civil Disobedience', 18 *Georgia Law Review* (1984) 929.

Reprinted: R.G. Wright (ed.), *Political Obligation* (1992).

'The Myth of State Intervention in the Family', 18 *University of Michigan Journal of Law Reform* (1985) 835.

'From False Paternalism to False Equality: Judicial Assaults on Feminist Community, Illinois 1869-1895', 84 *Michigan Law Review* (1986) 1518.

'Family Law', J. Janosik (ed.), I *Encyclopedia of the American Judicial System* (1987) 304.

'Feminism, Post-Modernism, and Critical Legal Studies', 5 *University College, London, Working Papers* (London, England, 1987) 29.

'Forældremyndighed og reproduktionsteknologi', 11 *Retfærd* (Copenhagen, Denmark, 1988) 61.

'Reductionism (Notes to Amuse a Legal Worker: Series 1, No. 1)', 1 *Yale Journal of Law and the Humanities* (1988) 157.

'Feminist Theory in Grand Style (Review of MacKinnon's *Feminism Unmodified*)', 89 *Columbia Law Review* (1989) 1147.

'Liberal Rights and Critical Legal Theory: A Feminist Perspective', in C. Joerges, D. Trubek (eds). *Critical Legal Thought: An American-German Debate* (Baden-Baden, West Germany, 1989) 241.

'The Supreme Court, 1988 Term – Comment: Unraveling Compromise', 103 *Harvard Law Review* (1989) 105.

'The Impact of Computerization on the Legal System and on Legal Reasoning', in A. Sajó, F. Petrik (eds), *High-Technology and Law: A Critical Approach* (Budapest, Hungary, 1989) 101.

'Comments on David Krell's "Lucinde's Shame: Hegel, Sensuous Woman, and the Law"', 10 *Cardozo Law Review* (1989) 1687.

'The Sex of Law', in D. Kairys (ed.), *The Politics of Law* (2nd ed., 1990) 453.

Reprinted: 'Feminism and Critical Legal Theory: An American Perspective', 18 *International Journal of the Sociology of Law* (1990) 199.

Translated: 'Das Geschlecht des Rechts', 3 *Kritische Justiz* (Germany, 1990) 303.

'In Memoriam: Mary Joe Frug', 11 *Harvard Women's Law Journal* (1991) i.

Reprinted: *CLS* (November 1991); 26 *New England Law Review* (1992) 659.

'A Finger to the Devil: Abortion, Privacy, and Equality', *Dissent* (Summer 1991) 377.

'The United Nations Convention on the Rights of the Child: An American Perspective', in P. Alston, G. Brennen (eds), *The UN Children's Convention and Australia* (Australia, 1991) 71.

'Children's Rights: Some Feminist Approaches to the United Nations Convention on the Rights of the Child, 6 *International Journal of Law and the Family* (1992) 192; symposium also published as book, P. Alston, S. Parker, K. Seymour (eds), *Children, Rights and the Law* (1992).

(with W. Weyrauch and S. Katz), *Cases and Materials on Family Law: Legal Concepts and Changing Human Relationships* (West Publishing Co. 1993)

(with W. Weyrauch and S. Katz), *Selected Readings in Family Law* (Anderson Publishing Co. 1993).

I. Introduction

This course is directed toward people interested in improving the role and status of women. It presents materials from the United States and Europe that deal with remedies for sex discrimination. The major focus of Parts II and III is employment discrimination.

The United States and Europe share a deep ambivalence about sex discrimination. On one hand, they oppose discrimination in a myriad of ways. The constitutions of several countries in Europe explicitly forbid sex discrimination and constitutions of other countries, like that of the United States, have been interpreted to forbid most instances of sex discrimination. Several federal acts in the United States forbid sex discrimination of various kinds; and United Nations documents, European Community provisions, and national laws in most European states recite their opposition to sex discrimination. Yet all countries practice discrimination, and strong opposition is raised against many policies that might end such discrimination.

The oppression of women is maintained by various forms of direct force, by economic coercion, by a culture of sexism, and by much more subtle forms of persuasion through ideology and mystification. The two most important sources of the oppression of women are (1) direct force and coercion of various kinds (which women may or may not resist to the full extent of their ability) and (2) patterns of ideas and expectations (in which women may participate and to which women more or less consent or in which they at least acquiesce). These two sources are interrelated in a number of ways. Although the two forms of oppression compliment one another – the more women are forcefully oppressed, the more they are likely to be also ideologically oppressed – the two forms can also relate to one another inversely. When the ideological oppression is effective enough, direct oppression by force may seem unnecessary. The more women accede to their subordinate role and the more fully they satisfy men's desires, the less reason any man has to use coercion or force against women. Approached from the other side, when direct force or coercion against women is pervasive enough, women may feel forced to accept many forms of ideological oppression. For example, the actual physical risk to women caused by widespread violent crime in the United States, and the relative acceptance of sex crimes against women as inevitable, make most women acquiesce in ideological notions that limit their movements, such as their freedom to be out at night, which limits their schooling and work opportunities. Similarly, if women are barred from better paying or more prestigious jobs (whether by exclusionary laws or by employment practices of private parties), they will more readily accept the idea that they find fulfillment in unpaid domestic work in the home and more readily 'prefer' to work in fields such as nursing or teaching, traditionally poorly paid and mostly done by women.

Rather than try to make any sweeping survey of the multiple forms of sex discrimination, this study focuses more deeply on one important field, employment discrimination. It is important that one not allow this focus to obscure or underemphasize the importance of other forms of discrimination. Women are discriminated against in housing, school and credit. Our culture is dominated my men, and the depiction of women continues to be belittling and offensive. Pornography and sexual violence impoverish the lives of many women in ways not experienced by men. Men would not put up with such disruptions to their lives, and if women were not subordinated, they would not either. Family law reinforces the inequality within families; domestic violence and sexual abuse within families affect females disproportionately and are all too tolerated by society. Women are discriminated against in social security and in welfare programs. There is sex discrimination in medical care, including access to medical care (especially abortion), quality of medical care received, and allocation of resources for medical research. Other forms of research also often focus attention differently on issues particularly affecting men or women, usually to the disadvantage of women. The particular manner in which child care is privatised harms many women. The tax system discriminates against women in a variety of ways; for example, it structures tax brackets in a manner that rewards pay gaps between husbands and wives. Additional areas of discrimination include the treatment of prostitution, the valuation of child bearing and rearing, the method of calculation of gross national product and the treatment generally of work typically done by women. In general, force (and physical coercion) and ideology (coercion, expectations, images and ideas) are deployed in a wide variety of ways that oppress women.

Employment discrimination is characterized by a complex interaction between these two forms of oppression. Ideology plays such an important role in employment discrimination that many forget that the basic mechanism of employment discrimination involves a form of force – the refusal of an employer to hire a woman or to pay her fairly. Until recently, force in the form of laws also prevented women and potential employers from entering certain employment contracts. For example, in the United States women were legally forbidden to work as attorneys at law during most of the nineteenth century. Until 1953, Harvard Law School forcefully excluded women from enrolling in the school or attending classes. While it may seem that legal changes have reduced the role of force and coercion in employment discrimination, it would be more accurate to say that the changes have redirected the force than that they have ended or even reduced it. Ideology obscures both the pervasiveness and the injustice of the force.

This course does not pretend to be simply an abstract intellectual enterprise, but is part of an effort to promote significant social change. I reject the fundamental support for the status quo, which is so often passed off as academic objectivity. Nor do I try to abstract myself from my own situation to present a 'view from nowhere.' I teach and write as a socially conscious and critical lawyer-turned-legal scholar from the United States.

From this perspective, it appears that law can be best understood as a social practice that 'cools out' social conflict and is designed to lead to political and social stability. Sex discrimination law in the United States, for example, appears to mediate a kind of unstated compromise between people who actually want to end discrimination and improve the role and status of women, on one hand, and, on the other hand, people who want to maintain or increase discrimination against women and continue the inferior status of women. The main purpose of the law seems to be to contain, limit and domesticate the conflict between these quite divergent positions.

It would be a misleading over-simplification to say that sex discrimination law is designed to end discrimination. Some people maintain that it is actually designed to perpetuate discrimination.[1] This alternative view is also an over-simplification. Yet sex discrimination law can be used to further either goal. Laws forbidding discrimination often reduce discrimination against women and open to women jobs that would otherwise be denied to them. Yet sex discrimination law can also stabilize and perpetuate discrimination. Moreover, in defining sex discrimination as a legal problem and giving the appearance of trying hard to end sex discrimination, the law can obscure the stark reality that sex discrimination keeps women relatively impoverished, keeps jobs segregated and maintains male domination. Thus, it has been said that anti-discrimination law in the United States serves to 'legitimate' discrimination. The law must hold sufficient promise of ending sex discrimination to placate persons seeking genuine reform and to convince them to struggle peacefully, keeping their efforts within the limits of the law. On the other hand, the laws provide sufficient loopholes and escape clauses to satisfy the misogynists and others committed to inequality. Much of the development of the law can be understood to reflect the ebbs and flows of influences between these two sides.

An interesting and more subtle problem with the role of law in this regard arises from the way in which these two sides wind up being consti-

1 See Powers, 'Sex Segregation and the Ambivalent Directions of Sex Discrimination Law', 1979 *Wis. L. Rev.* 55; Taub & Schneider, 'Perspectives on Women's Subordination and the Role of Law', in D. Kairys (ed.), *The Politics of Law* (1982) 118; Lacey, 'Legislation against Sex Discrimination: Questions from a Feminist Perspective', 14 *Journal of Law and Society* (1987) 410. Cf. Freeman, 'Legitimating Racial Discrimination Through Antidiscrimination Law: A Critical Review of Supreme Court Doctrine', 62 *Minn. L. Rev.* (1978) 1049 (arguing that racism and antidiscrimination law work together to legitimate the subordinate position of racial minorities).

tuted. Many of the people who most strongly support discrimination also support patriarchy and believe that the domination of women by men is a natural or good thing that should continue. This side is not really counterbalanced by any significant number of people who believe that the domination of women by men should be replaced by a domination of men by women. Although many such people may 'exist' as a fantasy in the minds of misogynist men to justify their fear of and hostility toward women, as a simple empirical matter the belief that women should dominate men is not widespread, nor does it seem to me to have any significant influence on the law of sex discrimination. Thus, the most 'extreme' position on one side is simply that women should be treated with as much fairness and concern as dominant men are treated. On the other side, however, are people who consider the paternalistic organization of families and society inevitable or desirable or both. Some of these people believe that the state should do nothing to reduce discrimination against women, or even that the state should actively maintain a patriarchal organization of society. Any compromise between these two 'extremes' – equality or male domination – is likely to leave women subordinate to men. If the conflict between these two end points is 'cooled out,' women remain oppressed, although perhaps a little less so. Thus, while discrimination law achieves significant benefits for the victims of discrimination, these benefits also bear a significant cost that should be recognized.

Social change comes from heating up the conflict. Although lawyers can consciously contribute to this process, the socialization process of most lawyers makes it seem counter-intuitive to do so. Perhaps the most common pattern is that the conflict is heated up by non-lawyers, and lawyers claim credit for the improvement in the status of women which the law grants in order to cool the conflict out again.

Some violence against women in the United States can be best understood as an effort by some men who oppose equality to heat up the conflict. This is a less misogynistic way of expressing the same sentiment intended by those who explain the seeming increase in violence against women as 'backlash' against women's gains in fields such as education and employment. Much sexual harassment, particularly but not exclusively 'hostile environment' harassment, is also best understood as a similar upping of the stakes by men who oppose women.

To conclude this introduction, I would like to note some of the reasons why I believe this is a particularly important time to focus attention on aspects of sex discrimination laws in Europe. It has become a commonplace to note that the countries of Central and Eastern Europe are in a state of extraordinary change. Less noticed are the complex and ambiguous effects of these changes on women.

One of the forces increasingly reflected in the politics of Central and Eastern Europe is nationalism. Nationalism has historically been associated with various forms of patriarchy and with attitudes hostile to feminism (and in some cases actually hostile to women in general). Although there is no necessary or inevitable connection between nationalism and anti-feminism, the rising nationalism in the 90s has had a number of negative effects on women. Hopes to increase the population of one's own national group and the rising influence of the Catholic Church in several countries, for example, have led to restrictions on abortion and to other forms of interference with women's medical needs. Moreover, some efforts have been made to use motherhood to excuse the heavier impact on women of increases in unemployment.

With the general demise of the former governments in the countries of Central and Eastern Europe, conditions for women have changed (often for the worse, at least at the moment) and it would seem to be at present an open question whether women will in the future have more or fewer opportunities to improve their conditions. Insofar as the former governments claimed to support women's advancement, there are significant ideological materials that could be mobilized to discredit those who today assert support for women's equality. Although it is mainly up to the women of Central and Eastern Europe to defend their position, it is also important for western feminists to keep informed and stand ready to help in those ways that we can. To whatever extent the new governments look to Western Europe or the United States as examples for economic and political development, it is important for feminists in these countries to ensure that women's rights (or, more precisely, reasonable treatment of and opportunities for women) are recognized as part of the liberal 'package' from the West.

Unfortunately, some of the men now governing Central and Eastern Europe sound very much like some Marxist theorists in their response to women's issues. Many seem to believe that economic reforms will semi-automatically solve the problems particularly plaguing women, just as some of their predecessors looked to communism as a solution to all women's problems. It would be ironic if the unpopularity of the former governments discredited the goal of women's equality more than it discredited the actual practices of these governments that all too much acquiesced in the continued oppression of women.

Finally, the increased role that racism seems to be playing in Europe makes anti-discrimination law more important. Racism and sexism are both based on the same kind of dynamic of the dominant group treating another group as 'other' and inferior. The treatment of the 'other' ties racism and sexism together; yet in a variety of ways, racism and sexism are quite distinct. The intimate relations claimed between the dominant and 'other' in sexism contrast with the more distant and instrumental relations that usually characterize relations between the dominant and 'other' races. A person can be on top of the sexual hierarchy and on the bottom of a racial hierarchy, or vice versa. Racism and sexism may or may not directly reinforce one another, but sex discrimination laws might well offer important insights for race discrimination law in Europe. The lessons of sex discrimination laws tell us much about how law can be utilized to oppose, moderate, legitimate or support race discrimination. In the United States, race discrimination law has often provided the model for sex discrimination law; perhaps in Europe sex discrimination law will provide a model for a future law of race discrimination.

As the European Community evolves over time, its laws and policies are likely to be increasingly important both because of their direct effect on the lives of residents of Member States and as an example for other countries. Such an example is particularly important as it provides to those countries an alternative to the example provided by the United States. It is also important to the United States as an alternative model. I intend by juxtaposing the developments in the United States and Europe to throw light on both.

II. Employment Discrimination: A Short History of Employment Discrimination on the Basis of Gender in the United States

A. Pre-Civil War

In the period before the American Civil War, the North was characterized by considerable job segregation on the basis of gender. On farms women tended to work at jobs considered domestic (which included work we might or might not today think of as domestic or women's work) and men did other, gender-specific work. In the cities and towns, and as work moved outside the home, the particular jobs created would generally be seen as either a man's job or a woman's job and be done primarily by members of that gender. Along with this rigidity, however, there was also flexibility. In cases in which a woman was widowed, for example, she might well continue her husband's work and thus, after his demise, perform tasks that would otherwise have been considered inappropriate for women.

In the South, a great deal of the labour was done by Black slaves, and a significant amount of the work done by slaves was not sex segregated. Women slaves worked in the fields alongside the men slaves. There was also, however, considerable sex segregation. Some jobs were seen as jobs to be done by men, and male slaves were considerably more likely to be 'hired out' to an employer. In some situations, male slaves were able to enjoy a degree of freedom regarding their 'hired out' work, including being allowed to keep a portion of the money they received, after handing over the major share to the person whom the law defined as their owner.[2]

Women slaves did a considerable amount of work that men did not do. Certain jobs in the houses – notably child care – were done by women and not men. Women slaves were also forced to do sexual and reproductive work. The law provided that any children born of a slave woman would be slaves owned by the woman's owner. Thus reproduction of the slave work force was part of the work required of slave women. Sexual intercourse between slaves was regulated in various ways, sometimes encouraged or required, other times forbidden or made difficult. Not infrequently slave women would be impregnated by their white owners or by friends of their white owners. The offspring, often relatively light-skinned, would be slaves with all the same legal disabilities as slaves kidnapped from Africa.[3] There were no laws to prevent men from forcing sexual intercourse upon slave women, and there seems to have been no effective social disapproval expressed against men having coercive or forced sexual intercourse with slave women whom the law defined as their property. There was no effective legal impediment to these 'owners' making any sexual demands they wished upon 'their' slaves. Moreover, as 'property' the slave women received no legal protection against sexual abuse. Attractive young female slaves brought a higher price on the slave market because of their status as sex objects.

B. Post-Civil War

The Civil War ended legal slavery in the United States. During the period of Reconstruction, there was considerable change in the South, but these changes had a greater effect on the relationship between whites and Blacks of both genders than upon the relationship between men and women of either race.

In the North, the period after the Civil War was marked by agitation and demands by women for their better treatment. There was an increased recruitment of women into (sex-segregated) factory jobs, especially of young women living at home. Many of the women were hired at very low wages, on which they were able to survive only because of their continued residence in the home of their parents. Nevertheless, many of the young women themselves reported that earning a wage gave them a sense of financial independence, in that they could contribute financially to the household and some-

2 F. Douglass, *Narrative of the Life of Frederick Douglass, An American Slave* (1845), Chapter XI, includes a description of his experiences with hiring out.

3 For a moving discussion of the social implications of these practices, see P. Williams, *The Alchemy of Race and Rights; Diary of a Law Professor* (1991).

times, with the permission of their families, spend some portion of their wages as they wished.

More women began entering professions, or trying to do so. In 1870, the University of Michigan admitted women to its law school, and a number of other law schools gradually followed suit. During the Civil War some women had been allowed to work in lawyers' offices as assistants, in essentially the same jobs previously filled by boys or young men studying to be lawyers themselves. Myra Bradwell, who had worked in her husband's law office, learned law on her own and edited the most influential law-oriented newspaper in Chicago, in 1869 applied to be admitted as a lawyer in the State of Illinois. The Illinois Supreme Court refused her petition, notwithstanding legislation that empowered the Court to license attorneys and made no reference to limiting the practice of law to men. The US Supreme Court upheld this decision in an infamous case discussed below.

Although women in the United States generally had no right to vote at this time, the women in Illinois were able to lobby the state legislature successfully to overturn the effects of the Court decision. The lobbying effort was led by Myra Bradwell and Alta Hewitt, a 19-year-old who became the first female lawyer in Illinois. Reform legislation, passed in 1872, permitted women to practice law and other professions and granted to women substantially equal employment rights with men. Many other states followed a similar pattern of conservative court decisions denying women employment opportunities, followed by reform legislation granting women the rights the courts had denied them. These reform bills were enacted by all-male state legislatures usually elected by an all-male electorate.

In general, during the last half of the 19th Century, all levels of American courts were more conservative than state legislatures or the national Congress. Judicial activism tended, as in the case of women applying to be lawyers, to be employed against the cause of equal opportunities for women. Although the legislatures would seem to have been at least as male-dominated as the courts, many of them passed a variety of laws that reduced the court-supported limitations on the options available to women. Reform legislation benefiting women typically received grudging and unsympathetic interpretation by the courts.

The role of trade unions, though complex, was generally not supportive of women's equality. Dating from the days of young women living at home being employed for less than survival wages, unions associated the employment of women with the depression of wages. And, of course, one reason employers initially chose to hire women was that the employers were generally able to pay women lower wages than they would have had to pay a male work force (much as industries now move to Mexico or Asia to reduce their labour costs). Thus the tendency of male unionists to see women's work as a threat to male wage rates was not without some justification. Yet the threat was considerably exaggerated; since work remained quite sex-segregated, there was only very limited replacement of male workers by lower-paid female workers.

Moreover, the response of many unions to this perceived threat was unjust, divisive and counter-productive. Women were excluded from many unions altogether; and even when unions were willing to accept women members, the unionization of female workers was not a priority. The generally negative attitude of the unions left women too often with no alternative except to agree to work for very low wages. Moreover, the sexism of many unions undermined possibilities for worker solidarity in many of the same ways as did union racism. Employers exploited this lack of solidarity in a variety of ways, including on occasion using women as strike-breakers.

The frequently short-sighted and negative response of unions to women workers complicated the movement for protective labour legislation. Women, less unionized than men and perceiving themselves to have less bargaining power than their unionized brothers, often supported efforts by legislators to enact into law minimum standards of work conditions, wages, and so forth. Some men also supported protective labour legislation. But many male unionists opposed such legislation, partly on the basis of political and economic theories suggesting that protection through a strong labour movement and collective bargaining agreements provided more security and more possibility for radical transformation of the economic system than state protection, and partly on the basis that protective labour legislation would benefit workers in non-unionized shops equally and thus indirectly undermine union recruitment efforts. Male unionists, justly viewed with suspicion by some women workers, could be charged with self-interest at the expense of women if they opposed protective legislation. They could also be suspected of self-interest, however, if they supported gender-specific protective labour legislation, mandating particular work conditions for women.

The issue of gender-specific labour legislation became particularly important after courts began overturning as unconstitutional most protective labour legislation while often upholding as constitutional and enforceable protective labour legislation limited to women workers. The politics of such legislation was complex. In some cases, gender-specific protective labour legislation was supported by the unions with the hope of actually improving the working conditions of women workers. In addition, unions sometimes supported such legislation because it could indirectly improve the conditions of male workers, either because of the interrelationships between the work done by women and men, or because some workers hoped that the protection of women would facilitate more broadly-based legislation. For example, toward the end of the nineteenth century, the Illinois legislature passed a law mandating the eight-hour day for women garment workers. If the bill had been enforced, it would have led to an eight-hour day for all garment workers unless employers could significantly change the way that they organized their work – which jobs they designated as 'women's' and which as 'men's.' Reformers familiar with the Illinois garment industry noted that factories that obeyed the law closed for the day for all workers after eight hours. Because the 'women's' work was essential to the 'men's,' the factories had little to gain in keeping the men at work longer than eight hours if they were required to let the women leave. State courts invalidated the act before it was widely implemented. Had the eight-hour day been established, the employers might have had a hard time taking it away. Even if the employers were able over time to reorganize their factories to make it possible for men to work longer hours than women, the purpose and likely effect of the gender-specific Illinois law was to improve work conditions, not to exclude women.

However, some gender-specific protective labour legislation was supported by unions as part of their efforts to reduce perceived competition from women workers, or to exclude women altogether from particular jobs. In addition, some labour legislation which had initially been enacted to improve the working conditions for women came to be used primarily to exclude women.

In recent years, the United States women's movement has been particularly sensitive to the misuse of protective labour legislation; but the more complex history of gender-specific protective labour legislation has not been well understood. Thus, some women believe that any legislation that serves to protect women (even if not gender-specific in terms!) will ultimately hurt women, as gender-specific and putatively protective legislation did when it was cynically enacted or enforced. As a result, the women's movement in the United States has been lukewarm in its support for maternity leave and employer-sponsored childcare. Any legislation that protects women will likely be compared to the old gender-specific protective labour legislation.

C. Racial Justice and the Women's Movement

In the United States, there has long been an important, if troubled, relationship between women's rights and concerns with the role and status of Black people. Sex discrimination law draws heavily upon race discrimination law. Constitutional developments in race discrimination greatly affect the constitutional treatment of sex discrimination, and the centerpiece of legislation against employment discrimination (Title VII of the Civil Rights Act) deals with race and gender together. Also, on the level of politics, women have been prominent in struggles for racial justice, and women's rights movements have generally followed on the heels of movements for racial justice. For example, the movement in the United States before the Civil War to abolish slavery provided many women with their first political experience. Women, Black and white, were active in the Abolitionist movement. What is often referred to as the 'first wave of the feminist movement' in the United States largely grew out of the work of women in the Abolitionist movement. And Abolitionists, men and women, were among the strongest supporters of women's rights. The first major women's rights conference was held before the Civil War at Seneca Falls, New York, in 1848. Some of the best known Abolitionists gave supporting speeches.

This alliance was badly undermined and damaged some years later when a split developed over the wording of amendments to the constitution that were enacted after the Civil War. Although women were generally not allowed to vote in the United States, there was no reference in the constitution forbidding women to vote or legitimating the refusal of particular states to allow women's suffrage. When an amendment was being drafted to enfranchise the freed slaves, many women's rights advocates preferred an amendment that would enfranchise Black and white women as well as Black men. At the least, they believed, the amendment should be silent on the question of gender, as much of the constitution was. Most supporters of racial justice suggested that they, too, would of course prefer such a broad, inclusive amendment; nevertheless, many of them – especially males – concluded that an amendment specifically limited to males would be more readily enacted and that the question of women's votes, Black or white, should be deferred until later. The split widened as some white women accused their old allies of betrayal and opposed the amendment limited to males because it would for the first time place a provision in the constitution that specifically favoured men. Some supporters of the limited amendment counter-charged that their old allies were racists. Eventually a split developed within the women's movement and some women argued that educated and cultured white women were at least as entitled to vote as Black men.

It is not certain what would have happened if supporters of the voting rights amendment had insisted on wording not specifically limited to men. It might well have been enacted, and the enfranchisement of Black women might have made the vote for Blacks more secure. Black women played a very active role in encouraging Black men to vote in the face a growing intimidation by the Ku Klux Klan and other racist organizations. Perhaps white society would have been less tolerant of terrorist acts against Black women voters than it was of such terrorism against Black men, and perhaps women's groups would have played a more active role in support of racial justice. On the other hand, the amendment might have been defeated because of the opposition of those opposed to women's suffrage. Some might have tried to discredit the amendment as a sly or opportunistic effort to obtain the vote for women. It is conceivable that the movement for racial justice could have been set back, and even that the franchise for women could possibly have been delayed even longer that the half century it was.

What did happen was that Black men obtained the vote by federal law, though after a few years it was effectively taken away by local laws and local practices. Women, Black or white, did not receive the right to vote in most jurisdictions until after the first world war and the enactment of the Nineteenth Amendment in 1920. The dispute over the exclusion of women from the amendment enfranchising Black males left a legacy of distrust and suspicion between many advocates of racial justice and of gender justice.

After the success of the women's suffrage movement, marked by the passage of the Nineteenth Amendment, the women's movement settled into decades of quiescence. The American Civil Rights Movement of the late 1950s and 1960s again saw the active participation of a considerable number of women. Although most of the major leaders were male, women played important roles and gained important political experience and confidence.

The so-called 'second wave of the feminist movement' in the United States came on the heels of the Civil Rights Movement. The relationship is made more complex, however, by the American anti-war movement that arose to oppose United States intervention in Vietnam and by the development of the Black Nationalist (Black Power) movement. Many feminists of the second wave gained their political maturity not in the Civil Rights Movement, but rather in the anti-Vietnam War and Black Power movements. It is often charged that these two movements particularly exploited and discounted women, and that the women's movement of the 1970s and 80s was a reaction against this sexism.[4] Therefore, it is argued, these feminists were generally disillusioned by and angry at their male colleagues in the anti-war and Black Power movements from an early stage. So far, however, in spite of occasional tensions, there has not been a repetition of the same kind of split between Black men and white women that occurred in the nineteenth century. Within law, the relationship between racial discrimination and gender discrimination is particularly close.

4 See, e.g., A. Dworkin, *Right-Wing Women* (1983) 94-99; A. Lorde, 'Learning from the 60s', in *Sister Outsider* (1984) 134-44; Williams, 'Why Women's Liberation is Important to Black Women', in W. Martin (ed.), *The American Sisterhood* (1972) 176-77; Combahee River Collective, 'A Black Feminist Statement' in C. Moraga & G. Anzalúaa (eds), *This Bridge Called My Back* (1983) 210.

D. Major Statutory Provisions

1. The Equal Pay Act

Enacted in 1963 as part of the Fair Labour Standards Act, the Equal Pay Act forbids sex discrimination in wages on the basis that such discrimination constitutes an unfair method of competition. To state a claim under the Equal Pay Act, an employee must prove that she (or he) is paid wages at a lesser rate than 'employees of the opposite sex' in the same establishment when such employees are doing 'equal' work, which requires 'equal skill, effort and responsibility' and is done under 'similar working conditions.'

A statute such as the Equal Pay Act, which is relatively limited in scope and effect, is among the easiest sex discrimination laws to enact. Male workers have long supported equal pay for equal work in order to prevent employers from exploiting women's weaker bargaining position to depress wage rates, thus perhaps affecting the men directly by depressing their own wage rates. In the nineteenth and early twentieth centuries, a number of male unionists who were generally opposed to legislative protection supported equal pay legislation in the belief that it would exclude women from most jobs. These men believed that employers would not hire women if they had to pay them as much as they would have to pay a man doing the same work. While this motive may seem quite ungentlemanly, an equal pay requirement would certainly seem to be a less offensive method to try to exclude women than gender-specific 'protective' labour legislation designed to exclude rather than to protect. The women's movement in the United States has never raised the concern that equal pay legislation will exclude women from jobs, although many in the movement express the fear that any employment benefit that might increase the cost of employing women is all too likely to be used to exclude them.

The Equal Pay Act is limited to pay discrepancy for equal work, and to state a claim a woman must find a man receiving a higher wage for essentially the same work with whom she can compare herself. Different work shifts could constitute different working conditions, relieving the employer of the equal pay requirement, unless the employer itself has in its own job classification treated the shifts as comparable. Similarly, if departments are sex-segregated and women workers in the department employing women are paid less than men in the department employing men, the act may be found to be violated, as long as the work is 'equal' and done under 'similar working conditions.'

Under the Equal Pay Act, once the plaintiff has established a prima facie case, the burden of proof shifts to the employer to establish a defence by a preponderance of the evidence. A pay differential may be justified on the basis of quality or quantity of production, seniority, a merit system, or 'any other factor other than sex.' A merit pay differential that favours male employees must not, however, be a mere subterfuge. Although a 'factor other than sex' is a broad catch-all, it does not include, for example, labour market conditions that depress women's wages. Employers have argued unsuccessfully that women's willingness to work for lower wages is a 'factor other than sex,' and courts have rejected employers' efforts to justify higher wages for men on the basis that the employer has to pay men more than women to get them to accept the job. Although a 'factor other than sex' must be more than a mere pretext, subjective evaluations of expected performance and other factors, such as prior salary, which are often themselves based on sex discrimination, have been allowed as defences.

2. Title VII of the Civil Rights Act

The most important anti-discrimination provision in United States law is Title VII of the Civil Rights Act of 1964. Unlike the Equal Pay Act, which deals with one particular form of sex discrimination, the Civil Rights Act deals primarily with racial discrimination. The Civil Rights Act of 1964 was enacted after years of growth in the Civil Rights Movement, a particularly persistent and effective social agitation by Blacks and supporters from all races. A massive movement involving protest marches, lawsuits and civil disobedience laid the foundation for the Civil Rights Act. Moreover, in the early 1960s the Black Nationalist movement was capturing the imagination of growing numbers of young people with talk of Black Power and self defence. Many whites felt threatened by this movement and feared it might lead Blacks to respond in kind to white violence, whereas a policy of non-violent resistance to white violence had dominated the Civil Rights Movement. All these factors contributed to the climate in which major civil rights legislation could be enacted. On one hand, the Civil Rights Act was supported by people who hoped to use it to promote racial justice. On the other hand, it was also supported by some people who hoped it would help to keep the ongoing social conflict within the confines of the law and minimize further unrest.

The story of how sex came to be added to the Civil Rights Bill as a forbidden basis of discrimination presents an interesting counterpoint to the story of how disputes over the voting rights amendment after the Civil War caused a split between supporters of racial justice and of gender justice. It also provides a classic example of the problems one can have determining legislative intent. The Civil Rights Act was originally drafted to protect against discrimination on the basis of race, colour, religion or national origin, without any reference to sex or gender as a protected class. After it had gone through the process of committee hearings and two days before Title VII of the Civil Rights Act was finally approved, a legislator who vigorously opposed the Civil Rights Act introduced the amendment that added 'sex' to the list of race, colour, religion and national origin, and thus forbad sex discrimination in employment. Earlier efforts, perhaps sincere, to add sex as a protected classification to other sections of the Act had consistently been rejected. Thus, many assume that the actual reason the amendment was proposed by such an opponent of the entire Civil Rights Bill, was that he hoped thus to sabotage the enactment of the Bill, believing that supporters of civil rights would rather give up having a law against race discrimination than give up the practice of sex discrimination. Yet, the Bill did pass, and it is likely that a significant number of the people who voted in favour of the amendment that added sex as a protected classification actually intended to end sex discrimination (or at least to place the question of sex discrimination before the courts and channel social disputes about such discrimination into the legal arena). A further amendment to modify the prohibition of sex discrimination to discrimination 'solely' on the basis of sex was defeated.[5] If the Bill's opponent in fact did support sex discrimination and was simply trying to defeat the Bill by the addition of sex as a protected class, his effort certainly backfired. Title VII of the Civil Rights Act of 1964 has become the most effective provision in United States law against sex discrimination in employment. It has also provided the foundation for sexual harassment law in the United States.

Title VII of the Civil Rights Act forbids covered employers from discriminating against any individual with respect to the terms, conditions or privileges of employment, hiring or firing or wages, on the basis of sex (or race, nationality, etc.). It has been interpreted to apply also to job advertisements, employment interview practices, working atmosphere, lay-offs or redundancies, post-employment references, and so forth. Most businesses that employ fifteen or more workers, including part-time workers, are covered by the Act, except Congress itself, Indian tribes and various tax-exempt clubs and religious groups. The Act covers foreign firms operating in the United States and protects aliens employed in the United States. One major loophole, however, is that the Act allows preference to be given in employment to military veterans, in spite of the long history of racial discrimination in the US military and its longer-lasting history of sex discrimination.

Under Title VII, a plaintiff states a prima facie case of sex discrimination if she can show that she was treated worse with regard to employment 'because of ... sex.' This includes both intentional discrimination (disparate treatment) and unintentional discrimination, both discrimination that is based on policies or employer classifications that make explicit reference to

5 For a nice, brief summary of this legislative history, see C. Thomas, *Sex Discrimination in a Nutshell* (2d ed. 1991) 217. This book, published by West Publishing Company, provides one of the best summaries I have ever seen of United States sex discrimination law.

gender and discrimination based on policies which, while gender-neutral in form, are gender-specific in impact (disparate impact).

Where the plaintiff establishes her prima facie case of disparate treatment by the preponderance of the evidence (and the fact-finder is allowed to infer unlawful discrimination from evidence that a woman, though qualified for a job, was not hired) the burden shifts to the defendant. The courts have held that once a prima facie case of discriminatory failure to hire has been made out under Title VII, the employer must 'articulate some legitimate, non-discriminatory reason' for not hiring the plaintiff. The employer does not, however, have the burden of proving that this non-discriminatory reason was the actual reason for the employment decision. The burden remains on the plaintiff, and she must try to show that the employer's articulated legitimate reason was merely a pretext for discrimination or at least that it is more likely than not that the actual motive of the employer was discriminatory.

The classic cases of disparate impact in the area of sex discrimination involve weight and height restrictions. An employer which hires only applicants six feet or taller is not making an explicit sex classification, yet could achieve a highly gender-skewed work force. Thus, unless the employer can show some business necessity for such a requirement, the employer would be found to discriminate on the basis of sex. More complicated are cases in which the practice or practices which have a disparate impact on women involve subjective personnel judgments or the exercise of employer discretion. In theory, proof of disparate impact of such decisions will establish a prima facie case of sex discrimination; in practice, such cases are generally not successful.

The affirmative defences available to the employer include both statutory defences and judicially created defences. First, the same defences available to employers under the Equal Pay Act are also available under Title VII. The burden of proof, however, remains on the plaintiff in Title VII; it does not switch to the defendant, as it does under the Equal Pay Act. Litigation has established that employers may use a seniority system that perpetuates past discrimination as long as it is facially gender neutral and can be said to be bone fide seniority system. In addition, Title VII provides as an affirmative defence to charges of discriminatory hiring or job assignment that sex is a 'bona fide occupational qualification [(BFOQ)] reasonably necessary to the normal operation' of the employer's particular business. Although such an exception could have destroyed the effectiveness of the act if courts interpreted it broadly, in most cases courts have kept the defence tolerably narrow. For example, courts have found it not to be a BFOQ that a state labour law forbids women from performing aspects of the job or limits the hours women may work at the job. Most such legislation has been ruled invalid under Title VII. Courts rejected efforts by employers to defend on the basis of BFOQ their refusal to hire women with pre-school age children. Similarly defeated were efforts by airlines to justify as BFOQ's, based on claims of customer preference, their refusal to hire male flight attendants or their requirement that female flight attendants retire at age 40. The BFOQ exception also cannot be used to exclude all women of child-bearing age from jobs suspected of endangering foetuses. The defence of BFOQ has, however, been accepted in a few cases in which it should not have been. For instance, a non-profit 'girls club' was allowed to fire an unmarried pregnant employee on the basis that in the particular narrow circumstances of the case, being a role model for girls in danger of unwed pregnancy could be considered a BFOQ.[6] In *Dothard* v. *Rawlinson*,[7] the United States Supreme Court allowed a prison to consider sex a BFOQ since the possibility that inmates might rape women guards would create a security problem for the prison. The Court emphasized that it was not paternalistically protecting the women job applicants, who could choose to take the employment risks they wished, but rather protecting prison security, because women were uniquely susceptible to rape. This decision perniciously reinforces the notion that the mere presence of women leads to rape. Women as prison guards, however, are safer than women on the street. What is particularly odd about the Court opinion is that of all places in America, jails are most associated with the rape of males (usually explained by the relative absence of women, whom men usually prefer to victimize). In a less clear-cut case, a hospital upheld its policy requiring female nurses in labour and delivery rooms on BFOQ grounds in the interest of privacy and the prevention of sexual abuse of female patients by male nurses. It seems to be a problem that sexual abuse is too readily accepted as an inevitable, perhaps even normal, aspect of any interaction between women and men in a setting in which sexual abuse might be possible. Sexual abuse certainly should be stopped, and it is important for courts to recognize that sexual abuse is a serious and pervasive problem. Yet one might hope that effective means could be found for stopping sexual abuse without placing unreasonable limits on the employment opportunities of innocent people; however, in barring the men nurses in this situation instead of the women guards in the other situation the court may at least be moving marginally in the right direction.

Courts created the affirmative defences of legitimate, non-discriminatory reason to claims of disparate treatment and of business necessity for disparate impact claims.

6 *Chambers* v. *Omaha Girls Club*, 629 F.Supp. 925 (D.Neb. 1986), aff'd, 834 F.2d 697 (8th Cir. 1987), reh'g denied, 840 F.2d 583 (1988); Austin, 'Sapphire Bound!', 1989 *Wisc. L. Rev.* 539.

7 433 US 321 (1977).

3. The Pregnancy Discrimination Act

The Pregnancy Discrimination Act of 1978 was enacted by Congress in response to a major lobbying effort to overturn a Court decision denying that discrimination based on pregnancy was discrimination 'because of ... sex.' Some years before, women had sued under Title VII to establish that an employment disability insurance program that covered virtually every medical condition that might disable a worker except pregnancy was a form of sex discrimination. A majority of the Supreme Court held that although only women were affected by it, not all women were affected and the exclusion was thus not gender-based.[8] Women and male supporters responded by deriding the decision and drafting legislation that would in effect overturn it. The legislation simply provided that discrimination based on pregnancy was sex discrimination and required employers to treat pregnancy like any other temporary disability. To facilitate the quick passage of the bill, its drafters excluded from its operation medical expenses in connection with abortion (unless necessary to save a woman's life), because the issue of abortion funding was considered too controversial (just as women's vote was considered too controversial in the middle of the nineteenth century).

After the enactment of the Pregnancy Discrimination Act, courts quickly established that if the employer provides disability expenses for employee spouses, male employees are entitled to coverage for their wives' pregnancy expenses.[9] It was considerably more controversial whether state laws could legally require employers to grant benefits for pregnancy that they did not grant equally to similarly 'disabled' employees. Because of the history of misuse of protective legislation to exclude women from particular jobs, a number of women's groups argued that the Pregnancy Discrimination Act should and did forbid any treatment of pregnancy that was not matched by identical treatment of any comparable disability that might afflict men. Other women believed that this position represented the 'use of a male model' run amuck. The Supreme Court eventually ruled in favour of treating the Pregnancy Discrimination Act as a floor, not a ceiling.[10] Thus state laws could treat pregnancy better than disabilities but could not treat it worse.

8 *General Electric* v. *Gilbert*, 429 US 125 (1976). See also *Geduldig* v. *Aiello*, 417 US 484 (1974) (pregnancy discrimination found not to violate fourteenth amendment).

9 *Newport News Shipbuilding and Dry Dock Co.* v. *EEOC*, 462 US 669 (1983).

10 *California Federal Sav. and Loan Ass'n* v. *Guerra*, 479 US 272 (1987).

E. Changing Role of Courts

1. Civil Rights

The United States Supreme Court's *Dred Scott Decision*,[11] upholding the Fugitive Slave Law, which required Northerners to return to slavery Black people who had successfully escaped from slavery in the South, was believed by many to be responsible for the American Civil War. It was not the Court's proudest moment, holding that Black people had no rights recognized by the Constitution. Nor did its decisions following the Civil War do much to redeem the Court. The Supreme Court gutted civil rights legislation enacted at the end of the war and refused to protect Blacks from the terrorism inflicted upon them. Especially in the South, terrorism was used by whites to subordinate and exploit the former slaves and their children and to prevent Black men from exercising their constitutional right to vote.

At the end of the nineteenth century, the Supreme Court decided *Plessy* v. *Ferguson*,[12] which upheld as constitutional so-called Jim Crow laws, state statutes and local ordinances which required segregation of Black people (defined in a racist manner to include virtually anyone who did not appear to be 'pure' white) in schools, public accommodations, and eventually virtually anywhere except where it served white interests for Blacks to be. The *Plessy* v. *Ferguson* case introduced into American constitutional law the infamous 'separate but equal' doctrine. The Court held that the Constitution was satisfied when separate accommodations were provided for people of different races, and that if Black people chose to view this segregation as a sign of their inferiority, that was their problem. And the Court accepted as 'equal' accommodations that were in virtually every regard inferior to the accommodations provided for whites. The 'separate but equal' doctrine was overturned in 1954 in the famous school desegregation case *Brown* v. *Board of Education*.[13] *Brown* was the culmination of a series of cases brought by the National Association for the Advancement of Coloured People (NAACP), in one of the most far-reaching and carefully planned-out litigation strategies in American legal history. Before *Brown*, the NAACP brought a case, for example, requiring a state law school to admit a Black student when there was no other law school in the state, and thus when it would be very hard to justify the student's exclusion even under the 'separate but equal' doctrine of *Plessy* v. *Ferguson*. The basic strategy was to start with the most sympathetic and 'easiest' cases to win and then proceed step by step to harder cases, each subsequent case requiring the

11 *Dred Scott* v. *Sandford*, 60 US 393 (1856).
12 163 US 537 (1896).
13 347 US 483 (1954).

Court to go just one step further.[14] The success of a litigation strategy that *Brown* v. *Board of Education* represented encouraged the Civil Rights Movement and later the women's movement to use the courts as part of their overall efforts at social change. In many ways, this was a significant break from the past, in which courts had often been seen as opponents of social change and as potentially an impediment to legislative reform. Until President Franklin D. Roosevelt, before the Second World War, threatened to 'pack' the Supreme Court by expanding its size and appointing sympathetic judges, the Court had invalidated as unconstitutional major portions of his 'New Deal' reform legislation. This judicial activism was a continuation of a process that had gone on for decades, in which courts had used the constitutional guarantee of 'due process' to invalidate most efforts at economic reform through legislation. For example, when workers were able to get state legislatures to enact labour protection, employers would turn to the courts and usually get the provision declared unconstitutional. This 'judicial activism' protected the status quo for the wealthy against the efforts of the less wealthy to bring about democratic reforms that would somewhat limit the power that property ownership gave to the owners to control the lives of others. 'Judicial activism' was condemned by many supporters of labour as elitist and undemocratic.

In the years after *Brown* v. *Board of Education,* a new form of 'judicial activism' developed. The Supreme Court (known as 'the Warren Court' after the Chief Justice, Earl Warren) interpreted the Constitution to protect the rights of citizens of minority races and women, who though numerically superior to men were politically relatively powerless. It became the turn of the conservatives to condemn 'judicial activism.' Although the charge of 'elitism' rang somewhat hollow, the Court was charged with being anti-democratic. It seems likely that during the next few years another switch will take place. Although conservatives still pay lip service to the value of 'strict constructionism' (often posed as the opposite of 'judicial activism') the once again conservative Supreme Court has in fact begun making quite a number of conservative decisions employing 'judicial activism.' One of the most interesting obvious examples is in the retreats made in Civil Rights, the precise field in which the Warren Court first came to be noted for its 'judicial activism.' There are strong arguments that the Court now ignores precedent (*stare decisis*) and apparent Congressional intent to reach the decision the Court's conservatives believe to be good social policy.[15]

14 See generally M. Tushnet, *The NAACP's Legal Strategy against Segregated Education,* (1987) 105-66; R. Kluger, *Simple Justice: The History of Brown* v. *Board of Education and Black America's Struggle for Equality* (1977).

15 See Kairys, 'Conservative Legal Thought Revisited (Book Review)', 91 *Colum. L. Rev.* (1991) 1847; Henderson, 'Authoritarianism and the Rule of Law', 66 *Ind. L. Rev.* (1991) 378, 434-47; Chang, 'Discriminatory Impact, Affirmative Action, and Innocent Victims: Judicial Conservativism or Conservative Justices?', 91 *Colum. L. Rev.* (1991) 790.

2. Women's Rights

The most famous nineteenth century case denying women rights was *Bradwell* v. *Illinois,*[16] the 1873 case upholding the refusal of the Supreme Court of Illinois to admit Myra Bradwell to the practice of law. Ms Bradwell, the editor of a major legal newspaper, was in every way qualified, except her gender. A concurring opinion by Justice Bradley is better known than the majority opinion (a somewhat technical and boring application of the decision of the *Slaughter-House Cases*[17] about the meaning of the 'privileges and immunities' clause of the fourteenth amendment, decided shortly before *Bradwell*). Bradley (who had dissented from the *Slaughter-House Cases* decision) argued that there was a 'wide difference in the respective spheres and destinies of man and woman' and that women's 'natural and proper timidity and delicacy ... unfits [the female sex] for many of the occupations of civil life.' He went on: 'The harmony, not to say identity, of interests and views which belong, or should belong, to the family institution is repugnant to the idea of woman adopting a distinct and independent career from that of her husband... The paramount destiny and mission of woman are to fulfil the noble and benign offices of wife and mother. This is the law of the Creator.'[18] Of course, by the time the *Bradwell* case was decided, the State of Illinois had already enacted legislation specifically authorizing women to engage in virtually all the 'occupations of civil life' and to adopt exactly such a 'distinct and independent career' as Justice Bradley considered 'repugnant.' Less than two months after the *Bradwell* case reaffirmed the Illinois Supreme Court's refusal to admit women, the first woman was admitted to practice in Illinois.

Muller v. *Oregon,*[19] a 1908 Supreme Court decision which also enjoys a prominent position in women's Rogue's Gallery of cases, was a politically complicated case. It was the case which upheld protective labour legislation limited to women, just three years after the Court had condemned protective labour legislation as paternalistic and a violation of workers' and employers' right to contract in *Lochner* v. *New York,*[20] a case involving legislation that was not gender-specific. *Muller* v. *Oregon* is properly criticized for its blatant sexism and offensive stereotyping. Yet, the case is also more complicated. On one hand, it was supported by liberals as part of the attack on the laissez-faire policies associated with the *Lochner* case and upon the *Lochner* case itself. *Muller* admitted what *Lochner* had tried

16 83 US (16 Wall.) 130 (1873).

17 83 US (16 Wall.) 36 (1873). For my extended discussion of these cases, see Olsen, 'From False Paternalism to False Equality: Judicial Assaults on Feminist Community, Illinois 1869-1895', 84 *Michigan Law Review* (1986) 1518, 1523-29.

18 *Supra* note 16, at 141.

19 208 US 412 (1908).

20 198 US 45 (1905).

to deny – that protective labour legislation can benefit workers and society. The Oregon legislation upheld in *Muller* directly benefitted many of the most exploited women by undermining employers' autocratic power and improving work conditions. On the other hand, *Muller* not only undermined women's equality, but paradoxically it also offered support for *Lochner*'s free-market principles by carving out a limited exception based on a view of women's physical weakness and family role. This limited exception both relieved some of the pressure for broader reforms and, by linking the need for protective labour legislation to women's frailty, offered ideological support for the notion that protective labour legislation was unmanly. Moreover, it provided a legal basis for gender-specific labour legislation which was protective in form but actually simply excluded women from relatively desirable jobs, often deliberately. Such legislation was not generally abolished until it was pre-empted by the federal anti-discrimination law, Title VII of the Civil Rights Act of 1964.

The Warren Court did not significantly improve the law of gender discrimination. As late as 1961 the Court continued to appeal to women's family role to justify discriminatory treatment. In *Hoyt* v. *Florida*[21] the Supreme Court upheld a provision in the State of Florida that automatically called men to serve jury duty but excluded women from jury service unless they volunteered. The Court justified the difference in treatment on the basis that women were 'still regarded as the center of home and family life.'[22] Thus, a woman convicted by an all-male jury of murdering her husband was found not to have been denied equal protection. (Ironically, some fourteen years later the Supreme Court overturned a nearly identical statute limiting women's jury service in Louisiana at the behest of a man charged with kidnapping and raping a woman.[23] The Court based its later decision on the Sixth Amendment right to a jury trial, rather than on equal protection.)

The first significant change in the Court's approach to gender discrimination came in 1971, after the retirement of Chief Justice Earl Warren, in *Reed* v. *Reed*.[24] The case arose when the mother of a deceased child objected to the gender-based statutory preference given to the child's father to be named executor under the Utah state law. Although the Supreme Court seemed to apply the lenient 'rational basis' standard of review, it scrutinized the means and ends of the statute more closely than it previously had in deciding cases involving gender. The Court concluded that giving the kind of absolute preference on the basis of gender did not bear a rational relationship to the state objective of eliminating the need for a hearing and

21 368 US 57 (1961).
22 Ibid. at 62.
23 *Taylor* v. *Louisiana*, 419 US 522 (1975).
24 404 US 71 1971).

avoiding intrafamily controversy. The Court later conceded that the *Reed* opinion marked a departure from its 'traditional' rational basis analysis.[25]

Reed v. *Reed* marked the beginning of an improvement, but a qualified improvement, in Court opinions for women. In 1973, the Court upheld women's right to have an abortion, but it limited the right and based its decision on a right to privacy, seemingly ignoring the fact that anti-abortion laws implicate questions of sex discrimination.[26] In 1974 and 1976 the Court decided two cases involving pregnancy that women have criticized especially strongly. In *Geduldig* v. *Aiello*[27] the Court upheld as constitutional under the fourteenth amendment a state medical program that excluded pregnancy coverage, holding that the exclusion was rationally related to the purpose of saving money and that no more stringent standard of review was required because pregnancy is not gender based. That case was followed by *General Electric* v. *Gilbert*,[28] which repeated the reasoning that pregnancy discrimination was not sex discrimination, this time in the context of a Title VII challenge. According to the Court, the employment disability insurance program was based on a classification between pregnant persons and 'non-pregnant persons,' not between men and women.[29]

Because of a tradition in the United States of recognizing little public responsibility for the welfare of pregnant women or the costs of childbirth, women were probably correct to conclude that comparing pregnancy to a heart attack or an appendectomy would improve policies toward and treatment of pregnant women. Yet, there is something odd about referring to pregnancy as a disability. A more complicated reason for the choice of most women's organizations to analogize pregnancy to medical disabilities relates to the historical use of so-called protective labour legislation to exclude women from segments of the work force. Women in the United States have been particularly sensitive to the possible incentive to discriminate against women that might be provided by any kind of pregnancy benefits that would be paid for, directly or indirectly, by an employer. This sensitivity also points up the extent to which women recognize that the present laws forbidding such discrimination are not really effective. Employers often encourage this fear by emphasizing how terribly inconvenient to them even limited right-to-leave-and-return protection for pregnant women would be.

25 *Frontiero* v. *Richardson*, 411 US 677 (1973).
26 *Roe* v. *Wade*, 410 US 113 (1973).
27 417 US 484 (1974).
28 429 US 125 (1976).
29 Ibid.

Unpaid pregnancy leave was at issue in the 1987 case *California Federal* v. *Guerra.*[30] The employer challenged a law of the State of California requiring most employers to grant unpaid pregnancy leave to their employees. The employer argued that the law discriminated unlawfully in favour of women and conflicted with the Pregnancy Discrimination Act of 1978 insofar as it required such leave for pregnant employees but not for workers suffering disabilities unrelated to pregnancy. The case evoked a good deal of controversy among feminists because the pregnancy leave provision seemed to some to violate certain notions of (formal) equal treatment and because of fear that such 'special treatment' of women would be detrimental in the long run. The Court upheld the California law in a much-praised opinion by Justice Marshall, who had as a lawyer played a particularly active role in the NAACP Civil Rights litigation. Interestingly, the same employers who bemoan the terrible disruption that will or would be caused by a requirement that they keep jobs open during pregnancy leave have rarely complained about a requirement to keep jobs open for men called into the military. Many employers hint that a pregnancy leave requirement will make discrimination against women of child-bearing age irresistible, yet during the years when only males were called into the military and women were not entitled to pregnancy leave, none of these employers seemed tempted to discriminate against men to avoid the disruption that might be caused when the men were called into the military. It is beside the point that wars seem beyond the control of individual workers. Indeed, such a call up would seem to be considerably more disruptive than the generally spaced and relatively predictable pregnancies of female workers. One aspect of sexism against women is the greater understanding many men instinctively show toward concerns that directly affect them or situations that they could imagine themselves in – like being called up for war – as opposed to being pregnant.

Craig v. *Boren,*[31] a 1976 case, established an 'intermediate' standard of review, stricter than 'rational basis' but less strict than 'strict scrutiny,' for analyzing the constitutionality of gender discrimination. Under this 'intermediate standard,' the Court asks whether a gender classification serves 'important governmental objectives' and whether the classification is 'substantially related to the achievement of those objectives.'[32] Like many of the successful sex discrimination cases, *Craig* v. *Boren* was a case brought by a male alleging that the law in question, here a different drinking age, 18 for females and 21 for males, unconstitutionally denied him equal protection of the laws. Many women supported these male-plaintiff cases as an effective way to expose the discrimination against women and

30 479 US 272 (1987).
31 429 US 190 (1976).
32 Ibid.

men embedded in the law and to dismantle the gender role stereotypes that the discrimination reflected and supported. It also reinforced the message presented by some segments of the women's movement that men too stood to benefit from ending the discrimination against women. A question that has not yet been answered, however, is whether women really did also benefit from the male-plaintiff cases. The mere fact that women as a group are more harmed than men as a group by gender specific laws and policies does not necessarily mean that women will benefit from each and every move toward gender neutrality or that moves toward gender neutrality that benefit men will necessarily be followed by further moves toward gender neutrality that will benefit women. Perhaps it should be seen as a strong demonstration of the extent of male domination that men can take advantage more effectively than women of anything society has to offer, even policies against sex discrimination.

Under the intermediate standard of review, courts are to ask whether a gender classification 'serve[s] important governmental objectives' and whether the classification is 'substantially related to the achievement of those objectives.'[33] Under this standard of review, the Court invalidated a provision of Mississippi University for Women, a public nursing school, that males could audit classes but not receive a diploma. Noting that women constitute 98% of the nursing profession and arguing that the exclusion of males tended 'to perpetuate the stereotyped view of nursing as an exclusively woman's job,' the Court found that the gender classification was not substantially related to an important governmental objective.[34] Thus gender is treated somewhat differently than race. Court decisions and statutory enactments have worked together to shape antidiscrimination law in the United States.

III. Employment Discrimination: European Community Law

A. Treaty Provisions and Directives

1. Treaty of Rome, Article 119

The Treaty of Rome, the founding instrument of the European Economic Community, provides in Article 119 that 'each Member State shall ... ensure and ... maintain the application of the principle that men and women should receive equal pay for equal work.' It requires specifically that piece work rates paid to men and to women 'for the same work' have to be calcu-

33 Ibid.
34 *Mississippi University for Women* v. *Hogan*, 458 US 718 (1982).

lated on the same unit of measurement, and that pay at time rates for men and women have to be 'the same for the same job.' 'Pay' is defined broadly to include in addition to the basic wage or salary 'any other consideration, whether in cash or in kind, which the worker receives, directly or indirectly, in respect of his employment from his employer.' The reason generally given for the inclusion of this provision was the fear by the French that they might otherwise be put at a competitive disadvantage *vis-à-vis* their community partners because French national legislation already required equal pay for equal work. This is the same kind of economic justification later used by the United States in the Equal Pay Act of 1963, which treated the practice of paying women lower wages for the same work men did to be an unfair method of competition. The economic problem is more pronounced in the case of the Common Market: if only a few of the trading partners required equal pay for equal work, it could distort competition in the Member States. For example, if employers in other countries could pay their women workers lower wages, they could produce at lower costs than French employers.

The Treaty of Rome required Member States to implement the equal pay provisions of Article 119 by 1 January 1962. Although some states did comply, at least on a formal level, many others did not. Two days before the deadline for compliance, and without going through the procedures necessary to amend the Treaty of Rome, the Member States adopted a Resolution purporting to delay the implementation of Article 119 and providing that by 31 December, 1964, both direct and indirect discrimination should be eliminated. Several Member States failed to observe even this later implementation date, and the European Commission eventually, by 1973, threatened to use its power under Article 169 to bring an enforcement action before the European Court of Justice.

2. Equal Pay Directive of 1975

In 1975 a Directive on Equal Pay was adopted defining 'the principle of equal pay' to be 'for the same work or for work to which equal value is attributed, the elimination of all discrimination on grounds of sex with regard to all aspects and conditions of remuneration.'[35].

The Equal Pay Directive of 1975 was enacted by the Council of the European Communities on the basis of Article 100 of the Treaty of Rome, which empowers the Council, acting unanimously on a proposal from the European Commission, to issue such directives in order to approximate the laws, regulations and administrative actions of Member States that 'directly affect the establishment or functioning of the common market.'

35 Article 1 EEC Council Directive 75/117, OJ 1975 L 45/19.

One reason the Council acted was 'to hasten the full implementation of Article 119',[36] which several Member States had still, by 1975, failed to implement. While Article 119 of the Treaty of Rome spoke in terms of 'equal work,' the 'same work,' and the 'same job,' the language of the Equal Pay Directive went further by adopting the language of the ILO Convention on Equal Remuneration. Article 1 of the Directive provided that 'for the same work *or for work to which equal value is attributed*'[37] there should be no 'discrimination on grounds of sex with regard to all aspects and conditions of remuneration' and that 'where a job classification system is used for determining pay, it must be based on the same criteria for both men and women and so drawn up as to exclude any discrimination on the grounds of sex.'

Article 2 requires Member States to enable wronged employees to pursue individual claims 'by judicial process after possible recourse to other competent authorities,' and Article 5 requires Member States to provide to employees who make complaints protection against retaliatory dismissal by their employers. Article 3 requires Member States to abolish all pay discrimination between men and women 'arising from laws, regulations or administrative provisions,' and Article 4 to ensure that discriminatory provisions appearing in 'collective agreements, wage scales, wage agreements or individual contracts of employment' be voided or amended. Member States are required by Article 6 to 'take the measures necessary' and 'see that effective means are available' to ensure the principle of equal pay. Finally, the Directive gave Member States one year to comply and required them to notify the Commission of what 'laws, regulations and administrative provisions' they had adopted to comply with the Directive; to make these laws, regulations and administrative provisions known to employees in their countries; and to report back to the Commission in three years' time.

3. Equal Treatment Directive of 1976

The Equal Treatment Directive[38] requires that men and women be treated equally 'as regards access to employment, including promotion, and to vocational training and as regards working conditions'[39] and regarding dismissal.[40] The Directive, which clearly goes beyond Article 119, finds its legal basis in Article 235 – the 'necessary and proper clause' – of the Treaty

36 Case 43/75, *Gabrielle Defrenne* v. *Société Anonyme Belge de Navigation Aérienne Sabena*, [1976] ECR 455 at 478, para. 53.
37 EEC Council Directive 75/117, OJ 1975 L 45/19 (emphasis added).
38 EEC Council Directive 76/207, OJ 1976 L 39/40.
39 Ibid., Article 1(1).
40 Ibid., Article 5.

of Rome, which empowers the Council to take additional measures that it deems necessary to attain the objectives of the Community beyond those powers otherwise provided for in the Treaty of Rome.

The Directive covers both public and private sectors of employment and includes as discrimination distinctions based on family status. '[T]here shall be no discrimination whatsoever on grounds of sex either directly or indirectly by reference in particular to marital or family status.'[41] Article 2 also provides that the Directive will be 'without prejudice to' provisions protecting women 'particularly as regards pregnancy and maternity'.[42] The Directive makes an exception and allows discrimination with respect to 'those occupational activities ... for which, by reason of their nature or the context in which they are carried out, the sex of the worker constitutes a determining factor.'[43] In Article 9(2), however, the Directive requires Member States 'periodically [to] assess the occupational activities' excepted from the equal treatment principle 'to decide, in the light of social developments, whether there is justification for maintaining the exclusions concerned' and to notify the Commission of the results of their assessment. Articles 3(2) and 5(2), which require Member States to revise laws and collective agreements that are contrary to the principle of equal treatment, each state in a subparagraph (c) that protective exceptions to the equal treatment principle be abolished 'when the concern for protection that originally inspired them is no longer well founded.' Article 2(4) also provides that the Directive will be 'without prejudice to measures to promote equal opportunity for men and women, in particular removing existing inequalities which affect women's opportunities...' In Article 6, the Directive requires Member States to introduce into their legal system remedies for persons wronged by the failure to provide equal treatment, and Article 7 requires Member States to protect employees who lodge complaints against retaliatory dismissal. Finally, the Directive gave Member States 30 months to comply with most provisions, 4 years to assess and abolish unnecessary discriminatory protective measures, and as in the equal pay Directive, required Member States to notify the Commission of what 'laws, regulations and administrative provisions' they had adopted to comply with the Directive; to bring these laws, regulations and administrative provisions to the attention of employees in their countries; and to report back to the Commission within two years after the 30-month implementation period.

41 Ibid., Article 2(1).
42 Ibid., Article 2(3).
43 Ibid., Article 2(2).

4. The Social Security Directives of 1978, 1986

Also important, though less within the scope of the present work, are two Directives on discrimination in Social Security, one enacted in 1978, which came into force in December 1984,[44] and the other in 1986, to come into force in 1993.[45] These Directives generally forbid discrimination based on sex, but make certain exceptions. The portion of these Directives that are important to this study are the provisions allowing Member States for the time being to exclude from their scope the 'determination of pensionable age for the purpose of granting old-age and retirement pensions'[46] and the possible implication for or consequences thereof to 'other benefits.'[47] As in the 1976 Equal Treatment Directive, the Member States are to 'periodically examine' their exclusions 'to ascertain, in the light of social developments ... whether there is justification for maintaining the exclusions concerned.'[48]

B. The Work of the European Court

The European Court of Justice, in Luxembourg, has jurisdiction *inter alia* to resolve disputes concerning the meaning of Articles of the Treaty of Rome and of so-called 'secondary Community Law' (regulations, directives, etc.). Issues involving sex discrimination reach the European Court of Justice through several different routes. First, officials of the Community may sue organs of the EEC if the organs fail themselves to uphold the anti-discrimination principles of the Community. More importantly, Article 177 of the Treaty of Rome authorizes national tribunals, including a country's lower courts, to apply to the European Court of Justice for rulings on the proper interpretation of Community Law where such a ruling might be relevant to cases before the national tribunal. If the proper interpretation of Community Law may be relevant to a case before a country's highest court, or before any national court or tribunal from which no further appeal is allowed, that national court or tribunal is obliged to apply to the European Court of Justice for such a ruling on the proper interpretation of European law. A third source of cases is actions brought by the European Commission against Member States for infringement of Community Law, as provided for in Article 169 of the Treaty of Rome.

Among the first sex discrimination cases the European Court of Justice decided were actions brought by officials of the Community under Article 179 of the Treaty of Rome. Women employees of the European Parliament

44 EEC Council Directive 79/7, OJ 1979 L 6/24.
45 EEC Council Directive 86/378, OJ 1986 L 225/40.
46 *Supra* note 44, at Art. 7(1)(a).
47 *Supra* note 45, at Art. 9(a).
48 *Supra* note 44, at Art. 7(2).

complained to the Court, in its capacity of an administrative tribunal, that they were denied expatriation allowances on the basis that their marriages terminated their status of expatriate because they did not, in the words of the Staff Regulations 'become the head of the family.' The expatriation allowances of most men would continue upon their marriages. The Court ruled that under the circumstances, the employer's decision to terminate the expatriate status of the complainants was illegal because it had not been made 'on uniform criteria, irrespective of sex.'[49]

The first lawsuit to result in a Court of Justice decision on sex discrimination outside the staff context was an action by a Belgium woman, Gabrielle Defrenne, against the state for refusing her a pension.[50] She brought a series of cases that challenged the state-owned Sabena Airlines' treatment of its stewardesses and kept raising the issue of European Community Law. In the process of her appeals, she presented to the Court for the first time three basic issues that the Court has later had to deal with repeatedly.

In her various lawsuits she demonstrated that she was paid less than her male colleagues, was forced to retire under the employment policies of Sabena Airlines which required its female, but not its male, flight attendants to retire at age 40, and was denied a pension because the government pension program for civil aviation air crews excluded airline stewardesses. It was fortunate that the airline happened to employ male stewards to whom Defrenne could compare her situation. Otherwise, she would not have had an equal pay claim, and in 1971 when the case arose, most of the (primarily male) decision-makers might not have recognized the (now) obvious sex discrimination involved in the (implicit, if not explicit) notion that women cease to be valuable employees whenever they get old enough that their role as sex objects begins to decrease.

1. The First Defrenne Case: The Relationship Between Social Security and Employment Discrimination

The first *Defrenne* case was her suit against the Belgium Government for refusing her a pension on the grounds of her sex. The Court easily dismissed her claim on the ground that Community Law at that time simply did not apply to pensions. The issue of what effects the permitted discrimination in social security matters, such as different pensionable ages, has or should have on employment discrimination generally has come before the Court on a number of further occasions.

49 Case 20/71, *Sabbatini-Bertoni* v. *European Parliament,* [1972] ECR 345; Case 32/71, *Chollet-Baudin* v. *Commission,* [1971] ECR 345; Case 21/74, *Airola* v. *Commission of the European Communities,* [1975] ECR 221.

50 Case 80/70, *Gabrielle Defrenne* v. *Belgium State,* [1971] ECR 445.

In *Worringham* v. *Lloyd's Bank*,[51] for example, an employer tried to use a discriminatory pension scheme that excluded women under 25 – and thus required no deductions from their salaries – as a justification for paying the men higher gross salaries than it paid the excluded women. The Court held that Article 119 was violated by the employer's policy of paying men a higher gross salary, even though their net salary would be equal to women's after deductions for retirement were made from men's wages but not from women's. The mere fact that discriminatory retirement programs might not violate the equal pay provisions (when they were state created, not completely the creation of the employer) did not mean that employers could pay men and women differently without violating Article 119. Women were prejudiced by the employer's procedure because the gross pay figure, lower for women, provided the basis for other salary-related benefits, such as unemployment benefits and credit facilities.

A similar issue of the relationship between social security and employment discrimination was raised in a factually more complex context in a 1982 case from The Netherlands. The *Liefting* case[52] involved the interpretation of the Equal Pay provisions. The Government of the Netherlands provided its civil servants with benefits for the spouse as well as the worker. The state was bound to pay the contributions on behalf of its employee, and it included the amount of these benefits in the calculation of the worker's gross salary. In the case of those civil servants who were married to a civil servant, the Government calculated the benefits in a sexually discriminatory manner. The husband and wife were treated as one person (in the finest Blackstonean tradition) and the contribution to the benefit scheme was based on their joint salaries. Where husband and wife were both civil servants, the benefits were paid primarily on behalf of the husband, and they were paid on behalf of the wife only insofar as the upper limit provided by law was not reached by the contributions made on behalf of the husband. Administrative convenience would seem to be the only justification for the practice, and since it had the same kind of negative effects on the actual pay (broadly defined) of women *vis-à-vis* men as in the case of *Worringham*,[53] the Court found it a violation of the Equal Pay provisions. This practice resulted in the women civil servants married to a civil servant receiving less gross salary than equivalent men. The practice had a variety of disadvantages for the women workers, in that it provided women with a lower salary for purposes of calculating a number of benefits that were salary linked.

51 Case 69/80, *Susan Jane Worringham and Margaret Humphreys* v. *Lloyd's Bank Ltd*, [1981] ECR 767.

52 Case 23/83, *W.G.M. Liefting and others* v. *Directie van het Academisch Ziekenhuis bij de Universiteit van Amsterdam*, [1984] ECR 3225.

53 *Supra* note 51.

In *Newstead*,[54] a 1987 case that arose in the United Kingdom, an unmarried man argued that the requirement that he contribute to a widow's pension fund as part of an occupational pension scheme while his female co-workers did not have to do so constituted sex discrimination in remuneration, although his payments would be returned, with 4% interest, upon his death or leaving employment still unmarried. The employee asserted that *Liefting* and *Worringham* had established that such disparities should be evaluated under the provisions of Article 119 of the Treaty of Rome. The Court easily distinguished between cases in which a social security deduction was used to try to justify a difference in the gross salaries of men and women, forbidden under Article 119, and the situation in *Newstead*, in which the gross salaries were identical but the provisions of a social security scheme, not covered by Article 119 and specifically exempted from the Equal Pay Directive, led to different net salaries for men and women.

The Court was asked for an opinion in a more complicated case involving voluntary redundancy benefits. In *Burton*,[55] the British Railway Board had made an agreement with the relevant unions for voluntary redundancy of workers five years before normal retirement age, in England 60 for women and 65 for men. A 58-year-old man, who was denied access to voluntary redundancy when, had he been a woman, he would have been granted it, complained to an Industrial Tribunal. He lost at the lower level and appealed to the Employment Appeal Tribunal, which referred to the European Court the question whether the agreement regarding voluntary redundancy violated the Equal Treatment Directive.

The Court concluded that the issue of conditions of access to voluntary redundancy benefits paid by an employer was covered by the Equal Treatment Directive, but that the scheme of the British Rail Board did not violate that Directive. The equal treatment principle of the 1976 Directive does not limit the rights of Member States to specify different retirement ages for men and women. The Court explained that Council Directive 79/7/EEC of 19 December 1978 on the progressive implementation of the principle of equal treatment for men and women in matters of social security provides that it is without prejudice to the right of Member States to exclude from the scope the determination of retirement age for purposes of old age benefits and the possible consequences thereof for other benefits.

Having held in *Burton* that basing access to voluntary redundancy upon pensionable age, when it was different for men and women, did not violate the Equal Treatment Directive, the Court decided in *Roberts*[56] that the Directive was also not violated by a plan for mass redundancy that granted

54 Case 192/85, *George Noel Newstead* v. *Department of Transport, and Her Majesty's Treasury*, [1987] ECR 4753.

55 Case 19/81, *Arthur Burton* v. *British Railways Board*, [1982] ECR 555.

56 Case 151/84, *Joan Roberts* v. *Tate & Lyle Industries Ltd*, [1986] ECR 703.

an early retirement pension to men and women based upon the single age of 55. In *Roberts*, the Court decided that a contractual provision was not discriminatory when it provided for a mass redundancy with an early retirement pension at a single age for men and women, although it was 10 years before normal retirement for men and only 5 years before normal retirement for women, as provided in the national pension provisions. Presumably the Court would have reached the same decision had the age of 60 been chosen, although that would have meant that only men and no women would be eligible for the benefit. Different retirement ages for men and women are allowed, but they are not encouraged. Although early retirement is often viewed as a special benefit for women, I have long suspected that men wanted an earlier retirement age for women so that their (often a few years younger) wives would not be working after they themselves retired. Not only did they want full-time care and companionship in their retirement, but they also did not want to start any bad habits of their working wives expecting an increased portion of housework to be done by their retired husbands.

On the same day that *Roberts* was decided, the Court also decided the *Marshall* case,[57] which involved a mandatory retirement scheme whereby women and men might be forced to retire upon reaching the pensionable age, 60 for women and 65 for men. The plaintiff complained that the state employer's policy of forcing retirement upon women at a younger age than men led to her earlier loss of work-satisfaction and to financial losses due to a shorter career span. The Court disapproved the policy, despite the employer's claim that it was basing the mandatory retirement upon pensionable age. The Court reaffirmed its characterization of the principle of equal treatment as of 'fundamental importance'[58] and insisted the Social Security Directive's allowance of different pensionable ages must be strictly interpreted. This opinion seems clearly correct. Whatever justification there may be for granting women earlier pensions than men, it would not justify an earlier forced retirement. It is somewhat difficult to justify any forced retirement, and a sexually discriminatory forced retirement is particularly unjust.

Beets-Proper,[59] raised essentially the same question in a case involving a private employer. There national legislation had been passed to implement the Equal Treatment Directive, and a court in the Netherlands asked for a preliminary ruling from the European Court on the question of how to interpret the Directive. The Court interpreted the Directive to require Member

57 Case 152/84, *M.H. Marshall* v. *Southampton and South West Hampshire Area Health Authority (Teaching)*, [1986] ECR 723.

58 Ibid., at 746, para. 36.

59 Case 262/84, *Vera Mia Beets-Proper* v. *F. van Lanschot Bankiers N.V.*, [1986] ECR 773.

States to forbid a term in employment contracts concerning termination of the contract on grounds of the age attained, where the condition related to the age at which the employee becomes eligible for a pension and would force women to retire earlier than men.

Thus, while the laws against employment discrimination do not prevent unequal treatment in social security, unequal treatment in social security cannot be piggy-backed into broadly unequal treatment in public or private employment.

2. The Second Defrenne Case: Direct Application of Community Law in the Courts of Member States

The second of Gabrielle Defrenne's cases to reach the European Court was the action against her employer. The important point established in this suit was that Article 119 was directly applicable in lawsuits within a Member State between an employee and employer, including a private employer. The *Defrenne II* case[60] held that domestic courts should apply Article 119 themselves in domestic suits.

Gabrielle Defrenne worked for Sabena Airlines from 1951 to 1968, when she was forced to retire (without a pension). During this time, she was paid less than male 'cabin stewards', which was permissible under Belgium law but which she asserted violated European law. Sabena Airlines admitted that its male 'cabin stewards' did the same work as its female air hostesses and that it paid its female employees less than its male employees for the same work. The only question was whether they could get away with it, insofar as Belgium, where the case arose, had failed to implement the provisions of Article 119 into its domestic law until late 1967, although Community Law required it to do so by 1 January 1962. The efforts the Member States had made at the end of December, 1961, to extend the deadline was without legal effect. The Court pointed out that Article 119 had a double aim – to avoid putting to a competitive disadvantage those countries that did provide equal pay for equal work, and to pursue the social objective of improving the living and working conditions of the people. It held that the principle of equal pay, with its economic and social objectives 'forms part of the foundations of the Community.'[61] That is why the Treaty required implementation by the end of the first stage of the transition

60 Case 43/75, *Gabrielle Defrenne* v. *Société Anonyme Belge de Navigation Aérienne Sabena* [1976] ECR 455.

61 Ibid., at 472, para. 12.

period, and why 'it is impossible to base any argument' on the delays due to 'dilatoriness and resistance'[62] in certain Member States. The Court established a distinction between on one hand 'direct and overt discrimination which may be identified solely with the aid of the criteria based on equal work and equal pay' and on the other hand 'indirect and disguised discrimination which can only be identified by reference to more explicit implementing provisions of a Community or national character.'[63] The Court suggested a broad understanding of indirect discrimination, including pay discrimination not only for the same work but within 'entire branches of industry and even of the economic system as a whole' which Community or national measures should properly try to eliminate. The Court asserted that the Equal Pay Directive had 'extend[ed] the narrow criterion of "equal work" [by adopting the International Labour Organization's] 'principle of equal pay for work "of equal value".'[64]

Recitals 21-24 of *Defrenne II* seemed to lay the foundation for a broad interpretation of Article 119. First, recital 21 provides that the forms of discrimination to which direct application should apply 'must ... include in particular those which have their origin in legislative provisions or in collective labour agreements'; and recital 23 seems to suggest that direct application should extend to any situation in which 'the Court is in a position to establish all the facts which enable it to decide whether a woman worker is receiving lower pay than a male worker performing the same tasks.' Recital 22 would seem to establish that direct application is not limited solely to 'cases where men and women receive unequal pay for equal work carried out in the same establishment or service, whether public or private', in that in such cases direct application 'applies even more'. Recital 24: 'In such a situation, at least, Article 119 is directly applicable and may thus give rise to individual rights which the courts must protect.' The only limiting language seems to occur in recital 21, which refers to discrimination 'which may be detected on the basis of a purely legal analysis of the situation.' There are aspects of the equal pay principle which do not have direct effect. Even with respect to these, however, the national legislatures did not retain exclusive regulatory powers, but rather Community and national measures together may implement equal pay. That would suggest that Community measures could be enacted which would then directly apply within the Member States.

The Court rejected arguments that there could be no direct effect because Article 119 referred expressly only to 'Member States.'[65] The Court argued that

62 Ibid., at 472, para. 14.
63 Ibid., at 473, para. 18 (emphasis added).
64 Ibid., at 473, para. 20.
65 Ibid., at 475, para. 30. Cf. *infra* at note 87.

> the fact that certain provisions of the Treaty are formally addressed to the Member States does not prevent rights from being conferred at the same time on any individual who has an interest in the performance of the duties thus laid down.[66]

The United Kingdom and Ireland submitted materials to the Commission in which they argued essentially that the equal pay principle had been so extensively violated after the date at which it was binding that the back claims of women who had been illegally underpaid could lead to multiple bankruptcies. The Court pointed out that the Commission's failure to take action against those Member States which delayed in implementing Article 119 may well have presented a misleading message to the employers violating the equal pay principle. The Court then remarked that '[i]n these circumstances, it is appropriate to determine that, as the general level at which pay would have been fixed cannot be known, important questions of legal certainty' make retroactive application of the direct effect 'impossible in principle.'[67] Although the Court may well be right that no one could now determine what salary levels would have been in the absence of sex discrimination, in most other contexts the Court has chosen to assume that the women's salaries would be raised to the level of the men's. It is probably more realistic to recognize that the employers who violated Article 119 probably did not keep all the profit from their violation, but paid their male employees some amount more than they otherwise would have. Yet, the original economic justification for the principle of equal pay is based on the assumption that employers who underpay women will produce goods cheaper, not that they will just pay their male workers more. As a result of

66 Ibid., at 475, para. 31. In 1967, when *Defrenne II* was decided, the Court was still flirting with the idea of directives, like the Treaty provisions themselves, having direct effect in the courts of Member States. Case 9/70, *Grad* v. *Finanzamt Traustein*, [1970] ECR 825, gave direct effect to the combination of a Treaty provision, two directives and a court decision; and Case 33/70, *SACE* v. *Italian Ministry of Finance*, [1970] ECR 1213, gave direct effect to a Treaty provision together with a directive. In 1977, in Case 51/76, *Verbond van Nederlandse Ondernemingen* v. *Inspecteur der Invoerrechten en Accijnzen*, [1977] ECR 113, the Court gave direct effect to a provision in a directive harmonizing turnover taxes, a directive made under the authority of Article 100, like the Equal Pay Directive. First in 1979 did the Court establish the distinction between direct effect against a Member State and direct effect against a third party. In Case 148/78, *Pubblico Ministero* v. *Ratti*, [1979] ECR 1629, the Court held that a 'Member State which has not adopted the implementing measures required by the directive in the prescribed periods may not rely, as against individuals, on its own failure to perform the obligations which the directive entails.' Ibid. at 1642. This holding was further clarified in Case 8/81, *Becker* v. *Finanzamt Münster-Innenstadt*, [1982] ECR 53:

> Thus, wherever the provisions of a directive appear, as far as their subject matter is concerned, to be unconditional and sufficiently precise, those provisions may, in the absence of implementing measures adopted within the prescribed period, be relied upon as against any national provision which is incompatible with the directive or in so far as the provisions define rights which individuals are able to assert against the State.

Ibid. at 71.

67 *Supra* note 60, at 481, para. 74.

the Court's ruling on retroactivity, discrimination in pay that was not forbidden by national law of the Member States is generally not actionable until after 1976, the date of the opinion. Nevertheless, for any workers who had already brought legal proceedings or made an equivalent claim, retroactive application would be provided. However realistic or practical the ruling on retroactivity may have seemed to the Court and to some observers, it may also be seen to treat Article 119 as insufficiently important and to discount the loss suffered by women in Member States which failed to implement the principle of equal pay. Moreover, the ruling overlooks the fact that the employers who paid their female workers less than their male workers achieved an unfair advantage over their economic competitors who obeyed European sex discrimination law.

In *Jenkins* v. *Kingsgate*[68] a female employee argued that paying less on an hourly rate to part-time workers constituted indirect discrimination in violation of the Equal Pay Directive of 1975 and of Article 119, and asked the Court to extend the principle of direct application to the 1975 Directive as well as to Article 119. The Court refused to decide about direct application of the Directive, arguing that Article 119 and the 1975 Directive were the same, and therefore it did not matter and the Court did not have to decide about direct applicability of directives. In recital 17, the Court spelled out the circumstances in which Article 119 could be directly applied against an employer.

> Article 119 of the Treaty applies directly to all forms of discrimination which may be identified solely with the aid of criteria of equal work and equal pay referred to by the article in question, without national or Community measures being required to define them with greater precision in order to permit of their application.

The 1982 case of *Garland* v. *British Rail,*[69] involved sex discrimination in the granting of post-retirement benefits in the form of special travel facilities. The British domestic court had found no violation of domestic sex discrimination law, but referred to the European Court the question whether the employer's policies violated Article 119 or either the Equal Pay Directive or the Equal Treatment Directive. Thus, the question was raised whether the Equal Pay Directive and the Equal Treatment Directive were directly applicable to Member States, as Article 119 had been found to be, and whether they too could be invoked by individuals before the national courts.

The Court was able to avoid the question of the direct applicability of the directives. The Court found that the special travel facilities were granted

68 Case 96/80, *Jenkins* v. *Kingsgate (Clothing Productions) Ltd,* [1981] ECR 911.
69 Case 12/81, *Eileen Garland* v. *British Rail Engineering Ltd,* [1982] ECR 359.

'directly or indirectly in respect of ... employment,'[70] and ruled that the discrimination against female workers thus violated the equal pay provision of Article 119. It stated that:

> [w]here a national court is able, using the criteria of equal work and equal pay, without the operation of Community or national measures, to establish that the grant of special travel facilities solely to retired male employees represents discrimination based on difference of sex, the provisions of Article 119 of the Treaty apply directly to such a situation.[71]

The Court thus found it unnecessary to decide whether either of the anti-discrimination directives were directly applicable to Member States.

The *Burton* case, discussed above,[72] also tried to raise the question of whether the Equal Treatment Directive was directly applicable to Member States. The voluntary redundancy scheme under scrutiny in the case was legal under the national law of Britain, which had not implemented the Equal Treatment Directive as required by European law. The Court was able to dodge the question of direct applicability of Directives because although it concluded that the issue of conditions of access to voluntary redundancy benefits paid by an employer was covered by the Equal Treatment Directive, the scheme of the British Rail Board did not violate the 1976 Directive. Thus, the Court was once again able to avoid the issue of direct application of Council Directives. Since the Court ruled that the voluntary redundancy scheme did not violate the Equal Treatment Directive, there was no need for it to decide whether the Directive had direct effect.

The next important case dealing with the issue of the effect of European sex discrimination law in domestic courts of Member States was *von Colson and Kamann*.[73] Two women social workers applied for jobs in a German prison for male offenders, and the social workers' committee identified the two women as the most qualified applicants and put them at the top of the list of candidates. The recruiting authority refused to hire the women and filled the posts with two less-qualified men. The women sued in their local labour court, which found that they had been discriminated against unlawfully, but concluded that German labour law provided no remedy beyond out-of-pocket expenses, as specified in Paragraph 611a of the *Bürgerliches Gesetzbuch*. The local court referred to the European Court detailed questions about the effect that European law, specifically the Equal Treatment Directive, should have upon its decision. For example, is an employer which has discriminated against a candidate on the basis of her sex required to offer that candidate a contract of employment, and if so, under

70 Ibid., at 369, para. 7.

71 Ibid., at 371-72 (holding para. 2).

72 *Supra* note 55.

73 Case 14/83, *Sabine von Colson and Elisabeth Kamann* v. *Land Nordrhein-Westfalen*, [1984] ECR 1891.

what circumstances – only if she is the best qualified candidate, or better qualified than the person hired in her place, or equally qualified, or even if she may have been less qualified but was not fairly considered because of unlawful sex discrimination? If the Directive does not require the employer to offer a contract of employment, what sanction does apply where there is an established case of discrimination in regard to access to employment, and does the Directive, as interpreted by the Court in its answers to the questions about remedies, constitute directly applicable law in Germany?

The European Court held that the Directive did not require the employer to offer jobs to the plaintiffs. (Although there is nothing in the opinion to suggest such a concern, it might be thought that the Court was troubled about what effect such a remedy might have on the men who had been placed in the posts, and who, though less qualified, may have come to rely upon their jobs.) The Court also refused to read into the Directive a requirement for the states to provide a specific type of remedy:

> the directive does not include any unconditional and sufficiently precise obligation as regards sanctions for discrimination which, in the absence of implementing measures adopted in good time may be relied on by individuals in order to obtain specific compensation under the Directive, where that is not provided for or permitted under national law.[74]

In the most important part of the decision, the European Court held that the Directive required Member States to provide an *adequate* remedy, and that 'if a Member State chooses to penalize breaches [of the Directive] by the award of compensation, then in order to ensure that it is effective and that it has deterrent effect, that compensation must in any event be adequate in relation to the damage sustained.'[75] The Court went on to rule that 'national courts are required to interpret their national law in the light of ... the directive in order to achieve the result referred to.'[76] This has been referred to as the doctrine of 'indirect effect.'[77]

A second case decided the same day raised identical issues in the context of a woman denied employment not by an organ of the state but by a private employer. In *Harz*[78] another lower labour court in Germany had

74 Ibid., at 1892 (headnote 2). Josephine Shaw has argued that the prison, as a public employer, is not even covered by the act dealing with private employment, but rather with other provisions, which in fact allow for a court order that the employer must conclude a contract of employment with the victim of sex discrimination. See Shaw, 'Sex Discrimination Law in Germany,' 13 *Comp. Labor L.J.* (1991) 18, 34.

75 *Supra* note 73, at 1910 (holding para. 3).

76 Ibid., at 1909, para. 26.

77 See Shaw, 'Recent Developments in the Field of Labour Market Equality: Sex Discrimination Law in the federal Republic of Germany,' 13 *Comparative Labor Law Journal* (1991) 18, 26. See also Fitzpatrick, 'The Significance of EEC Directives in UK Sex Discrimination Law,' 9 *Oxford J. of Legal Studies* (1989) 336.

78 Case 79/83, *Dorit Harz* v. *Deutsche Tradax GmbH*, [1984] ECR 1921.

concluded that the only damages it could award were 'damages in respect of the loss incurred by the worker as a result of his [sic.] reliance on the expectation that the establishment of the employment relationship would not be precluded'[79] by discrimination, and asked the European Court for an opinion. The Court again held that Community law did not require that the victim of discrimination be offered the job she was refused, but that mere out-of-pocket damages were insufficient. The European Court emphasized that it was up to the national courts to interpret their own law, but added that the obligation of Member States to implement the Directives extended to 'all authorities of Member States including, for matters within their jurisdiction, the courts.'[80] In applying its national law, a court must 'interpret its national law in the light of the wording and purpose of the directive.'[81] Thus the Court refused to draw the distinction between private and public employers which had been suggested by the Commission in its *amicus curiae* brief.[82]

These decisions establish that in suits both against an organ of the state and against third party employers, national courts have an obligation to interpret national legislation so as to accord with the meaning of Directives. Presumably, this requirement can apply only when the court can assert at least that the national legislation is ambiguous.[83] A court that is seeking to do justice, however, may be creative at finding ambiguity in a national law that seems to conflict with the anti-discrimination principles of the European Community. Lower courts are empowered, under Article 177 of the Treaty of Rome, to apply to the European Court of Justice for rulings on the proper interpretation of Community Law where such a ruling might be relevant to a case before the court. If the lower court then creatively interprets its national law to be consistent with European law, as articulated by the European Court, the national appellate court might be faced with a difficult choice: either it must uphold the lower court ruling or, in the process of challenging the lower court's interpretation of national law, the higher court must thereby assert that the national law is in direct conflict with the provisions of European law. In this way, lower courts can make an 'end-run' around their own appellate courts. This end-run is particularly important in countries in which the lower court judges often seem to be more sensitive to issues of sex discrimination than the higher court judges are.

Finally in 1986 the European Court of Justice held in *Marshall*[84] that aggrieved employees can enforce the sex discrimination directives against

79 Ibid., at 1936, para. 4 (quoting Paragraph 611a(2) of the *Bürgerliches Gesetzbuch*).
80 Ibid., at 1942, para. 26.
81 Ibid.
82 Ibid., at 1934.
83 See, e.g., *Duke* v. *G.E.C. Reliance Ltd.* 2 WLR (1988) 359, 371.
84 *Supra* note 57.

organs of the state, though not against individuals. The Court based its view upon Article 189 of the Treaty of Rome, which makes directives binding only in relation to 'each Member State to which it is addressed.' The Court reasoned that it would be wrong to allow Member States to rely on their own failure to implement directives as a defence in a legal proceeding, since the directives impose on Member States an unconditional requirement to implement the terms of the directive in domestic law. Thus, the individual may rely upon the directive in cases in which the state is acting in the role of employer, no matter whether the state acts in its realm of public authority or as a market participant. '[W]herever the provisions of a directive appear ... unconditional and sufficiently precise,' individuals may rely upon them against the State, where the State fails to implement the directive within the period prescribed.

On the question of direct application of the Equal Treatment Directive, the appellant argued, citing *von Colson and Kamann*,[85] that national courts must interpret their domestic law so as to give effect to European directives whenever possible and argued that moreover, in the case of conflict, national courts should declare the national provision inconsistent with a directive inapplicable. The Commission argued that the provision involved was sufficiently clear and unconditional that it could be directly relied upon before a national court. The UK tried to distinguish between the Member State qua public authority, against whom a sufficiently clear directive could be directly applied, and Member State qua employer, against whom it argued a directive could not be directly applied without establishing an unjustified distinction between the rights afforded to employees who happen to be working for the Member State and employees who happened to be working for private employers, but whose situation was otherwise identical. The Court had already decided in *Becker*[86] that directives could be relied upon against Member States themselves where the provision in question was 'unconditional and sufficiently precise' and the state had failed to implement the directive as required. Against this argument of 'arbitrary and unfair' distinction between classes of employees, the Court suggested that it could be 'easily avoided' by the Government of the UK implementing the Equal Treatment Directive, as it was legally required to do. This is a satisfactory answer to the UK's argument against protecting public employees, although it of course provides no comfort to the victims of non-implementation – the private employees who may be subjected to continuing sex discrimination as long as the UK and other Member States fail to implement the antidiscrimination directives. The Court, in what common law countries would consider dicta, since it was not relevant to the actual decision before

85 Case 14/83, *supra* note 73.
86 Case 8/81, *Becker* v. *Finanzamp*, [1982] ECR 53.

it, limited its holding on direct effect to actions against state defendants and not private employers. The Court emphasized that Article 189, the basis for direct effect, made Directives binding only upon 'each Member State to which it is addressed' and asserted that 'a directive may not of itself impose obligations on an individual and that a provision of a directive may not be relied upon as against such a person.'[87] This opinion gives greater protection to public employees, but it takes nothing away from the requirement in *von Colson and Kamann* and *Harz* that in actions brought against either public or private employers, national courts must interpret their law 'in the light of the wording and purpose of' the Directives.

In *Beets-Proper*,[88] which raised essentially the same question as *Marshall* in the Netherlands in a case against a private employer, national legislation had been passed to implement the Equal Treatment Directive. The Supreme Court in the Netherlands asked for a preliminary ruling from the European Court on the legal meaning of the Directive, to help it in its interpretation of its domestic implementing legislation. The case involved only the interpretation of the Directive and was not treated as raising the issue of direct application of the Equal Treatment Directive.

In *Francovich*,[89] the European Court of Justice held that individuals may bring direct actions for money damages against their own governments for losses they suffer as a result of their country's failure to implement a Community directive. The case arose in Italy in the context of a bankruptcy. A worker of a company that went bankrupt sued the Italian government for failing to implement a Community directive which would have protected him with a preference in bankruptcy for his wages. In a ruling that should be broad enough to protect individuals injured by the failure to implement Community directives on sex discrimination, the Court found against Italy. This ruling means that the Courts of each Member State are obliged to entertain actions against them brought in their domestic courts by citizens alleging a failure to implement a Community directive. Thus, while non-implemented directives still cannot be enforced against private employers, the victims of the non-implementation now have the opportunity to claim damages from the state. If properly followed, this ruling should give Member States a strong economic incentive to implement Community directives and thus eliminate many of the worst aspects of the Court's refusal to make non-implemented directives directly applicable against private employers.

87 *Supra* note 57, at 749, para. 48.
88 Case 262/84, *supra* note 59.
89 Joined Cases C-6/90 and C-9/90, *Francovich* v. *Italy*.

3. The Third Defrenne Case: How Broad a Concept is Equal Pay?

The third *Defrenne* case[90] involved her complaint about the mandatory retirement provision of women at age 40, while men were not forced into such an early retirement. Since the case arose in the 1960s, long before the Equal Treatment Directive of 1976, the Court found against the applicant. Article 119 forbade discrimination only with regard to pay, and not in the context of hiring or firing or forced retirement. The Court held that:

> Article 119 of the Treaty cannot be interpreted as prescribing, in addition to equal pay, equality in respect of the other working conditions applicable to men and women.[91]

Defrenne had argued that aside from Article 119, Community Law also contained general principles, including respect for fundamental personal human rights, which included the elimination of sex discrimination, the observance of which the Court had a duty to ensure. The Court responded that:

> at the time of the events which form the basis of the main action there was, as regards the relationships between employer and employee under national law, no rule of Community law prohibiting discrimination between men and women in the matter of working conditions other than the requirements as to pay referred to in Article 119 of the Treaty.[92]

In rejecting Defrenne's argument that in light of the social provisions of the Treaty of Rome, Article 119 should be given a wide interpretation, the Court suggested that

> [i]n contrast to the provisions of Articles 117 and 118, which are essentially in the nature of a programme, Article 119, which is limited to the question of pay discrimination between men and women workers, constitutes a *special* rule, whose application is linked to precise factors.[93]

Women have a good reason to wince any time they hear the word 'special'. It is almost always invoked in the context of denying women something given to 'people' – real people, that is, men. More explicit is the statement in recital 22. Here the Court explains that whereas men and women are on an equal footing when they do the same work or provide comparable services, and should therefore receive equal pay, 'an assessment of the other conditions of employment and working conditions involves factors connected with the sex of the workers, taking into account considerations af-

90 Case 149/77, *Gabrielle Defrenne* v. *Société Anonyme Belge de Navigation Aérienne Sabena*, [1978] ECR 1365.

91 Ibid., at 1377, para. 24.

92 Ibid., at 1379, para. 33.

93 Ibid., at 1377, para. 19 (emphasis added).

fecting the *special position* of women in the work process' (emphasis added). As over half the population, women should not really be considered the exception, in a 'special position'. If either sex is to be considered to be in a special position, it makes as much sense to consider men in a special position. Men are in the 'special position' of never giving birth to children and often being able to get someone else to do most of their domestic and human maintenance work for them. Although men are paid considerably more for the work they do, women do more work than men. Unless one arbitrarily eliminates from 'the work process' a disproportionate amount of the work done by women in Europe, because it is unpaid, most studies suggest that women as a group do considerably more work than men as a group do and should certainly thus not be considered the 'special' exception.

Of course, defenders of the Court might try to explain the Court's position by the fact that the Member States have transferred to the Community only those regulatory powers which are expressly provided for in the Treaty of Rome. Thus, because the issue of equality in the workplace was outside the scope of Article 119 and there was a consequent absence of secondary legislation before 1976, the Community simply lacked any authority to legislate in this area. But such an argument misses the point. The Court relied upon the 'specialness' of women's position in the work process to conclude that Article 119 should receive narrow interpretation and that Sabena's mandatory retirement policy involved the issue of equality in the work place, not of equal remuneration.

Finally, the Court ruled in *Defrenne III* that although it had the duty to ensure the observance of the general principles of Community Law, including respect for fundamental personal human rights, and that '[t]here can be no doubt that the elimination of discrimination based on sex forms part of those fundamental rights',[94] nevertheless since at the time Sabena discriminated against Gabrielle Defrenne 'the Community had not ... assumed any responsibility for supervising and guaranteeing [in employer-employee relationships subject to national law] the observance of the principle of equality between men and women in working conditions other than remuneration'[95] the employers should not be liable under Community Law.

Yet, if a degree of employment security is one of the benefits of working (that is, 'directly or indirectly in respect of ... employment'), it could be considered part of remuneration. Men are effectively paid a good deal more for the same work if they are given a degree of employment security until age 65 while women are given the same degree of employment security only until age 40. Perhaps this is clearest if one imagines a 39-year-old man and

94 Ibid., at 1378, para. 27.
95 Ibid., at 1378, para. 30.

a 39-year old woman each offered a small per week bonus in exchange for relinquishing all job security. The woman's one year of job security is worth much less than the man's 26 years of job security. In addition to paying its male employees a higher basic wage than its female employees, Sabena Airlines provided its male employees 'other consideration' in the form of a degree of job security worth more than that provided to its female employees for the same work.

Fortunately the Court did not continue to limit so sharply its understanding of remuneration, at least after secondary Community law had been adopted. The Court was asked for its opinion in *Garland* v. *British Rail*[96] a case involving post-retirement benefits which were provided by the employer railroad, although it was not contractually bound to do so. The railroad continued to provide for its retirees special travel facilities it provided to its employees, and in the case of male but not female retirees, provided the facilities also to the retiree's spouse and dependent children.

Because the Court found that the special travel facilities were granted 'directly or indirectly in respect of ... employment,'[97] it ruled that the discrimination against female workers violated the Equal Pay provision of Article 119. Moreover, the Court concluded that a national court should be able 'using the criteria of equal work and equal pay, without the operation of Community or national measures, to establish that the grant of special travel facilities solely to retired male employees represents discrimination based on difference of sex,'[98] making the provisions of Article 119 of the Treaty directly applicable.

In *Macarthys* v. *Smith*,[99] a woman sued her employer who had paid her predecessor, a man, higher wages than the employer paid her. The Court ruled that Article 119 was not limited to those 'contemporaneously doing equal work for the same employer' but also ruled that 'comparisons are confined to parallels which may be drawn on the basis of concrete appraisals of the work actually performed by employees of different sex within the same establishment or service.'[100] The underpaid woman tried to introduce the concept of a 'hypothetical male worker' with whom women should be able to compare themselves, so that they would not be limited to actual cases in which there was a real man with whom to compare. This notion was not rejected outright by the Court, but it would not employ the concept in the case of direct application of Article 119.

96 Case 12/81, *supra* note 69.
97 Ibid., at 369, para. 7.
98 Ibid., at 370-71, para. 15.
99 Case 129/79, *Macarthys Ltd* v. *Wendy Smith*, [1980] ECR 1275.
100 Ibid., at 1289, paras. 13 and 15.

In *Murphy* v. *Bord Telecom Eireann*[101] the Court decided that work did not have to be of precisely equal value. The Court rejected the employer's argument that because the plaintiff receiving lower wages was doing work of greater value, rather than of equal value with the higher-paid male to whom she was comparing herself, the equal pay principle was not violated. This was not the only case in which the Court avoided making a decision that could have seriously undermined the effectiveness of Community anti-discrimination provisions.

4. Other Cases in Which the Court Turned Down an Invitation to Gut European Sex Discrimination Law

In *Commission* v. *United Kingdom*,[102] the Court upheld the Commission's action challenging for failing to implement the Equal Pay Directive, the equal pay law of the United Kingdom, Equal Pay Act 1970, as amended by the Sex Discrimination Act 1975, under which the requirement that man and women receive equal pay for work to which equal value is attributed was limited to situations in which the employer chose voluntarily to agree to a job classification system or a job classification study. The Court emphasized that Community Law required equal pay for work of equal value and that under the Directive, a job classification scheme was only one of several methods of determining when what work should be considered 'work to which equal value is attributed'. The national law fell short of the Directive requirement. The United Kingdom was required to endow some national authority with the jurisdiction to decide when work has the same value as other work so that individuals who were denied equal pay could seek redress.

The Commission brought an action against Luxembourg for failing to implement the Equal Pay Directive with respect to sex discrimination in the conditions for the grant of head of house-hold allowances for civil servants, *Commission* v. *Grand Duchy of Luxembourg*.[103] The Court rejected Luxembourg's defences that it had failed to comply because of (1) the need to enact legislation, (2) the need to assess budgetary consequences, and (3) the need to make changes in the rules applicable to part-time work, which would require discussions with civil service representatives. The Court restated 'the well-established case-law of the Court' that 'a Member State

101 Case 157/86, *Murphy* v. *An Bord Telecom Eireann*, [1988] ECR 673.

102 Case 61/81, *Commission of the European Communities* v. *United Kingdom of Great Britain and Northern Ireland*, [1982] ECR 2601.

103 Case 58/81, *Commission of the European Communities* v. *Grand Duchy of Luxembourg*, [1982] ECR 2175.

may not plead provisions, practices or circumstances existing in its internal legal system' to justify a failure to comply with Community directives.[104]

The Commission's second action against the United Kingdom challenged certain provisions in national law for failing to implement the Equal Treatment Directive.[105] Specifically, the United Kingdom's anti-discrimination law applied only to employers with more than five employees and excluded employment in a private household, regardless of the number of employees. The Commission charged that the UK law failed to provide for amending or nullifying collective agreements or other provisions contrary to the principle of equal treatment and exempted the occupation of midwife altogether, allowing only women to practice the profession.

The Court found that the UK law was too limited. Section 2 of Article 2 of the Equal Treatment Directive provides for an exception for an occupational activity if by reason of its nature or the context in which it is carried out, 'the sex of the worker constitutes a determining factor.'[106] While this exception might apply to many forms of employment in a private household, it would not apply to all such forms of employment. Regarding the exception for employers with 5 or fewer workers the Court stated:

> the United Kingdom has not put forward any argument to show that in any undertaking of that size the sex of the worker would be a determining factor by reason of the nature of his activities or the context in which they are carried out.[107]

The law regarding midwives did provide for limited access by males to the profession, and the UK justified the limits on the access in terms of 'respect for the patient's sensitivities'.[108] The Court allowed this defence, emphasizing the provisions of Article 9(2), which require periodic review of such exempted fields. Finally, the Court rejected the UK's defence that their collective agreements were not legally binding; in the Court's view the Directive applied to all agreements, legally binding or not, on the basis that such agreements can nevertheless have important de facto effects.

Perhaps the most insidious effort by a Member State to destroy the effectiveness of sex discrimination law was Germany's implementation of the Equal Treatment Directive through the addition of paragraph 611a to the *Bürgerliches Gesetzbuch* which led to ECJ cases *von Colson and Kamann*[109] and *Harz*.[110] As pointed out above this law limits damages for

104 Ibid., at 2181, para. 3.
105 Case 165/82, *Commission of the European Communities* v. *United Kingdom of Great Britain and Northern Ireland*, [1983] ECR 3431.
106 Ibid., at 3448, para. 12 (quoting Equal Treatment Directive, *supra* note 38, at Article 2(2)).
107 Ibid., at 3448, para. 15.
108 Ibid., at 3449, para. 18.
109 *Supra* note 73.
110 *Supra* note 78.

proven sex discrimination to the plaintiffs' out-of-pocket expenses, 'the loss incurred by the worker as a result of his reliance on the expectation' that the employer would not discriminate against him.

The Court held that mere out-of-pocket damages were insufficient. Against the argument of the Government of Germany that the EEC Treaty Article 189 left the 'form and methods' of achieving compliance with Community Law to the discretion of each Member State, the Court stated that:

> the sanctions must be of such a nature as to constitute, for the candidate discriminated against, appropriate compensation and, for the employer, a means of pressure which it would be unwise to disregard and would prompt him to respect the principle of equal treatment.[111]

In *Harz*, the Court asserted that Article 6 of the Equal Treatment Directive, 'by granting applicants for a post who have been discriminated against recourse to the courts, acknowledges that those candidates have rights of which they may avail themselves before the courts.'[112] The German Government had argued in both cases that the law in Germany did already allow for more than the nominal damages provided for in the employment law itself because the refusal of a better qualified female applicant purely on grounds of sex would constitute a tort under a different section of German law. *Harz* and *von Colson and Kamann* did much to promote this interpretation, and many German courts have accepted it. The fact that the lower courts had refused damages beyond out-of-pocket expenses shows the situation in Germany to be at least ambiguous and thus raises questions about effective implementation and enforcement of Community sex equality law.

The experience of most plaintiffs, even in countries such as the United States and the United Kingdom which may issue an injunction requiring the defendant to hire the plaintiff or grant substantial money damages, suggests that 'appropriate compensation' should be interpreted generously. The laws against sex discrimination are most successful when they do not have to be invoked. The process of actually bringing a sex discrimination lawsuit is expensive, time-consuming and to many, emotionally draining. Studies have suggested that even when damages may be substantial, most women bring such suits only in cases that seem to them extreme and in which they feel that they must carry out their (implicit or explicit) threat to sue for the sake of others. As Richard Townshend-Smith puts it:

> Throughout the process [of bringing a sex discrimination case in England] claimants are subjected to tremendous stresses. If they win, which is statistically

111 Ibid., at 1939, para. 14.
112 Ibid., at 1941, para. 22.

> unlikely, the gains will be limited. They may have difficulty in obtaining the money. The costs at work are likely to be enormous. Yet the majority of successful applicants considered it worthwhile to establish a principle and to expose the employer as a discriminator. It is beyond doubt that the law utterly fails to protect those courageous and principled women who are prepared to use the law despite tremendous odds.[113]

In those countries in which sex discrimination actions can effectively be brought only with union backing, the quality of sex discrimination law will depend on the sensitivity and commitment of the unions. Damages may have to be quite substantial to change long-entrenched employment practices.

In *Commission* v. *Germany*,[114] the Commission accused Germany of failing to implement either the 1975 or the 1976 Directive. Germany had long taken the position that its constitutional provision on equality of the sexes was sufficient to counter discrimination and refused to enact legislation required by the European Community. Finally, however, it passed legislation to implement the Equal Treatment Directive, but it limited the act to employment in the private sector, and it did not cover the independent professions. Germany initially denied that the Equal Treatment Directive applied to public service at all, but it also asserted that its constitution and pre-existing legislation adequately protected those in the public service and in the private professions against discrimination. The Commission also objected that the German law did not provide sufficient clarity to limit the exceptions allowed under Article 2(2) of the Directive for activities where sex is an essential element of the activities carried on. Moreover, Germany failed to provide an adequate basis to enable the Commission to supervise this exception, as is required by Article 9(2).

The Court rejected most of the Commission's complaints because the Commission failed to show that Germany in fact permitted discrimination. The single complaint it upheld was Germany's failure to implement 9(2). The Court pointed out that despite a clear indication in the Directive that Member States should periodically assess the justification for the exceptions allowed under Article 2(2), Germany never adopted 'the necessary measures to create even a minimum of transparency with regard to' the activities which they exempted from the principle of equal treatment of the sexes mandated by the Equal Treatment Directive.

113 R. Townshend-Smith, *Sex Discrimination in Employment: Law, Practice and Policy* (1989) 209.

114 Case 248/83, *Commission of the European Communities* v. *Federal Republic of Germany*, [1985] ECR 1459.

Johnston v. *Chief Constable of the Royal Ulster Constabulary*,[115] provides another useful example of a case in which the Court was invited to gut sex-discrimination law. During unrest in Northern Ireland, the police began carrying guns. The defendant refused to arm the women on the force and limited their work to that which could be done without guns. As a result, the Constabulary cut back on the number of women it employed, and refused to renew the plaintiff's contract after six years of duty. Ms. Johnston's sex discrimination action was obstructed by the Secretary of State issuing a certificate stating that the refusal to renew her contract was done in order to safeguard national security and to protect public order and public safety, which under local law had the effect of withdrawing the issue from the consideration of courts and tribunals altogether. The defendant argued that the alleged sex discrimination was done to protect public safety in a particularly difficult situation and that with respect to measures taken to protect public safety, the equal treatment provisions of European law simply do not apply. The Commission took the position that Article 224 of the Treaty of Rome, while allowing a Member State to derogate from the principle of equal treatment 'in the special conditions envisaged by that article and subject to judicial review'[116] did not exempt the derogations from judicial review. The Court rejected the broad defence of the defendant and decided that 'acts of sex discrimination done for reasons related to the protection of public safety must be examined in light of the exceptions to the principle of equal treatment for men and women' in the 1976 Directive.[117] It also decided that it did not have to deal with the issue of the interpretation of Article 224, because it accepted the derogation under the exception of Article 2(2) of the Directive itself. The Court's approach was to determine 'whether, owing to the specific context in which the [policing of Northern Ireland] is carried out, the sex of the person carrying out that activity constitutes a determining factor.'[118] The reasons the Chief Constable gave for his anti-armed women policy, according to the Court, were that

> if women were armed they might become a more frequent target for assassination and their fire-arms could fall into the hands of their assailants, that the public would not welcome the carrying of fire-arms by women, which would conflict too much with the ideal of an unarmed police force, and that armed policewomen would be less effective in police work in the social field with families and children in which the services of policewomen were particularly appreciated.[119]

115 Case 222/84, *Marguerite Johnston* v. *Chief Constable of the Royal Ulster Constabulary*, [1986] ECR 1651.
116 Ibid., at 1684, para. 25.
117 Ibid., at 1684, para. 28.
118 Ibid., at 1686, para. 34.
119 Ibid., at 1686, para. 35.

The Court added,

> the possibility cannot be excluded that in a situation characterized by serious internal disturbances the carrying of fire-arms by policewomen might create additional risks of their being assassinated and might therefore be contrary to the requirements of public safety.[120]

In rejecting the broad argument that public safety overrode anti-discrimination, the Court avoided making a decision that might have seriously undermined sex discrimination law. Leaving the issue of equal employment opportunities to the security people's discretion could be disastrous. Nevertheless, the opinion has serious problems.

The exceptions provided in Article 2(2) must be very narrow. This is why it was fortunate that in the Commission's action against Germany the Court at least agreed that Article 2(2) exceptions had to be identified in such a way that the Commission could carry out its function envisioned by the 1976 Directive.

There is nothing in the Court's opinion to suggest that the decisions of the Chief Constable were actually based on anything more than typical male prejudices against women. Firearms would seem to reduce, not increase, the different capabilities of men and women. If men are on average larger and perhaps on average stronger than women, this does not make them any more effective with guns.[121] It would seem to me that the assumption that unarmed women are more effective in their 'womanly' work with families and children reflects mainly a particular sexist attitude. Of course, the assertion in this context of women's particular effectiveness in this branch of work is characteristic of a sexist understanding of gender roles that is frequently employed to the disadvantage of women. One could equally well assume that armed women could be more effective with families and children – in such a violence prone society they might be taken more seriously. Moreover, why are women thought to be more likely assassinated than men? Armed women are not any easier to assassinate than armed men. Is the assertion that women might be more likely target of assassination some recognition that men are prone to kill women, or that the death of women is somehow more acceptable than the death of men? Or might not either chivalry or politics make men more likely targets of assassination. Would anyone actually believe that had the Royal Constable concluded that men were more prone to be assassinated he would have barred men and used only armed women? Surely the ease with which the Chief Constable could decide on the remedy of refusing to arm women

120 Ibid., at 1686-87, para. 36.

121 Moreover, the difference in average size does not tell us whether the female police hired by the Chief Constable are any smaller or less strong than their male colleagues. It is quite likely that some of the women were larger and stronger than some of the men.

should raise serious questions regarding the factual basis for his asserted justifications.

It should be obvious that leaving the issue of equal employment opportunities to the discretion of security people would be disastrous. While less obvious, it might be almost as disastrous to leave the issue of equal employment opportunities to the unions. That may be what lay behind the Commission's action against Denmark. In *Commission* v. *Denmark*[122] the Commission complained that Danish law provided equal pay only for equal work or the same work, rather than providing equal pay for work of equal value, as required by the Equal Pay Directive. Denmark's defence was that the law, specifying equal pay for *samme arbejde*, meant equal pay for work of the same value. Most employment in Denmark is covered by collective agreements, which, according to the Danish Government, all specified equal pay for work of equal value. Moreover, the Danish representative had entered a declaration in the Council minutes during the preparatory work that led to the Equal Pay Directive specifically asserting that 'Denmark is of the view that the expression "same work" can continue to be used in the context of Danish labour law.'[123] What is interesting about the Court's decision rejecting Denmark's arguments is its failure to express any concern with the truth of Denmark's assertions about the meaning of *samme arbejde*. This contrasts with the Court's treatment in *Commission* v. *Germany*, in which the Commission's failure to show actual discrimination was fatal to part of its case. Neither, however, is it obvious why Denmark clung so tenaciously to its language. Denmark in general preferred collective agreements to legislation, but once it had acquiesced in legislation, the wording seems to have been treated as peculiarly significant by both parties to the action. The history of sex discrimination by unions in the United States makes it easy to support the Commission's unwillingness to leave sex discrimination issues to the unions. This is similar to the problem that arises from the reality that in many countries only if the union backs a discrimination claim can a worker realistically afford to bring it.

122 Case 143/83, *Commission of the European Communities* v. *Kingdom of Denmark*, [1985] ECR 427.

123 Ibid., at 435, para. 12.

IV. Substantive Examples

A. Maternity Leave Provisions

The first enforcement action the Commission brought under the Equal Treatment Directive, *Commission* v. *Italian Republic*,[124] was somewhat trivial, but the results were disappointing.

The Commission's most specific complaint against Italian law was that in the case of adopted children under the age of six, the mothers, but not the fathers, could claim up to three months maternity leave after the child entered the family. In general Italian law provided for two month maternity leave prior to birth and three months subsequent to birth. This could be taken only by the mother, ordinarily the parent who gave birth.

However, with regard to child care leave, Italian law provided that the father could take the leave in lieu of the mother. Child care leave was limited to a child under three, and provided for six months leave in which the worker's job would have to be kept open. Further, the mother or father of a child under three is also entitled to a leave when the child is sick, upon submission of a medical certificate. Apparently the father could take the leave only if the mother were working outside the home and chose not to take it, while presumably the mother could take the leave even if the father were not working outside the home. This discrimination is probably of greater ideological and theoretical than practical importance.

Italy's justification for its rule that the mother but not the father of an adopted child could take the three-month 'maternity' leave, though a bit odd, was accepted by the Court. The Court referred to Italy's 'legitimate concern to assimilate as far as possible the conditions of entry of the child into the adoptive family to those of the arrival of a newborn child in the family during the very delicate initial period'.[125] The 'delicacy' of the initial period after adoption would seem, if anything, a good reason to provide an adopting family as much flexibility as possible in parenting options. It would seem rather an overstatement, in the case of a toddler to six-year-old, to claim that granting a three-month 'maternity' leave assimilates the conditions of the child's arrival into an adoptive family with that of a newborn baby. There would seem to be little or no justification for a government to prevent parents from choosing that the father rather than the mother be the primary care-taker of their children, newborn or older. To the extent that the three-month post-birth maternity leave period is intended to facilitate parent-child bonding, there would seem to be no justifiable reason for limiting it exclusively to mothers, whether in the case of adoption or

124 Case 163/82, *Commission of the European Communities* v. *Italian Republic*, [1983] ECR 3273.

125 Ibid., at 3288, para. 16.

childbirth. The experience in countries that do allow the parents to allocate the leave to either the mother or the father seems to suggest that while the option of the father taking child-care leave is not often utilized by parents, neither is it abused or misused.

The *Commission* v. *Italy* case was followed by a case which is considerably more problematic, *Ulrich Hofmann* v. *Barmer Ersatzkasse*.[126] The first clear indication of the conservatism of the opinion comes in the second paragraph, in which the Court specifies that the action was brought by the father of an 'illegitimate child.' In a case in which the parents seemingly agreed that the father would care for the child while the mother returned to work, the Court endorsed Germany's refusal to allow the father to claim the financial benefits that the law would have granted to the mother, had the couple acquiesced in the Government's preferred parental roles (mother caretaker, father bread-winner). German law provided a mandatory 8-week period following childbirth, during which the mother may not be employed, presumably to provide a period of rest – whether the mother wants it or not – after the strain of giving birth. In addition, mothers, but not fathers, can claim leave until the child is 6 months old and will receive up to 25 Marks a day from the government in salary replacement. The leave after the initial 8 weeks would seem clearly to be related to child care, not to physical health, insofar as the mother must choose whether to take the leave four weeks before the end of the initial period, before she is likely to know her physical condition, and the leave is terminated if the child dies (three weeks after the death). Germany defended its position with arguments to the effect that benefits are good for mothers, but Germany did not make any serious attempt to justify why the mother should be bribed or coerced to care for the child herself instead of the father caring for the child after the initial eight weeks. It requires little imagination to think of reasons that a mother might prefer for the father to take a child-care leave, and nothing was argued why it should not be allowed. The Government claimed that it was trying, in the words of the Court, 'to reduce the conflict between a woman's role as a mother and her role as a wage-earner.'[127] Germany admitted that 'there are differing views on the length of time for which a woman should enjoy special treatment following pregnancy and childbirth.'[128] The Court did not seem to notice that the German law is likely to ensure that the treatment of women remains 'special', and to ensure that for a person to be both a child's primary care-taker, *and* a serious participant in the work force should not come to be seen as any kind of norm. The male worker with no significant child-care tasks continues to be the norm, and women receive 'special' exceptions. Efforts by governments 'to reduce the conflict between

126 Case 184/83, *Ulrich Hofmann* v. *Barmer Ersatzkasse*, [1984] ECR 3047.
127 Ibid., at 3072, para. 14.
128 Ibid.

a woman's role as a mother and her role as a wage-earner' never seem to extend far enough actually to provide equality or independence to women.

The Court quoted from Article 2(3) that the Directive should be 'without prejudice to provisions concerning the protection of women, particularly as regards pregnancy and maternity.' It goes on to quote Article 2(4), which provides that the Directive is also without prejudice to affirmative efforts to bring about equal employment 'by removing existing inequalities which affect women's opportunities in the areas' of access to employment, promotion and other working conditions. The Court, however, made no attempt to explain the relevance of this passage. The Court ruled simply that:

> It is apparent from the above analysis that the directive is not designed to settle questions concerned with the organization of the family, or to alter the division of responsibility between parents.[129]

This is of course the wrong question. No one argued that the Directive was designed to alter the division of responsibility between parents. The question was whether the Directive promoting equality of employment left Member States free to restrict and financially punish efforts by members of a family to divide child-care responsibilities more evenly, or in a way that might reduce the 'existing inequalities which affect [the woman's] opportunities'.[130]

Article 2, paragraph 4 might properly justify a provision that allowed the mother to choose to take a parental leave in preference to the father in the case of a dispute between them, but it provides no justification for a government restricting a parental benefit to those cases in which the parents acquiesce in the government's choice to discourage paternal responsibility for child care and to encourage mothers to stay out of the work force.

The Court asserted that it was legitimate for a government 'to protect the special relationship between a woman and her child over the period which follows pregnancy and childbirth, by preventing that relationship from being disturbed by the multiple burdens which would result from the simultaneous pursuit of employment.'[131] It should be noted that 'the period which follows pregnancy and childbirth' provides very little limit. Would the Court really allow a Member State, if it chose, to limit all child benefits – let's say from tax deductions, to *Kindergeld*, to free university education – to children whose mothers stayed out of paid employment, as long as the Member State characterized the benefit as a benefit to the mother to protect her special relationship to her child, which might be dis-

129 Ibid., at 3075, para. 24.
130 Ibid., at 3075, para. 23 (quoting Equal Treatment Directive, *supra* note 38, at Article 2(5)).
131 Ibid., at 3075, para. 25.

turbed by the burdens of raising the child and simultaneously pursuing employment?

The Court fails to deal adequately with the question of why the parental leave pay for children should be limited to situations in which the mother, not the father, takes care of the child. The only real effort occured when the Court stated that 'it is only the mother who may find herself subject to undesirable pressures to return to work prematurely.'[132] The father of an infant may well find himself subjected to pressures to continue full-time work, which may well in turn subject the mother to pressures to do most of the child care and to remain out of work. These pressures seem to me to be quite 'undesirable.' The question of what is a 'premature' return to work should be decided by the worker, not by the government. In the absence of any showing that women suffer by allowing them to decide upon an allocation of family responsibilities that leaves the father taking care of the child, the Court is simply endorsing the Member States' freedom to use economic bribery or coercion to enforce a particular role allocation within the family – a role allocation that seems systematically to undermine women's employment opportunities.

B. Part-Time Work

Some of the important issues that lie at the heart of questions about part-time work and whether discrimination against part-time work should be forbidden as a form of sex discrimination include whether part-time work is voluntary or mandatory, available or unavailable, and how women do and should deal with the double burden of home and career.

In the United States, there has been a strong bias within the women's movement against part-time work. The predominant attitude is that for women to accept part-time work is to accept the unequal division of labour within the family – an unequal division that should be challenged, not accepted. This attitude may reflect a middle-class bias. The second wave of American feminism was strongly influenced by middle-class women rebelling against the meaninglessness of housework and demanding career opportunities. It may also relate to the strong acceptance within the United States of the protestant ethic, or the notion that if one works hard enough one achieves salvation. Women seem to believe that if they work 20-hour days until they have a nervous breakdown this will somehow liberate them.

An interesting alternative view of the double burden of home and work is that housework will only be automated and made easier if and when women refuse to work unreasonably long hours. If they have to do home

132 Ibid., at 3075, para. 26.

care work, they can refuse to do more than part-time work outside the home. A serious problem with any such approach is that the work world is structured to prejudice part-time work. Even if equality demands are successfully raised by part-time workers, full-time work continues to be the model and part-time work a reasonably rare, usually temporary exception. Part-time work is easily exploited, and this exploitation is difficult to end. Some promising efforts have been made in European law, however, to challenge discrimination against part-time worker as indirect sex discrimination.

In *Jenkins* v. *Kingsgate*,[133] the Court refused to find the employer's practice of paying part-time workers a lower hourly wage a *per se* violation of the Article 119 equal pay requirement, but where the part-time workers are disproportionately female, left it to the employer to show that the pay difference was not in reality an indirect way to reduce the pay of women workers. Moreover, if the national court is able to establish that the lower pay for part-time work is discriminatory 'using criteria of equal work and equal pay without the operation of Community or national measures'[134] then the Court can directly apply Article 119 to find a violation without having to depend on domestic law.

Bilka-Kaufhaus v. *Weber von Hartz*,[135] went further. There the Court ruled that an occupational pension scheme established in accordance with statutory provisions to supplement social benefits paid under national legislation but based on agreement between employer and employees, is part of pay and subject to the equal pay principle. Women sued to obtain pension benefits denied to part-time workers. The company rules required 15 years of full time work out of twenty years to qualify for a pension. Company officials tried to justify their rule on the basis that they wished to encourage full-time work in order to utilize efficiently their work force. (Part-timers were allegedly reluctant to work on Saturdays and late afternoons.) They also claimed that 81% of their pensions went to women, while only 72% of their employees were women. The Court suggested that there might exist economically justifiable economic grounds to allow the discrepancy between full- and part-time workers, but put the burden of proof on employers. Further developments can be expected in the area of part-time work.

C. Comparable Worth

Comparable worth arguments become important in the face of a persistently sex-segregated work place. Comparable worth has both radical and less

133 Case 96/80, *supra* note 68.
134 Ibid., at 927, para. 18.
135 Case 170/84, *Bilka-Kaufhaus GmbH* v. *Karin Weber von Hartz*, [1986] ECR 1607.

radical aspects. On the more radical side, an objective measure of work value decreases the autocratic power of employers (especially in the United States, where unions are quite weak). A more conservative understanding of comparable worth is that it facilitates leaving the work place sex segregated. By removing some of the economic injustice, comparable worth can throw a few more crumbs to women to keep them willing to stay in 'their place'.

In the United States, comparable worth arguments have had more success politically than legally, with legislatures revising the pay structures of public employees in response to comparable worth studies showing unjustly low pay for employment categories with a high percentage of women. Courts have been quite reluctant to endorse comparable worth arguments.

The interpretation of the Article 119 equal pay requirement endorsed by the Equal Pay Directive of 1975 provides for equal pay for work to which equal value is attributed. To the extent that job classification systems are used, this could significantly affect the disparate wages in sex segregated employment fields. One important case suggests the potential value of this provision.

In *Rummler* v. *Dato-Druck*,[136] the Court allowed a job classification system which used a criterion of muscle demand, muscular effort or heaviness of work, for which men as a group sometimes show greater performance, but insisted that in such cases the system as a whole must preclude sex discrimination by also taking into account other criteria for which women may show greater aptitude. The Court ruled that:

> the use of values reflecting the average performance of workers of one sex as a basis for determining the extent to which work makes demands or requires effort or whether it is heavy, constitutes a form of discrimination on grounds of sex, contrary to the directive [and] in order for a job classification system not to be discriminatory as a whole, it must, in so far as the nature of the tasks carried out in the undertaking permits, take into account criteria for which workers of each sex may show particular aptitude.[137]

D. Positive Action

Affirmative action is necessary for a number of reasons, including the role that employers play in creating images of jobs and worker expectations.[138] Much of the affirmative action that was practiced in the United States during the past quarter century was the result of remedial consent decrees which

136 Case 237/85, *Gisela Rummler* v. *Dato-Druck GmbH*, [1986] ECR 2102.

137 Ibid., at 2119 (holding para. 2, b and c).

138 See Schultz, 'Telling Stories About Women and Work: Judicial Interpretations of Sex Segregation in the Workplace in Title VII Cases Raising the Lack of Interest Argument', 101 *Harvard Law Review* (1991) 1749.

settled class action lawsuits, often against employers who showed a pattern and practice of intentional discrimination. Presidential executive decrees and municipal set-asides preferring businesses owned by women or minorities, or businesses with a certain percentage of women or minority workers, have also been effective.

In any employment field in which there is considerable hiring discretion, such as executive jobs or teaching positions in universities, prejudice is pervasive and difficult to prove. My experience on several faculties involved in dozens of hiring decisions has been that only if we consciously set out believing we are engaging in affirmative action do we begin to counteract our unconscious biases.

Affirmative action may be necessary, but it is sometimes not sufficient. Formal efforts at affirmative action may be counterbalanced or sabotaged by male or majority resistance. In many dominantly male fields, the few women who try to find employment are so harassed that work becomes intolerable. In certain skilled jobs affirmative action requirements may be cynically obeyed by employing a woman or a minority who will satisfy an affirmative action guideline or goal, but who is considerably less well qualified than other women or minorities who might have been hired. In this way the male and majority decision-makers can also satisfy their own prejudices and may avoid the threat that they might feel from having a highly qualified woman or member of a minority group in the job. In any situation in which a minimum quota for women is adopted, it is important that the quota be high enough that it cannot be filled with unthreatening tokens. For example, if 10% of the delegates from a political party must be women, the men could afford to choose relative incompetent, unthreatening women. But if 50% must be women, the men will not be able to satisfy their prejudices without threatening the party to an imprudent degree, and thus such a quota may be effective.

The politics and ideology of positive action are complex and important. Affirmative action has come under increasing attack in the United States. The more conservative Supreme Court resulting from Reagan and Bush appointments has imposed limits on affirmative action and the Republican Party has recently used affirmative action as the centerpiece of its attack on civil rights.

The question of affirmative action cannot be fully distinguished from the question of burden of proof.[139] Generally, once a prima-facie case of sex discrimination has been made, the burden of proof shifts to the employer. In the United States, the employer may counter the plaintiff's prima facie case of discriminatory failure to hire by showing that it had some legitimate,

139 See Olsen, 'The Family and the Market: A Study of Ideology and Legal Reform', 96 *Harvard Law Review* (1983) 1497, 1549-55.

nondiscriminatory reason for rejecting the applicant. If the employer makes such a showing, it is still available to the plaintiff to show by a preponderance of the evidence that the employer's stated reason for rejecting her was merely a pretext.

Under European law, the situation is somewhat ambiguous. A 1988 draft directive that would have specified a burden of proof was vetoed by the United Kingdom. The European Court has placed the burden on the employer to show that its pay practices are not discriminatory in a case in which the average pay to women was lower than to men and the system was so non-transparent that the worker would be unable to prove discrimination directly.[140] Such reasoning should apply equally to cases involving equal treatment as to cases involving equal pay.[141]

Unless the burden of proof is shifted to the employer, employers would be free as a practical matter to discriminate and hide behind an opaque personnel system. As Evelyn Ellis puts it, it would be 'highly unusual' for an employer 'to broadcast the fact that it has arrived at a decision on discriminatory grounds.'[142] Yet, as conservatives in the United States have argued, if statistics alone can make out a prima-facie case, employers have an incentive to try to achieve a fair statistical representation of women (and minorities) at all job levels and to ensure that on average women are paid as much as men. (Conservatives often ignore the fact that employers have a similar incentive to achieve some balance unless both sides are barred from admitting any such statistical evidence, which would seem arbitrary and counter-productive.) For an employer to try to achieve a fair representation of women and for women to be paid on average the same as men may be one of the best ways to counteract unconscious discrimination.

E. Sexual Harassment

Among the most interesting and exciting developments of American employment discrimination law is the development of a legal cause of action against sexual harassment. It has taken a private, hidden problem that individual women dealt with often at great personal expense and made it into a public cause of action. In the process, it has given victims of sexual harassment incentives to publicise their experiences and has transformed societal understanding of the nature and pervasiveness of the problem. In the United States, the EEOC guidelines on sexual harassment provide:

140 Ellis, *European Community Sex Equality Law* (1991) 156-61 (an excellent book).
141 Ibid., at 160-61.
142 Ibid., at 160.

Unwelcome sexual advances, requests for sexual favours, and other verbal or physical conduct constitute sexual harassment when
1. Submission to such conduct is made either explicitly or implicitly a term of condition of the individual's employment,
2. Submission to or rejection of such conduct by an individual is used as the basis for employment decisions affecting such individual, or
3. Such conduct has the purpose or effect of unreasonably interfering with an individual's work performance or creating an intimidating, hostile, or offensive working environment.

It is still the case, as in other forms of sex discrimination, that the law against sexual harassment is really effective only when it does not have to be formally invoked. But the development of the law has also given women considerably more tools with which to deal informally and more effectively with sexual harassment. In this sense, sexual harassment law can be said to work well.

Yet sexual harassment law can also be said not always to work well. Sexual harassment law primarily protects those women who are least in need of protection. The more oppressed a women is, the less she feels she is able to resist sexual imposition, and the less likely she is to be successful if she brings a sexual harassment action.

Sexual harassment law is not as well developed in the European Community yet as it is in the United States, but perhaps it will develop to be more effective. Efforts are underway to enact Community provisions against sexual harassment, and arguments have been advanced that sexual harassment violates the Equal Treatment Directive.

Section 5 of the Equal Treatment Directive certainly could be interpreted to forbid sexual harassment, but most national legislation implementing the Equal Treatment Directive has not been interpreted to forbid sexual harassment.[143] There have been efforts to create a Directive on sexual harassment. In 1990 the Council of Ministers passed a resolution on the dignity of women and men at work,[144] which, while not as effective as a directive, seems clearly to be a step in the right direction. The resolution defines sexual harassment reasonably broadly to include harassment by co-workers as well as by supervisors and to include hostile environment as well as quid-pro-quo harassment. It asserts that sexual harassment may, in particular circumstances amount to a violation of the Equal Treatment Directive, and it

[r]emind[s] employers that they have a responsibility to seek to ensure that the work environment is free from:

143 The exceptions are the UK and Ireland. See Rubenstein, *The Dignity of Women* (1988), cited in Ellis, *supra* note 140, at 149.

144 OJ 1990 C 157/3, cited in Ellis, ibid., at 151.

(a) unwanted conduct of a sexual nature or other conduct based on sex affecting the dignity of women and men at work;
(b) victimization of a complainant or of a person wishing to give, or giving, evidence in the event of a complaint...

The resolution calls on Member States to develop awareness on the part of employers and employees of the problems of sexual harassment, to develop measures against sexual harassment in the public sector that can serve as a model for the private sector, and to encourage the inclusion of anti-sexual harassment clauses in collective agreements.

The two major forms of sexual harassment, quid-pro-quo harassment and hostile environment harassment, can both be viewed in a variety of ways. On one hand, sexual harassment may be seen as an inappropriate importation of the personal into the marketplace. It may be seen as an unprofessional abuse of a position of power. Work is work and sex is sex. Sexual harassment can happen to men or to women and it can be committed by men or by women.

A more radical view of sexual harassment sees it as an important part of male oppression of women. While women can sexually harass men, the rarity of this form of harassment is no accident. The hostile environment harassment imposed on women who try to 'invade' a male-dominated work place is a good illustration of the domination and hostility involved in harassment.

V. Conclusion

It is popular to think of inequality as being caused by society and that the State if acquiescent is merely ratifying societal inequality, or that the State does make attempts to overcome the old inequality that pervaded social norms years ago. In fact, however the State reinforces inequality in numerous ways. Sex discrimination law mediates a complex compromise between conflicting views of the proper role and status of women in society. It also seems clear that women and men who support equality must use other forms of political struggle in addition to law if they wish to get beyond a mere compromise that leaves women partially oppressed.

The Political Culture of Liberalism and the Prospects for Eastern and Central Europe

PANEL DISCUSSION
of

RONALD DWORKIN & STEVEN LUKES

Academy of European Law (ed.),
Collected Courses of the Academy of European Law, Volume II, Book 2, 269–287.

Biography of Ronald Dworkin

Education. I received a BA degree from Harvard College, and was a Rhodes Scholar at Oxford University. I served on the Harvard Law Review, and thereafter clerked for Judge Learned Hand on the Second Circuit Court of Appeals. I was associated with a law firm in New York (Sullivan & Cromwell) for four years.

Appointments. I was a professor of law at Yale University Law School from 1962-1969. From 1968-1969 I was Wesley Hohfeld Professor of Legal Philosophy there. I have been Professor of Jurisprudence at Oxford and Fellow of University College since 1969. From 1975 I have also been a professor of law at New York University, as a joint appointment with Oxford. I am a member of the British Academy and of the American Academy of Arts and Sciences.

Other. I was the co-chairman of the Democratic Party Abroad. I am a member of the Council of Writers and Scholars Educational Trust, of the editorial committee of its journal, Index on Censorship, and of the Programme Committee of the Ditchley Foundation. I have been a consultant on human rights to the Ford Foundation.

Principal Publications of Ronald Dworkin

In addition to articles in philosophical and legal journals, and more popular articles on legal and political subjects in the New York Review of Books, I have published the following books: *Taking Rights Seriously* (1979), *A Matter of Principle* (1985), *Law's Empire* (1986), *Philosophical Issues in Senile Dementia* (a monograph commissioned by the United States Congress) (1987) and *A Bill of Rights for Britain* (1990). I will shortly publish a new book on abortion and euthanasia. *Law's Empire* won a number of awards, including the American Association of Law School's Coif award for the best work on a legal subject in a three year period, and the Harvard Law School's Ames Award for the best work on a subject connected with law in a five year period. Books have been translated into French, German, Spanish, Italian, Hungarian, Japanese and Chinese.

Biography of Steven Lukes

Fellow in Politics and Sociology, Balliol College, Oxford 1966-87.

Professor of Political and Social Theory, European University Institute, Florence 1987 – at present.

Fellow of the British Academy.

Principal Publications of Steven Lukes

Emile Durkheim: His Life and World

Individualism

Power: A Radical View

Essays in Social Theory

Moral Conflict and Politics

The Political Culture of Liberalism and the Prospects for Eastern and Central Europe

Panel Discussion

Dworkin: I'm going to talk in a rather general and abstract way at the beginning about liberalism as a kind of political thought, a kind of approach to the central problems of politics. I think of liberalism as a very general abstract set of impulses and I think of particular liberal theories as conceptions detailing interpretations of that general impulse. So there are many different liberal philosophers, and some of them have very different theories from others, but I want to suggest to you that each of them, in spite of the differences, is offering us an interpretation of a few central, important ideas.

What I want to do is to tell you what I think those central abstract fundamental ideas are and then to describe to you a conception, a particular interpretation, of those ideas that – it seems to me presently – are particularly compelling. Then I want, in accordance with the general theme this year, to attempt to raise some questions about this particular interpretation which I call 'liberal equality'. I want to raise some questions about the feasibility of that in Eastern Europe.

So back to the beginning, the most abstract part of what I want to say. To my mind liberalism as a general impulse or attitude is the idea that picks on two historical virtues of political society: liberty and equality, and regards those two large ideals as parts of a single ideal, as aspects of each other. Now, I put it that way because I want to suggest that liberalism as a historical impulse is to be distinguished from a kind of conservatism which says that liberty and equality are antagonistic ideas, that in order to protect liberty, equality must be rejected, that we can have equality only if we reject liberty. And conservatives who say this of course point conspicuously to the Eastern European and Soviet experience to say that there equality was pursued at the cost of liberty.

On the other side of liberalism, there is the 'left' or 'radical' position that says liberty and equality are antagonistic ideas, in this way agreeing with what I call conservatism, but maintaining that we must instil equality and when necessary we must abridge liberty. This view on the left has been progressively rejected in our decade. Now, liberalism rejects both of these. That is why it is convenient to think of liberalism – people often do – as in one way in the middle. But there is another way to think of that. You might say liberalism is not in the middle, is not between a left and a right. For liberalism is in a philosophical sense opposed to both left and right because liberalism rejects the idea that liberty and equality are separate ideals and insists that they are fused. Well I hope in discussion we'll explore the question of how far this very abstract description can be supported. But my way of supporting it is to try to offer you a more detailed account of how these two virtues, liberty and equality, can be understood as part of the same virtue, as complimentary rather than antagonistic. And in doing that I must tell you that what I am going to be describing now is work that I myself have done. As I say, this is a particular conception of liberalism. I cannot say that everybody who is a liberal accepts what I am about to say because they have other ways of uniting these two ideals. But just to give you an example of the kind of way in which they might be united, I will describe this idea.

Any political theory and therefore any conception or interpretation of liberalism must answer the question 'in what does equality consist?' Now, you might say that I'm beginning too far along the road because the first question is 'do we want equality?'. I believe that we all accept the following very important, though very abstract, principle which we might call *the abstract principle of equality*. That is the principle that says: government must treat all those subject to its dominion, all those over whom government exercises authority, with equal concern. That is, from the point of view of government or the collective power of the community, it is just as important what happens to each citizen as what happens to any of us. That abstract principle has been rejected more often in the history of the world than it has been accepted and I suppose it is rejected in more places around the world even now than it is accepted. But that does not matter because we all accept it, don't we? and we can imagine that any respectable political community, any structure of government must accept this very basic idea, must treat its citizens as equals, with equal concern. That is what I mean when I say that any political theory fit for us, fit for a democracy, must be one that answers the question, given that the government must show equal concern for each citizen: what system of the distribution of property brings that about?

The answer that liberalism gives, I believe, is this: it must be a system of the distribution of property which recognizes that, in principle, each person is entitled to an equal share of the resources that in some way are collectively available to everyone. An equal share. What does an equal share mean? Liberalism says an equal share is one defined in the following way: how much one person has must be measured by the opportunity costs of those resources to others. So if I occupy certain property or consume certain goods, the question of whether I have a fair share or not is to be answered by asking a further question: what is the proper price of those goods? How much would others pay for them? In order to illustrate, this may be a rather difficult idea to grasp immediately but it might be helpful to you to tell a story that I have used in the past. Imagine that we all are shipwrecked and have to redistribute the resources that we find on a desert island that we wash up on. The appropriate method to use is the method of auction. Here is how it would go. If we were carrying this experiment out, I would give everyone in the room an equal pile of little chips, worthless things, and then an auction consists in taking each resource, property, food and so forth, and holding it up and saying how much am I bid, and each of you says 'I bid three chips', another says 'I bid four chips'. The one who bids the most wins. And then having auctioned my sun-glasses, I auction the water and I auction everything there is, all resources, all property. And if at the end of the auction someone says 'I'm not happy, I did not spend my money in the way I wanted' – we all start with the same money – then we do it all over again. It may take a whole day. When we finish the following is true: nobody envies the property of anybody else because if you would prefer anyone else's bundle of goods, you could have had it yourself. That is a feature of the auction. Now this in a very abstract way is my suggestion as to what a fair distribution is.

Two points I want to make about this. First, the equality that we arrive at in this way is not an equality of welfare or well-being or happiness or success. None of those words that belong to the vocabulary of welfare economics would be appropriate. Steven Lukes is, let us say, a much happier kind of person than I am and gets much more pleasure out of simple things. In a fair equal distribution of resources I might be very unhappy, he might be very happy but we are equal because we have got a fair share of resources. The first point I want to make about this conception of equality is that it is one that gives us equality over things, resources, but not equality over the psychological aspects of life, that is well-being, happiness, pleasure and so forth.

The second point I want to make is that this way of looking at equality shows the centrality of liberty to equality, because the auction that I described will only give us a distribution that we can say treats people with equal concern, will only give us that if people are free to make up their own minds about what they want from life, to do that as individuals, and are free to the extent this is possible compatibly with other people's freedom and are free to spend their life as they want, buy what they want and so forth. That is, in the story I am telling, liberty is not something we add on to equality or we contrast with equality, it is a pre-condition of equality. Now, another way to put this, a more concrete way to put this would be this: there can be no fair egalitarian distribution of property without a free economic market. A command economy is an inherently anti-egalitarian economy. Now that will strike many of you as paradoxical and no doubt that is why I put exactly that way. I want it to strike you as paradoxical because I want you to reflect on the depth of the point that I am trying to make.

Of course, it does not follow that an absolutely free market will produce an egalitarian or indeed even a defensible distribution. We need taxation, redistribution. We need to pay attention to the fact that some resources are in the nature of things unequally distributed, such as talents. In a market economy, some people will turn out to have certain abilities, be a good baseball player or a pop singer or a brilliant surgeon, or a skilful banker. These will be resources those people have and true equality of resources requires that the distribution in the end be sensitive to these differences in talent so that we do not just have a free market. We have to correct in certain ways through taxation and redistribution. We probably won't have much time to discuss the mechanics of that, or the effect of that, on economic efficiency but I just might call your attention if you want to pursue it to two articles I wrote exploring that problem called: 'What is Equality', part 1, and 'What is Equality', part 2, in *Philosophy and Public Affairs* (1981). So I want to say that this morning mainly by way of a footnote to show you that I recognize this problem.

I want to emphasize not the adjustments that have to be made but the central idea that there must be in place a free market with freedom of choice as to how you want to spend your time and what you want to buy. You can adjust it through taxation. In principle the choices must be free for individuals. Of course there is much more to any particular interpretation of liberalism than just equality and liberty. We have to have a theory about political equality – about democracy. We have to have a theory about human rights and the protection of human rights in a constitution. Those are all centrally important matters. But just now I want to emphasize that connection. I will say a bit more though about liberty. So far I have only defined liberty as an offshoot of equality, I have been stressing a paradoxical idea that in order to have any kind of defensible equal concern there has to be a free market.

But now I want to say more about the dimensions of liberty, thinking of liberty as an important subject on its own. I'm going to offer you again what may seem to many of you to be a rather suspiciously interconnected definition of liberty. But here it is. But I will say something first. There is a certain strong tradition among liberal writers. I have in mind, for example, John Stuart Mill, Isaiah Berlin and John Rawls, three very well known liberal philosophers. That tradition defines liberty in this way: liberty means the power to do whatever you might want to do unhindered or unchecked by external authority, like government. Now I do not like that definition of liberty. My main reason for disliking it is this: it does not tell us what is good about liberty. It does not capture the idea that liberty is something crucially important that we must fight for if necessary, because on that definition when the city of Florence introduces a pedestrian zone in the centre and stops people from driving cars, it has limited liberty and though one can speak that way, it seems to me an unattractively broad notion of liberty. So I offer you this different idea: liberty properly understood is the power to do what one could do in a just society or you might say an ideally just society. Now that might seem unhelpful but if you bear in mind the account I gave a few moments ago of what a perfectly just society would be like, then perhaps it won't seem so strange.

Two illustrations: first, suppose government now in our present condition puts constraints on monopoly power and says 'no-one will be allowed privately to own all of an important raw material and charge whatever price that person wants to charge', that is, anti-monopoly legislation. Is that, as conservatives say, an invasion of liberty? The answer is that on the account I have given to you it is not, because in a society in which distribution is fair, no-one would have the economic power to do that. Anti-monopoly legislation then should not be regarded as a constraint on liberty but should be regarded instead as an attempt to increase liberty just as it increases equality. Now consider, however, someone who says 'we would organize the economy better and have a more efficient society if we reduced political activity, if we allowed only one political party, or maybe a small number of political parties; then we would not have so much division and strife and the people would produce more and so forth'. Well now that argument is a very different one from the argument about monopoly because, exactly on the contrary, people would have the right in an ideally just society, people would certainly have the right and indeed it would be central to the fairness of the society if they did have the right, to speak out as they wanted on political and moral issues.

The distinction then that this approach to liberalism makes between invasions of liberty and protections of liberty is different from what some of you might have expected. I say that because some people have thought that there are two kinds of liberalism in the world. First, there is economic liberalism thought to be a rather conservative idea, the sense of liberalism that I encounter very often in Europe. People say to me 'if you are a liberal, that means you are in favour of letting the rich increase their wealth'. And then there is the American sense of liberalism in which one associates liberalism with economic reform with the protection of civil liberties, with the attempt to combat racial discrimination and so forth. These seem like two very different theories and people have said 'well, it is just that the word: liberalism means one thing in Europe and means something entirely different in America.' What I am suggesting is that the division between economic liberties on the one hand, and civil liberties on the other, is not the important distinction. Economic liberties and civil liberties are both important, they are both aspects of liberty but it is crucial to get straight when some economic constraint is a constraint on liberty and when, on the contrary, it increases liberty, and if you begin to think about liberalism as the theory that 'equality and liberty are part of the same idea', then I think you find a more helpful division and one that explains that there are not two kinds of liberalism; there might just be disagreements about what the one understanding of equality and liberty properly intertwined would reveal.

Now, what have I offered you? I said at the beginning I was going to offer a general account of what liberalism is. Well, I said liberalism is the idea, put in the most abstract, that liberty and equality have to be understood as complementary parts of a set of ideas. I said I'd try and explain in the broadest outline a particular interpretation of liberalism and I have tried to do that by describing liberal equality. Just to summarize, liberal equality has two features: first, that equality is defined on the space of resources rather than welfare and defined in such a way that people's tastes, differences in taste, enter the calculation of what a fair distribution is through something like an auction. Secondly, that liberty in liberal equality must be understood not just as the power to do anything you might want but as itself refracted through the idea of fair distribution.

The third part of what I said I wanted to do this morning was to attempt to become a bit more concrete about the possibilities of realizing liberalism in various places. I will start with a general thought about the responsibilities that scholars have or students have about political theories that appeal to them. As you can tell perhaps by my tone of voice, this notion of liberal equality very much appeals to me. When I see it described, it seems to me true and important and worth fighting for. But I accept that I have two intellectual responsibilities or intellectual responsibilities of two different kinds that follow from my enthusiasm and just to give a kind of image to this, I want to distinguish these kinds of responsibilities as horizontal and vertical. In both cases my responsibility is to try and connect my enthusiasm for this political theory to other things I believe to be true.

So, horizontally I have to ask 'does liberalism so understood fit well with what I think about sociology, social psychology, economics, geography, climatology.' In short, given what we think about human beings from these more or less empirical social sciences, is liberalism possible? That is the horizontal question. The vertical question is: 'given what we think, not about these empirical matters, about the right way for human beings to live, given what we think about subject we might call philosophical ethics, what the good life is for people, is liberalism a good way, a good political organization, is it the kind of political organization that people who have views of the good life, some of them given by religion, could properly choose'. What one wants both on the horizontal dimension and on the vertical dimension is integrity. You want your political theory to fit with what you believe is true about human beings as a matter of fact, but you also want it to fit vertically: you want it to fit with your ideals about what human beings are around for and what kind of life counts as a decent successful life. You want to do both those things.

We might talk vertically, we might talk about ideals, we might talk about whether somebody with a religious conviction could accept the kind of liberalism I am talking about. But I suppose mainly we are going to be concerned with the horizontal dimension. Now, I want to ask, what kind of a society in terms of the sociology of it all could reasonably be expected to move in the direction of the particular kind of liberalism that I have been describing. What has to be true about a society in order for it to be on the cards, a possibility. Well, you might say if a society is divided in some fundamental way as, for example, the communities of Northern Ireland are divided by religion, then you might say liberalism is not possible in such a society. Or you might say on the contrary if a society is homogeneous, if it is monolithic, if it is all given over to certain religious traditions that are unquestioned, liberalism is not fit for that society either, a society of that sort cannot accept one feature of liberalism which I have not mentioned but which I now want to bring to the surface and that is the *neutrality* of liberalism. You remember that I said that it is essential in a fair society that people have the freedom to form for themselves ideals about what the good life would consist in and make their economic and social choices in a price mechanism against a background of their own convictions, that is essential. Now an egalitarian society is one that respects people's liberty to do that and therefore a liberal society will be one that says 'no-one must be at a special disadvantage because that person's conception of religion or morality of the good life is in a minority, or is disapproved by the majority'. If anyone is at a special disadvantage for that reason, then the fundamental basis of liberal equality, equality as well as liberty is destroyed because that person is not allowed to bid in the auction as it were as herself or himself. That person is forbidden to try and enter the civic community as somebody concerned to do what he or she wishes with her fair share, but somebody who is regarded at the beginning as an outcast. Liberalism, therefore must be neutral in matters of religion and in matters of personal ethics. Now people therefore say 'but a community which is monolithic, which is dedicated, which is conceived on the assumption, say, that there is a particular God and that God's peoples existence on earth is entirely a matter of the grace of that God and for the purposes of that God, cannot possibly accept this kind of liberal neutrality.' That is why I say that it is quite common to say that a theological monolithic state could not be a liberal state.

If a community, on the other hand, as I said, is too divided, if the community feels itself two communities, say Catholic and Protestant, then the equality of concern that I described, the feeling that it matters just as much what happens to each member of the community, will be absent because people will have the sense that they are not one community but two. I do not want to suggest the terribly pessimistic conclusion that Iran cannot become a liberal society but just to say it would have to change so fundamentally to become a liberal society that it would really of course be a different country. If one were to say 'let us set out to realize liberalism in post-Khomeini Iran', then I think one would say this is not on. It may be. I do not want to be pessimistic about Northern Ireland though living in England as long as I have does tend to make one pessimistic about that. Or one might take the case of Israel, the Arab minorities. In order for liberalism to have a chance in a society like that, so polarized and divided, then something also not perhaps as dramatic as what would have to happen in the religious monolithic states, but something pretty dramatic would have to happen – namely they would have to begin to think of themselves as a political community within which the idea of equal concern took hold in order to become, to have any chance of realizing a genuine liberal society. Once we separate out as very problematic, on the one hand, monolithic societies and, on the other hand societies so riven that they are really two societies trying to live together, then we have left out most of the societies represented by people in this room.

In the case of Eastern Europe, I would have thought as a viewer from the outside that the schisms, the divisions, are different from the cases I have been speaking about. Is it possible for people who have a sense of a different culture to live together in a liberal society? Well, I want to suggest to you that the answer to that very important question might turn on two distinctions. The first is a distinction within the idea of liberal tolerance. I said we can understand that goal in two ways. We can understand the goal as saying whatever the political society decides on will be equally convenient to all the national groups within the larger communities, will please them equally. That is not possible. It is not what liberalism promises. Liberalism promises something different and sometimes we lose sight of the difference. Liberalism promises that no structure, no tax system, no geographical division, will be set up because of a desire to please one ethnic group rather than another. Liberalism cannot promise that when, for example, decisions are made about what language to teach in schools, the result won't be more in keeping with the desires of one group than another. I emphasize this because part of the question whether can liberalism succeed in Eastern Europe or anyplace else concerns the great threat of ethnic nationalism. Part of the answer is the question of what the legitimate expectations of different groups are. The second question that I would ask you in connection with this is this one: does liberal neutralism, liberal neutrality, the idea that liberalism has got to be fair, that we have got to accept equal concern, do we understand this to say each person must be able within the boundary set by a fair division of resources to lead the life in the culture, speaking the language with the associations that person wants, is that what we mean? If it is, then I do not see why that is not available under the kind of scheme that I have been describing. Or do we want something more, namely that each person will be in a position to have that person's convictions realized by how other people should live. That is very different. Third-person convictions, the convictions of one ethnic group for example as to conformity by others is not part of what liberalism promises to respect. Liberalism offers a guarantee of first-person neutrality. A liberal government is not hostile to the ambitions, cultures, traditions of any group within it but liberalism does not promise to respect third-person morality. Liberalism is hostile to the very idea that one group should be in a position to dictate to others. Is liberalism, the kind of liberalism that I described, is that on the cards, is that a possibility in Eastern Europe? I see two dangers: one short-term and one long-term. The short-term may be fatal. Liberalism requires, as I said earlier, a move from a command to a market economy. It demands much else, it demands fairness in the market economy but it does demand movement from command to market. And as you all know better than I do, that means a period of tremendous political instability as people's lives are rearranged and some people's lives fractured as a result. That is a short-term problem I would hope. But I cannot say anything about that at all – you all know more about that than I do.

The other kind of threat, one I have been talking about just now, lies in the wrong sense of community. I have been talking this morning about liberal ideals of equality and liberal ideals of liberty and I will close by speaking about the third ideal of the French Revolution which I left out. I won't insult you by calling it fraternity, but I will call it community. Liberalism, the picture that I have been trying to create, carries with it a certain answer to the question – how are we united in community? And the answer is: we are united by equality of concern understood to have the distributional implication that I described, understood to have the dimension of liberty but also understood to have this idea that if I belong to one ethnic group and there is a rival ethnic group within my political community, I must understand the importance of not attempting that I run the life of anyone else in the community. Not simply out of a kind of scepticism but out of a sense that it is part of that person's inherent worth to make decisions about the character of life for themselves. That is an ideal of community. It says I have a special relationship with other people in my political community. It is a different connection than the connection of ethnic genetic derivation. It is a different connection from the connection of religion. It is quintessentially and specially a political connection. We are in a joint venture together. This person is somebody for whom I must have concern not because he is a fellow Serb, not because he is a fellow Catholic, not because he is a fellow human being but because he is a fellow member of my political community engaged with me in the attempt to bring justice to our community. Now that is the liberal ideal of community. Is it available?

Lukes: Ronnie Dworkin has characterized liberalism for us and also situated it and I first want to say a few things about that characterization and situation and then turn our discussion back to the very interesting question of liberalism's prospects in Eastern and Central Europe.

The characterization which he offered us began with this very abstract principle of equality of concern of which he then offered us a specific interpretation in terms of equality of resources. The abstract principle of the equality of concern together secondly with the idea that the cardinal values, the central values of liberty and equality, are not inherently or necessarily conflicting but rather, as he put it, fused. And then a third idea which emerged later in his remarks, essentially connected with these first two ideas, is the idea, which has to be defined very precisely, of neutrality – the idea that in some way or other liberalism embodies a set of principles that require some kind of neutrality or, I would prefer to say, impartiality between different conceptions of what is valuable in life.

Now, I have got no quarrel, indeed I am very sympathetic, to this way of thinking about liberalism. I just want to make one comment about one thing that Ronnie Dworkin said about the particularity of this set of principles. He said no-one in this room would disagree with him, he hoped, but that nevertheless they were not universally accepted, indeed he said these principles have probably not been accepted in most times and places. Now I just want to ask here a question about what it is to accept a set of principles. After all these ideas, the ideal of the State having a general principle of equal concern for citizens, the idea of liberty being essential to what equality is, being a precondition of it and the idea that the State must somehow stand back from imposing a particular way of life...

Dworkin: May I just say it is only the first of those that I said I thought everyone in this room would agree to. The second two are I think more particular, more controversial – it was the abstract principle I was hoping everyone would agree to.

Lukes: But even you are committed to the idea that the first is also controversial in that it is only accepted in a small part of the world and a small part of history.

Dworkin: That is right. It is just that the most I would claim is that everybody here agrees with that.

Lukes: But nevertheless in the large span of time and space, it is controversial. Well, this is something I wanted to specify a little bit because of course you do not want to say that these principles are put into effect, or fully put into effect, by our societies but not elsewhere. I want to really just raise the question: what it is to accept a principle? I mean you could say that anybody when asked will accept the principle that everyone should be treated with equal concern. But what is the meaning of that acceptance? In what sense do we, let us say in this room, accept these principles, whereas let us say in Chile, or Paraguay or Iran, the principles are not accepted. Do you mean that they are put into effect somehow – that the political and economic system *embodies* these principles or do you mean that in some sense they are accepted by the culture or the citizens of a given society even if they are not actually exemplified or fully realized in the practice of those societies? I think that what you mean to say, and I would agree with this, really is that there is a kind of culture of liberalism or culture in which these principles, the most abstract one and then the others also, actually have a force, a cultural force in political and social life in some societies but not in others, even though one would also want to say that in those societies where they do have this force they are not of course fully implemented. They represent a kind of critical standard which counts in some places but does not count in others, even if in those places where you may say these principles count you can then criticize the societies and the economies for not living up to them. I hope this point does not sound pedantic but it seems to me somewhat important. We do not want to imply, I certainly would not want to imply, that liberalism thus understood is anywhere actually realized. It may be more realized in some places than others but the distinction that is important is that in some times and places these principles count in the sense that they represent a standard or a principle that people take seriously, whereas in other places and times, and you would argue and I'd agree, in most places and times they are not even referred to, or if they are referred to, it is in a very empty or rhetorical way.

Secondly, I wanted to say something about how you situated liberalism. You said that there was some kind of left-right continuum and that liberalism was somehow in the middle. You said that for those on the right the principle that liberty and equality are essentially in conflict was a kind of principle, dogma, or something which was somehow commonplace but this was also something that was accepted though for different reasons and in a different way on the left and that liberalism was somehow in the middle because it asserted something that both the left and the right deny. Now, my first remark is, and I imagine that those of you from Eastern Europe will probably agree with this, that in Eastern Europe there is a problem about this very topography, this very distinction between left and right. I have for a long time noticed friends from Eastern Europe and those writing from Eastern Europe observing the very distinction between left and right no longer seems to make sense. And indeed it seems to correspond with one's observations. Is Boris Yeltsin on the left or the right, or Gorbaciov, or Watesa? I do not find those questions easy to answer. And I am inclined to think that the very way we think about the whole political spectrum has been thrown into a kind of confusion by the events, the world-historically important events of the last two or three years. More particularly, though, the very meaning of liberalism in Eastern Europe has I think even more than in Western Europe a very particular meaning, and not the meaning which you've been eloquently expounding to us today. I think generally in Eastern Europe liberalism tends to mean economic liberalism, it tends to mean essentially the spread of the market and market principles together with a general commitment to the rule of law. But the main force, the central idea, that is thought of as liberal is, if you want to put it in terms of names, represented by Hayek rather than John Stuart Mill or John Rawls. And that is actually important in the context of the argument you've advanced because, on that view of the matter, certainly, if you take Hayek or let us say Milton Friedman or, to take another name, Jerry Sachs, one cardinal principle of liberalism as it is generally understood in Eastern Europe, is precisely that liberty and equality are in fundamental and inevitable conflict. In other words if you want to promote a liberal society you have to give up on equality. And that is because on this view of the matter equality is seen as a principle of distribution in which essentially what is distributed (the answer to the question, equality of what?) is income, wealth and conditions of life. And the whole experience of Eastern European Communism has basically turned people off the idea of equality as such. So I think your argument today that we should be liberals and that means we should be egalitarian faces a problem with East Europeans for whom not only the very idea of Communism but also of I think of Socialism and I suspect of equality are suspect, contaminated notions.

Now I would like, having said something about how you characterized liberalism and how you situated it, to raise a question of a very general sort. The question I want to ask is: to what problem is liberalism a solution? I mean why do we need liberalism? Liberalism as you have expounded it, as it is expounded in the great texts of liberalism and most notably in our own day by John Rawls in his book *A Theory of Justice*, proposes or offers a set of principles that could be accepted after due reflection, after reasonable reflection, by citizens of a political community as a basis on which to distribute resources and powers in any given community. That is to say it is a principle of distribution, a set of principles which are to govern economic life but also constitutional and political life, on the assumption that these principles can be given a kind of coherent structure. Now why should you need such a set of principles? I think there are a number of very fundamental, let us say four very fundamental features of the human predicament or the human situation which make such principles necessary.

The first is scarcity. Not everything is available for everybody; we do not live in a world of total abundance. You need to have a set of principles on which people, citizens, can regard distribution of the benefits and burdens of living but more particularly the resources that are available in any given community, as fair.

The second feature of the human situation to which liberalism can be thought of as a response is the fact that people are not all, as the French revolutionaries might have said, brothers. That is to say, there is a limit to the degree of altruism or benevolence that you can assume to exist.

Thirdly, there are limits to the degree of, to the extent of human rationality. Even if people were universally benevolent, and they were concerned with distributing resources and powers and so on in society in a fair way, they are very likely to get it wrong or to make mistakes, to fail to understand how society and nature work because of lack of information but also because of limits to human intelligence.

And fourthly, and this is perhaps the most important in relation to what I want to say in a moment, people differ and they differ fundamentally about what is valuable in life. There are differences about what the nature of the good life consists in and how people should live their lives. And for this reason it becomes important to think of ways of organizing life together in which those differences, differences about what is important and valuable, are recognized and allowed to continue to survive. In other words, people can, if they recognize this fact as an important fact, the fact that people differ about what is important and what is valuable, then try to find ways of living together without suppressing those differences or by suppressing them to some minimal degree.

If those are, very speedily said, the conditions which make a liberal set of principles or a set of principles which we could call liberal needed, I now want to make some remarks about Eastern Europe because I want to suggest to you that liberalism defined very much as Dworkin did is both highly relevant to Eastern Europe but also highly precarious. It is relevant firstly I think for straightforwardly historical reasons, I mean reasons that have to do with very recent history. As I see it, the revolutions of 1989 were revolutions which recognized that these facts of the human predicament which I just referred to are indeed necessary facts of human life. If you consider the regimes against which these revolutions were directed, they were of course regimes that embodied massive economic failures and indeed failures of many other kinds. The Revolutions which brought the collapse about were also a rejection of a certain set of assumptions about social life, about how societies work and about human history. To be more precise, Marxism-Leninism is distinctive in many ways, but it is distinctive among other things I think precisely in that it always denied that these four facts that I just referred to are indeed facts of the human predicament. Scarcity in the first place, Marxism always promised, was going to be overcome through the historical development of the forces of production. Capitalism was going through its development to point towards and socialism eventually would become societies of abundance. Communism is the name for a society in which benevolence, the overcoming of selfishness and social antagonism, would indeed be realized. Human irrationality or limits of human rationality would become overcome by a completely planned or plannable, organizable, thinkable society in which there would no longer need to be failures of rationality in the end and above all at the level of economic planning. Lastly and most importantly, divergences between ways of life or conceptions of what is important in life would cease to matter. Religion, nationality, ethnicity, all these various things which divide people and indeed other kinds of moral difference would no longer matter because under a Communist society these would become marginal and eventually wither away.

I think that the revolutions of 1989 were not revolutions of rising expectations; they were revolutions of fallen expectations. That sort of expectation of prospects for human life was decisively rejected and you could say that these revolutions embodied a kind of expectation or hope for justice, for the implementation of rights, for fairness, for the establishment or institution of citizenship, and this very interesting little word 'civic' and citizen was very central at that time. So I think that liberalism can be thought of as very relevant to our times and in particular to the experience of Eastern and Central Europe because liberalism offers a set of principles that answers to a situation which became visible again at the time of the fall, the rejection of a whole political culture, a whole political morality if you like which precisely denied it. I also think therefore, that liberalism remains in principle extremely relevant precisely because the problem of scarcity and the problem of managing social conflict and the problem of organizing production, and above all the problem of finding ways of living together in a single political community are acute in Eastern Europe today and what liberalism offers is a set of principles that can be offered as reasonably acceptable to and by citizens of a political community as a basis on which to run their lives, a set of principles which citizens can offer themselves as reasonable but which also offer or promise a certain kind of coherence.

But I'd like to draw your attention to one clause or phrase in the sentence I just uttered. I said 'a set of principles which the citizens or the members of a political community can offer themselves' and that is the point which I want to move to – the precariousness of liberalism in Eastern Europe today. What Ronnie said earlier was that liberalism is a doctrine that is or a set of principles that are relevant to the members of a political community. But liberalism has nothing, I think, to say about what we might call the boundary question. *Who* are the members of the political community? I noticed particularly that you did not mean a particular nation or a particular ethnic group and you did not mean humanity in general. You meant the citizens of a political community. But the citizens of which political community? The question of *who* they are to be and where the boundaries lie is of course one of the most acute questions that are now ravaging not only Eastern and Southern Europe but also of course the Soviet Union. I agree with the remarks you made towards the end. I think that to the extent to which this question, this problem is put into question a problem of a very fundamental sort is set for the implementation of the acceptance of liberal principles, precisely because what would have to be a settled condition for liberalism to work, to be accepted, is itself unsettled. So that is the first reason I think for regarding liberalism as precarious – the most serious threat that I think is posed by present events, by present prospects, at least in some places. But the second and final reason I think that liberalism might be thought to be precarious is more paradoxical. It is posed by the very success of liberalism understood in the economic sense, à la Sachs, Milton Friedman or Hayek. To the extent that this becomes, as it were, the new ideology, the new ideological force that fills the ideological vacuum, to the extent to which, in other words, people believe in, or governments and opinion leaders and the leaders of the intellectuals get committed to, the implementation of an ideology in which liberty is understood very narrowly to be economic freedom, freedom of choice in the marketplace and everything that is thought of as Socialist or Social-Democratic or even social is rejected because it smacks of equality. That represents, if you like, the threat which liberalism understood in the narrow sense poses to liberalism understood in the broader and richer sense that we have been offered today.

Index of Decisions of Transnational Courts

A. Judgments of the European Court of Human Rights (in alphabetical order)

B. Decisions and Reports of the European Commission of Human Rights (in alphabetical order)

C. Resolutions by the Committee of Ministers of the Council of Europe (in alphabetical order)

D. Judgments of the European Court of Justice (arranged by case number)

E. Reports by the United Nations Human Rights Committee in the Framework of the Covenant on Civil and Political Rights (in alphabetical order)

MIX
Papier aus verantwortungsvollen Quellen
Paper from responsible sources
FSC® C105338

If you have any concerns about our products,
you can contact us on
ProductSafety@springernature.com

In case Publisher is established outside the EU,
the EU authorized representative is:
Springer Nature Customer Service Center GmbH
Europaplatz 3, 69115 Heidelberg, Germany

Printed by Libri Plureos GmbH
in Hamburg, Germany